APPROACHING YEHUD

Society of Biblical Literature

Semeia Studies

Gale A. Yee, General Editor

Editorial Board:
Roland T. Boer
Tat-Siong Benny Liew
Sarojini Nadar
Erin Runions
Fernando F. Segovia
Ken Stone
Caroline Vander Stichele
Elaine M. Wainwright

Number 50

APPROACHING YEHUD
New Approaches to the Study of the Persian Period

APPROACHING YEHUD
New Approaches to the Study
of the Persian Period

Edited by

Jon L. Berquist

Society of Biblical Literature
Atlanta

APPROACHING YEHUD
New Approaches to the Study of the Persian Period

Library of Congress Cataloging-in-Publication Data

Approaching Yehud : new approaches to the study of the Persian period / edited by Jon L. Berquist.
        p. cm. — (Society of Biblical Literature Semeia studies ; no. 50)
    Includes bibliographical references.
    ISBN: 978-1-58983-145-2 (paper binding : alk. paper)
    1. Jews—History—586 B.C.–70 A.D.—Historiography. 2. Judaism—History—Post-exilic period, 586 B.C.–210 A.D.—Historiography. 3. Bible. O.T.—Historiography. 4. Yehud (Persian province)—Historiography. 5. Judaea (Region)—Historiography. I. Berquist, Jon L.
    DS121.65.A82 2007b
    933'.03—dc22   2007035327

15 14 13 12 11 10 09 08 07   5 4 3 2 1
Printed in the United States of America on acid-free, recycled paper conforming to ANSI/NISO Z39.48-1992 (R1997) and ISO 9706:1994 standards for paper permanence.

Contents

RESPONSES

ABBREVIATIONS

AB	Anchor Bible
ABRL	Anchor Bible Reference Library
ABD	*Anchor Bible Dictionary.* Edited by David Noel Freedman. 6 vols. New York: Doubleday, 1992.
AfO	*Archiv für Orientforschung*
AJA	*American Journal of Archaeology*
AOAT	Alter Orient und Altes Testament
AOS	American Oriental Series
ATD	Das Alte Testament Deutsch
BBET	Beiträge zur biblischen Exegese und Theologie
BBR	*Bulletin for Biblical Research*
BEATAJ	Beiträge zur Erforschung des Alten Testaments und des antiken Judentum
BETL	Bibliotheca ephemeridum theologicarum lovaniensium
Bib	*Biblica*
BibInt	*Biblical Interpretation*
BIS	Biblical Interpretation Series
BJS	Brown Judaic Studies
BN	*Biblische Notizen*
BO	Bibliotheca orientalis
BTS	Bible et terre sainte
BWANT	Beiträge zur Wissenschaft vom Alten und Neuen Testament
BZAW	Beihefte zur Zeitschrift für die alttestamentliche Wissenschaft
CANE	*Civilizations of the Ancient Near East.* Edited by Jack Sasson. 4 vols. New York: Scribner, 1995.
CAT	Commentaire de l'Ancien Testament
CBQ	*Catholic Biblical Quarterly*
CBQMS	Catholic Biblical Quarterly Monograph Series
CurBS	*Currents in Research: Biblical Studies*
ErIsr	*Eretz-Israel*
FAT	Forschungen zum Alten Testament

FCB	Feminist Companion to the Bible
FOTL	Forms of the Old Testament Literature
Fort.	Persepolis Fortification Text
FRLANT	Forschungen zur Religion und Literatur des Alten und Neuen Testaments
HAR	*Hebrew Annual Review*
HAT	Handbuch zum Alten Testament
HKAT	Handkommentar zum Alten Testament
HR	*History of Religions*
HSAT	Die Heilige Schrift des Alten Testaments.
HSM	Harvard Semitic Monographs
HUCA	*Hebrew Union College Annual*
IBC	Interpretation: A Bible Commentary for Teaching and Preaching
IBT	Interpreting Biblical Texts
ICC	International Critical Commentary
IEJ	*Israel Exploration Journal*
Int	*Interpretation*
JANESCU	*Journal of the Ancient Near Eastern Society of Columbia University*
JAOS	*Journal of the American Oriental Society*
JBL	*Journal of Biblical Literature*
JCS	*Journal of Cuneiform Studies*
JRAS	*Journal of the Royal Asiatic Society*
JSOT	*Journal for the Study of the Old Testament*
JSOTSup	Journal for the Study of the Old Testament Supplement Series
JSS	*Journal of Semitic Studies*
KAT	Kommentar zum Alten Testament
LCBI	Literary Currents in Biblical Interpretation
MdB	Le monde de la Bible
NCB	New Century Bible
NCBC	New Century Bible Commentary
NEAEHL	*The New Encyclopedia of Archaeological Excavations in the Holy Land.* Edited by Ephraim Stern. 4 vols. Jerusalem: Israel Exploration Society and Carta; New York: Simon & Schuster, 1993.
NIB	*The New Interpreter's Bible*
NICOT	New International Commentary on the Old Testament
OBO	Orbis biblicus et orientalis
OBT	Overtures to Biblical Theology

OEAANE	*The Oxford Encyclopedia of Archaeology in the Near East.* Edited by Eric M. Meyers. New York: Oxford University Press, 1997.
OIP	Oriental Institute Publications
Or	*Orientalia*
OTG	Old Testament Guides
OTL	Old Testament Library
OtSt	Oudtestamentische Studiën
PSB	*Princeton Seminary Bulletin*
RB	*Revue biblique*
REA	*Revue des études anciennes*
RES	*Revue des études sémitiques*
ResQ	*Restoration Quarterly*
SB	Sources bibliques
SBLDS	Society of Biblical Literature Dissertation Series
SBLMS	Society of Biblical Literature Monograph Series
SBLSemPap	Society of Biblical Literature Seminar Papers
SBLSymS	Society of Biblical Literature Symposium Series
SBS	Stuttgarter Bibelstudien
Sem	*Semitica*
SemeiaSt	Semeia Studies
SJOT	*Scandinavian Journal of the Old Testament*
SSN	Studia semitica neerlandica
TBC	Torch Bible Commentaries
TDOT	*Theological Dictionary of the Old Testament.* Edited by G. Johannes Botterweck and Helmer Ringgren. Translated by John T. Willis et al. 15 vols. Grand Rapids, 1974–2006.
Transeu	*Transeuphratène*
UF	*Ugarit-Forschungen*
VF	*Verkündigung und Forschung*
VT	*Vetus Testamentum*
VTSup	Supplements to Vetus Testamentum
WBC	Word Biblical Commentary
WMANT	Wissenschaftliche Monographien zum Alten und Neuen Testament
ZA	*Zeitschrift für Assyriologie*
ZAW	*Zeitschrift für die alttestamentliche Wissenschaft*
ZTK	*Zeitschrift für Theologie und Kirche*

Approaching Yehud

Jon L. Berquist

The recent emphasis on the Persian Empire within biblical studies is not new. A century ago, a number of Persian-period studies were at the forefront of ancient Near Eastern and biblical studies (Strassmeier 1890a; 1890b; Tolman 1908; Cowley). Throughout the early parts of the twentieth century, scholars recognized the influences of the Persian Empire on the social setting and politics of fifth- and fourth-century Jerusalem and speculated about the connections between Zoroastrianism and nascent Judaism and Christianity. However, these studies did not greatly influence the mainstream of biblical studies. Instead, critical biblical studies reflected the Wellhausenian view that Israel's prime occurred earlier, during the monarchy, and that the postexilic period was a lesser, derivative era. Theologically, this reflected an understanding of the period as legalistic (in comparison with earlier periods of Israel's history). At its worst, the disregard of the Persian period participated in a denigration of Judaism that still runs throughout much biblical scholarship.

Biblical studies' interest in the Persian period diminished, although the middle of the twentieth century witnessed the publication of several books that became standards of Persian-period scholarship (Olmstead; Kent). In biblical studies, the Persian period was often depicted as a "dark age" or, at the best, as a "silver age"—a diminished time that eluded historical analysis and that offered little theological or literary innovation. This flowed, in part, from an erroneous assumption about the high degree of historical certainty with which earlier periods could be known. The Persian period was considered an unknown territory in comparison to periods such as the monarchy, at a time when scholarly certainty about the monarchy was at an unsustainable peak. Inherent in the scholarly construction of a "postexilic" era were the assumptions that the preexilic times could be known securely and that the times afterwards were logical extensions of earlier historical events and situations. Biblical scholarship has now lost much of its faith in the older views of great historical certainty in the monarchy, and theories of history now emphasize both continuity and discontinuity of any historical period with its past.

By the 1960s, English-speaking scholarship developed a broad consensus about Israel's exile and restoration (Ackroyd 1968). This consensus view advanced several theses: the Babylonian deportations of 587 B.C.E. substantially emptied the land of Israel; the deported community in Babylonia was the generative inheritor of earlier Israelite tradition; the exilic period (i.e., the Babylonian deported community) was instrumental in the writing and standardization of most older literary and theological traditions; the deportees were united in their desire for a rebuilt temple in Jerusalem to serve as the core of religious experience; this desire expressed itself in some messianic expectations; in 539 B.C.E. the ascension of the Persian Empire allowed for the mass return of these Babylonian deportees; and these people became community leaders in Jerusalem who reshaped the city into a temple-centered community based on the desire to restore First Temple religion in an improved cult. This consensus was rarely questioned for a quarter century.

During this time, studies in Achaemenid history and society continued to grow. The groundbreaking work of Muhammad Dandamayev became available in western Europe and in North America. In Groningen, an Achaemenid History Workshop began meeting in 1983, eventually publishing thirteen volumes of essays that advanced Persian-period studies. Eventually, the rise of new Persian-period historians such as Pierre Briant began to change the field and make the work of a new generation more accessible. In biblical studies, the rise of social-scientific studies of ancient Israel became more prominent through the work of the Society of Biblical Literature's Sociology of the Monarchy Section and the publications of series such as Social World of Biblical Antiquity. Perhaps the most important change in this sociological advance was the shift in attention away from the exile and restoration paradigms to concepts of empire and colony. This provided a different conceptual framework for understanding Jerusalem and its environs in the time of the Persian Empire, and sociological attention led to a new set of understandings about the Persian period. This rise of scholarship produced a number of new insights about Yehud, the Persian colony that included Jerusalem.

These new perspectives influenced several commentaries (Petersen; Meyers and Meyers 1987; Blenkinsopp 1988) and became the basis of several monographs (Smith-Christopher 1989; Hoglund 1992; Berquist 1995a). An increasing number of major scholarly publications also reflected these new views. The development of the so-called Copenhagen or minimalist school of historiography also shifted attention from earlier periods to the Persian and Hellenistic periods as crucial contexts for understanding the construction of all Hebrew Bible literature (Lemche; P. R. Davies 1992). Scholars began to talk of the exile as a "myth of the empty land" and thus began to imagine the postexilic period from a different starting point (Carroll 1992; Barstad). A number of groups arose in the SBL to study the Second Temple period's history, literature, and society. In the last twenty years, a variety of new publications and new scholars have pushed forward the sociological and historical study of Yehud, as well as new analyses of the literature and theology of the period.

Of course, the rise in Persian-period studies was also an attempt to deal with Jerusalem and Yehud in their own terms, apart from a chronological-ideological framework that depicted it as a devolved precursor to the New Testament or to early Judaism. The creation of "Persian-period" studies gave the field a way to speak of itself not in terms of preparing for a new messianic age or in terms of hearkening back to a previous monarchy.

Through these changes in scholarship, a new image of Yehud has emerged. It may still be too soon to refer to this image as a consensus, but much of the last decade's scholarly work has shared a number of these working assumptions:

- ▶ The Babylonian incursions of the early sixth century B.C.E. removed a minority of the population of Jerusalem.
- ▶ Only a small minority of the descendents of these deportees migrated from Babylonia to Yehud in 539, and they migrated over a period of several decades.
- ▶ The population of Jerusalem and its environs in the Persian period was much smaller than earlier estimates (and these estimates have continued to decline from tens of thousands to perhaps a few thousand).
- ▶ The exilic period produced little of the literature that became the Hebrew Bible, but much of the literature may have been assembled in a relatively short period of time in the fifth century (and some would identify a later period).
- ▶ The community of Yehud was not unified but experienced substantial social conflict. This included diverse opinions about the construction and function of the Second Temple as well as cultic practices.
- ▶ Yehudite culture was strongly influenced by Persian imperial politics. The empire utilized methods of social control in Yehud similar to those that the empire employed in other colonies, and the Hebrew Bible shows the evidence of this social and ideological intervention.
- ▶ The economics of Yehud as a Persian colony are crucial to the understanding of the society and literature of the period.

▶ Yehud was a site for ethnic conflict and ethnic definition, perhaps setting the stage for later understandings as well.

This new perspective on Yehud has become widespread in biblical scholarship, but the ramifications of these changing assumptions are yet to be seen.
The essays in this volume reflect many of these assumptions and contribute to
the ongoing process of analyzing Yehud, but they also call into question the
methodological issues embedded in these very assumptions.

The first essay in this volume focuses on society and religion. Melody
Knowles concentrates on pilgrimage, a key feature of Persian-period religion,
treating pilgrimage as a religious practice as well as a social phenomenon.

The next pair of essays examines textuality and intertextuality. Richard
Bautch explores the methodological bases of intertextuality, with suggestions about how these methods will influence Persian-period studies. Donald
Polaski's essay on power and writing advances the discussion about what texts
existed at the end of the Persian period and how Yehud viewed those texts.

Historiography forms the theme for the third set of essays. David Janzen
scrutinizes the interpretation of Ezra 9–10, a key passage for understanding
ethnicity as well as cultic practice in Yehud. Christine Mitchell discusses the
role of identity in the creation of history, attending to the book of Lamentations. Both of these essays suggest new ideas about how and why history is
understood and written.

Three essays illuminate issues of prophecy. Brent Strawn's work demonstrates the role of iconography in understanding Isa 60. Jean-Pierre Ruiz uses
postcolonial reading strategies to interpret Ezekiel. John Kessler's treatment of
Zech 1–8 places this prophetic writing within the context of Yehudite society.

Wisdom literature also receives treatment from two authors. Herbert
Marbury focuses on Proverbs, examining the ethnic rhetoric about the
"strange woman." Jennifer Koosed's exploration of Qoheleth deconstructs the
book's presentation of women. In a final chapter, I offer an exploration of
identity in Psalms.

Taken together, these twelve chapters represent a range of studies that
push forward new perspectives on Yehud. They treat a range of biblical genres
and a variety of textual and historical problems. Several of the essays deal with
issues of ideology and power, advancing the study of these concepts. Gender
and ethnicity run throughout these chapters, treated in a more sophisticated
manner than in earlier works. Economics and imperial politics inform the
results of several of these chapters. Issues of empire and colonialism appear in
most of the essays, with some moving toward explicitly postcolonial perspectives. Methods of social history, critical theory, and deconstruction also run
throughout these approaches. The methodological variety of these chapters

show that Persian-period studies are moving beyond the historical roots and the sociological studies of twenty years ago. The growing consensus about the Persian period is not only a result of changes in scholarship but has become a catalyst that, through interaction with different critical methodologies, is creating prolific new scholarly approaches.

These chapters not only reflect the new perspectives on Yehud but also raise a number of matters that scholarship is only beginning to address: (1) imperialism and its effects, including postcolonial interpretation sensitive to the multiple encodings of agency and resistance; (2) bodies and sexualities as constructed in the Persian period; (3) economics, including food, migration, trade, and class; (4) identity, in particular ethnicity and perceptions of the other in the setting of pluralism; (5) scribalism and canonization, as well as the proliferation of texts; (6) regional differences between Yehud and its neighbors, within the imperial context; (7) relations and influences between Yehud and its non-Persian contacts, including peoples of the Mediterranean; (8) the reintegration of social history with religious practices of the period; and (9) understanding the production and uses of texts within the period, including the history of different writings now extant and the intertextual relations between texts.

This book's essays demonstrate how Persian-period studies can move forward to address these and other questions, building upon the work of the past and integrating a variety of new methods to produce a more fulsome picture of society and religion in Yehud.

Pilgrimage to Jerusalem in the Persian Period*

Melody D. Knowles

What was the practice of religion in the Persian period, and how did it reflect YHWH's return to Jerusalem? Given that most of the biblical literature of this time emphasizes that YHWH is again dwelling in the city (YHWH is "the God who is in Jerusalem," according to Ezra 1:3), is it possible to detect this emphasis on sacred geography in the people's worship? According to Safrai, pilgrimage is a feature of the Hasmonean period and later; there is no good textual evidence for Persian-period pilgrimage, and the few biblical examples are only exceptions that prove the rule: "There are various cases of pilgrimage from the Diaspora, but this only proves that there was no kind of widespread need."[1] Although most evidence indicates that the practice of pilgrimage to Jerusalem was not widespread until the Hasmonean period and later, it is possible to trace its earlier manifestations in the biblical texts from the Persian period, including the prophets, the historical narratives, and Pss 120–134. Yet the different genres maintain different emphases when describing the practice of pilgrimage. The prophets emphasize eschatological pilgrimage and include both the Diaspora and the nations as participants. Although the Chronicler recounts pilgrimage as a past event, the nations are included as participants. In Ezra and Nehemiah, however, pilgrimage occurs in the present day and mostly includes only the chosen community in Yehud. Finally, Pss 120–134 speak little of the ethnic categories of the participants, but these "Songs of Ascent" incorporate several themes that relate to and encourage pilgrimage to Jerusalem. I will discuss the evidence for each genre in turn and then present

---

* Another version of this essay appears as chapter 4 in Melody Knowles, *Centrality Practiced: Jerusalem in the Religious Practice of Yehud and the Diaspora in the Persian Period* (SBLABS 16; Atlanta: Society of Biblical Literature, 2006), 77–103.

1. "Vereinzelte Fälle von Wallfahrt aus der Diaspora gab es wohl schon immer, aber es lässt nachweisen, dass es sich um keinen verbreiten Brauch handelte" (Safrai: 8 n. 45).

two models for understanding the practice of pilgrimage to Jerusalem in the Persian period based on the biblical texts and the archaeological evidence.

For the purposes of this essay, I define pilgrimage as travel outside one's sphere of daily activity to a site designated as holy by the community in order to worship or communicate with the divine. This is similar to other scholars' definitions, such as "paying a visit to a sacred site outside the boundaries of one's own physical environment" (Dillon: xviii) or "sacred journey and arrival to the temple, with the prayers and sacrifices which ensue" (Smith and Bloch-Smith: 16). In ancient Israel and Greece, pilgrimage was probably not an infrequent event: Exod 23:17; 34:23 and Deut 16:16 command every male to appear before Yhwh three times a year, and journeys to a central cult site were also made on other occasions, such as the birth of a child (Lev 12:6–8). In ancient Greece, the festival at Olympia was celebrated once every four years, the festivals at Nemea and Isthmia were celebrated every two years, and spectators and participants could attend festivals at various other sites (Dillon: 99). Given the frequency of ancient pilgrimage (at least as a desideratum), there was not the same emphasis on the penitential hardship requiring a long or arduous journey as is found in Late Antique, Middle Ages, or Muslim practice. Further, not specifying a particular geographical distance in the definition of pilgrimage (only that the worshiper must leave the confines of her daily world) allows both those coming from within the province of Yehud as well as those who traveled from farther away to be designated pilgrims. This definition differs from more modern conceptions of pilgrimage that predominantly focus on once-in-a-lifetime treks involving a great distance. Such pilgrimages require a radical break from regular social conditions (Turner 1969; 1973a; 1973b; Turner and Turner). Given that ancient pilgrimage often occurred more often than once in a person's lifetime, and given that people from the local communities could worship together at the cult, such radical breaks do not seem as relevant to the ancient world.

Although pilgrimage in the Hebrew Bible is sometimes designated by the terms חגג or חג ("to make a pilgrimage," and "feast, pilgrim-feast," so BDB), journeys to a sacred place are also designated by other terms of travel. In this aspect, Hebrew is similar to Greek, where pilgrimage is designated with the terms such as "those going" and "those coming." Other terms for pilgrimage in Greek texts include "the watchers" (θεαταί), "those attending a panegyris" (πανηγυρίζοντες), and those who wish "to go, to sacrifice, to seek an oracle and to watch" (see Dillon: xv–xvi.) For instance, בוא ("to go in, enter") describes the journey to the place where Yhwh or other gods are worshiped,[2]

---

2. The verb בוא is used to describe the journey to the place where Yhwh is (Isa

oftentimes in the explicit context of a חג (Deut 31:11; Isa 30:29; 2 Chr 30:5). In addition, the H form of בוא designates the bringing of offerings and sacrifices to YHWH.[3] The root הלך often designates the journey to a sacred area,[4] as does עלה (Exod 34:23–24; 1 Sam 1:3, 7, 24; Isa 2:3).

Prophetic Biblical Texts

Foundational to the desire to make a pilgrimage to Jerusalem is the acknowledgement that YHWH has once again taken up residence there, and this fact is emphasized throughout the prophetic texts of the Persian period. In Zechariah, YHWH proclaims "I have returned to Jerusalem" (1:16) and subsequently calls the temple "my house" several more times throughout the book (1:16; 3:7; cf. 2:10, 11). In Haggai, the temple is also predominantly called YHWH's "house" (1:2, 9, 14) or "YHWH's temple" (2:15, 18). Although Trito-Isaiah reminds the reader that YHWH "dwells in the high and holy place" (57:15), Jerusalem and the temple are also designated by YHWH as "my holy mountain" (56:7; 57:13; 65:11, 25), "my house of prayer" (56:7), "my house" (56:7), "my glorious house" (60:7), and "my sanctuary … [the place] where my feet rest" (60:13). Additionally, YHWH promises to "come to Zion as Redeemer" in Isa 59:20.

Since Jerusalem and its temple is where YHWH resides, it follows that worship of YHWH includes pilgrimage to the holy dwelling and the prophets envision this predominantly as a future practice that includes the community along with foreign nations. Zechariah 6:9–12 recounts exiles coming (בוא) to Jerusalem from Babylon bearing gold and silver. For the prophet, this act

---

27:13), where other gods are worshiped (Judg 9:46; 1 Sam 5:5; 2 Kgs 10:21 [3x]; 2 Chr 23:17; Ezek 20:29; Hos 9:10), or where a prophet resides (1 Kgs 14:3, 5; 2 Kgs 4:42; Ezek 20:1, 3; cf. Ezek 14:4, 7).

3. So Gen 4:3, 4; Num 15:25; Mal 1:13 (2x). It also designates the bringing of offerings and sacrifices to the priests (Lev 2:2; 5:11, 12; 2 Kgs 12:5 [2x; Eng. 12:4]) or into the temple (2 Chr 31:10; 34:9), and to YHWH's storehouse (Mal 3:10).

4. The verb הלך is used when Jephthah's daughter and her companions went and mourned on the mountains for two months (Judg 11:37) and when, subsequent to her death, the daughters of Israel went out (תלכנה) regularly to lament her (11:40). Other examples of this term used to describe a journey to a place of worship and/or sacrifice are found in Gen 25:22 (Rebekah); Exod 3:18, 19 (the Israelites wanting to take a three-day journey into the wilderness); Deut 14:25 (Israelites who live far from Jerusalem), 26:2 (the nation); 1 Chr 21:30 and 1 Kgs 3:4 (David and Solomon going from their home to worship and sacrifice at Gibeon); Qoh 4:17 (Eng. 5:1); Ps 55:15 (Eng. 55:14); Isa 30:29; and Jer 3:6. Examples from outside the Hebrew Bible include the letter from Mari when Kiru, the daughter of Zimri-lim, asked her father permission to leave her situation to "go" (*lu-ul-li-ka-am-ma*) and sacrifice (ARM X 113.20–22; see Batto: 128).

initiates future pilgrimage—immediately following this account is a prophecy that this pilgrimage will be repeated both by the Diaspora and by Gentile nations: "Those who are far off shall come [יבאו] build the temple of Yhwh" (6:15). In addition, Yhwh will bring (הבאתי) people from the east and west to live in Jerusalem (8:7). Others will come at their own initiative, with Jews, "strong nations," and "the inhabitants of many cities" issuing their own call to pilgrimage: "Come, let us go [נלכה הלוך] to entreat the favor of Yhwh, and to seek Yhwh of hosts; I myself am going [אלכה]" (8:21). Further, the prophet declares that in days to come, "ten men from nations of every language shall take hold of a Jew … saying, 'Let us go [נלכה] with you, for we have heard that God is with you'" (8:23). Return to Jerusalem is also part of the later prophecies of Third Zechariah. In chapter 10 Yhwh promises to bring back the people scattered among the nations (והושבותים in 10:6 of the Leningrad Codex; השיבותים in 10:10). They will return (שבו, 10:9), and Yhwh will bring them back (אביאם, 10:10) to the land of Gilead and to Lebanon (10:6–12). Note also Zech 14:16–19, where the nations will go to Jerusalem annually to keep the festival of Booths.

Haggai and Third Isaiah also prophesy such future and/or eschatological pilgrimage, although it is primarily the nations and their wealth that are in view. In Haggai, Yhwh promises to shake the heaven, the earth, the sea, the dry land, and all the nations, "so that the treasure of the nations shall come [ובאו], and I will fill this house with splendor" (2:6–8). In Third Isaiah, foreigners who keep the Sabbath and the covenant will be brought (H of בוא) to Yhwh's holy mountain to offer burnt offerings and sacrifices (Isa 56:6–7). The text also has the promise that "nations shall bring [להביא] you their wealth … to beautify the place of my sanctuary" (60:9, 13; cf. 60:6–16). Taken together with the texts in Zechariah, these texts emphasize both the future expectation of pilgrimage and the inclusion of foreigners with the nation in worshiping Yhwh in Jerusalem.

Chronicles, Ezra, and Nehemiah

Similar to the nomenclature in the prophets, the Jerusalem temple in Ezra and Nehemiah is called Yhwh's "house" no less than sixty-four times and Yhwh's "temple" eight times.[5] The royal decrees in Ezra further stipulate that

---

5. For Yhwh's "house," see Ezra 1:2, 3, 4, 5; 2:68 (2x); 3:8 (2x), 9, 11, 12; 4:3, 24; 5:2, 8, 9, 11, 12, 13, 15, 16, 17; 6:3 (2x), 5, 7 (2x), 8, 12, 16, 17, 22; 7:16, 17, 19, 20, 23, 24, 27; 8:17, 25, 29, 30, 32, 36; 9:9; 10:1, 6, 9; Neh 6:10; 8:16; 10:33, 34, 35, 36, 37, 38, 39, 40 (Eng. 10:32, 33, 34, 35, 36, 37, 38, 39); 13:4, 7, 9, 11, 14. For Yhwh's "temple," see Ezra 3:6,10; 4:1; 5:15; 6:5; Neh 6:10 (2x), 11.

Y<small>HWH</small> is "the God who is in Jerusalem" (Ezra 1:3) and that God's "dwelling is in Jerusalem" (7:15). In Chronicles, the expressions "house of Y<small>HWH</small>" or "house of God" occurs over one hundred times.[6]

When compared to the prophetic texts, Ezra and Nehemiah handle pilgrimage quite differently. Not only is the practice actualized in the present (the accounts describe pilgrimage feasts and additional assemblies in Jerusalem); it also does not generally include foreigners.

The first pilgrimage feast mentioned is the Festival of Booths in Ezra 3:1–6a. No year is given for this first celebration of the festival of booths by the returnees, and with such an omission the author implies that it is still the "first year of Cyrus" (Ezra 1:1; Schneider: 105). For this pilgrimage, the "sons of Israel" left their towns in the seventh month and gathered in Jerusalem (3:1). After the altar was set on its foundation, the burnt offerings for the חג־הסכות began (3:3, 4).

After this celebration for the foundation and the Festival of Booths, Ezra 6 recounts the celebration of the rebuilt temple, and, like the foundation celebration, a pilgrimage festival follows the dedication of the temple. The temple dedication was attended by "the people of Israel, the priests and the Levites, and the rest of the returned exiles" (6:16), and the festivities included the offering of burnt sacrifices (6:17) and a sin-offering of twelve male goats "according to the number of the tribes of Israel" (6:17). Finally, the priests were set in their divisions and the Levites in their courses "for the service of God at Jerusalem" (6:18). With the temple built and dedicated, the sin of Israel atoned for, and the clerical orders arranged, all was ready for the worship of Y<small>HWH</small> in Jerusalem, and specifically the pilgrimage feasts. Consequently, the author directly follows the temple dedication with the celebration of Passover (הפסח) and the seven-day Feast of Unleavened Bread (חג־מצות; 6:19–22). The single time in the texts of Ezra and Nehemiah that foreigners participate in a pilgrimage feast is in the Passover described in Ezra 6:19–21: "It [the Passover lamb] was eaten by the people of Israel who had returned from exile, and also by all who had joined them and separated themselves from the pollutions of the nations of the land to worship Y<small>HWH</small>, the God of Israel."

Nehemiah adds another pilgrimage festival to those recounted in Ezra. According to Neh 8:13–18, the Festival of Booths was kept in Jerusalem. During the celebration the returnees made booths, "kept the festival [חג] seven days," and concluded with a solemn assembly on the eighth day.

---

6. See also the expressions "temple of Y<small>HWH</small>" (2 Chr 26:16; 27:2; 29:16), "sanctuary of Y<small>HWH</small>" (1 Chr 22:19; 2 Chr 30:8), and "his [Y<small>HWH</small>'s] dwelling place" (2 Chr 36:15). See Japhet 1989:69–71.

By confining the celebration of both Passover and Booths to Jerusalem, the texts emphasize worship in Jerusalem. This is in contrast to the purpose given for other celebrations of these festivals: in 2 Chr 30:1–27 they were intended to appease Yʜᴡʜ ("come to his sanctuary ... and the fierceness of his anger will turn from you," 30:8), and in Deuteronomy they are to remind the community of how Yʜᴡʜ brought the people out of Egypt at night and how they left in haste (Deut 16:1–8). In contrast to the venerable tradition of celebrating Passover in the home (Exod 12:1–20; Num 9), Ezra maintains the Deuteronomistic centralization program (Deut 16:1–8) and locates the festival in Jerusalem. If one wanted to keep Passover, at least according to Ezra, one had to travel to Jerusalem.

There is a similar emphasis in the celebration of Booths in both Ezra 3 and Neh 8. In the two accounts, the Jerusalem location for the festival is specified: while the people are still in Jerusalem to set the altar on its foundation in the seventh month ("the seventh month came, and the Israelites were in the towns, the people gathered together in Jerusalem," Ezra 3:1), they subsequently celebrated the Festival of Booths ("and they kept the Festival of Booths [ויעשׂו את־חג הסכות], as prescribed," 3:4). Likewise, the location for the celebration in Neh 8 is Jerusalem: the text specifies that the people gathered branches and made booths for themselves, "each on the roofs of their houses, and in their courts and in the courts of the house of God, and in the square at the Water Gate and in the square at the Gate of Ephraim" (8:16). Although some have argued that these several locations indicate that the festival was celebrated both within Jerusalem and locations outside of the city (Fishbane: 111; Rubenstein: 79–80; W. R. Scott: 116–17, 120), the text allows the interpretation that it was kept by the community that gathered together in Jerusalem. According to Neh 8:17–18, Ezra read the law to the celebrants, a detail that assumes that the whole community was together in one large place. Further, as Michael Duggan (132) points out, the H of בוא in Neh 8:15 and 16 ("'Go ... and bring branches ... to make booths.' ... So the people went out and brought them") suggests that the branches were brought to a central location. Finally, because most of the locations named for the booths are in Jerusalem (the courts of the house of God; the squares at the Water Gate and at the Gate of Ephraim), it is probable that the other two locations (the roofs of their houses and in their courts) also were in Jerusalem. Although the festival ordinances in Exod 23 and 34 (cf. Lev 23:39–43) instruct the people to celebrate the festivals "before Yʜᴡʜ," a centralized sanctuary is not specified (Fishbane: 110). The authors of Ezra and Nehemiah are more clear, and, in keeping with the ordinance in Deut 16:16, they confine both the festivals of Passover and Booths to Jerusalem: in the holy city the returned community reinstitutes the centralized pilgrimages.

The two books also include additional cultic festivals and more secular gatherings. As I have argued elsewhere, the returns to Yehud recounted in Ezra 1–2 and 7–8 may be read as separate pilgrimages to Jerusalem (Knowles: 57–74). Nehemiah 12:27–43 describes the dedication of Jerusalem's wall: after a grand march upon the wall, the assembly "sacrificed … great sacrifices" (זבחים גדולים ... ויזבחו; Neh 12:43), and then the temple responsibilities were established (12:44–47). Besides these pilgrimage and temple feasts, Ezra and Nehemiah refer to other gatherings of the community in Jerusalem. These gatherings show that the city was not only a cultic center but also an assembly place where noncultic concerns could be addressed. In Ezra 10:6–44 all of the people of Judah assembled at Jerusalem within three days of a summons to deal with the marriages with foreigners. To deal with the economic troubles of the Jews, Nehemiah called a great assembly of the people (עליהם קהלה גדוכה; Neh 5:7). Since the people within the city "were few and no houses had been built" (7:4) when Nehemiah "assembled [ואקבצה] the nobles and the officials and the people to be enrolled by genealogy" (Neh 7:5), a gathering of 42,360 people (7:66), it seems most likely that the crowd came from outside Jerusalem. When "all the people" (כל־העם) again assembled in Jerusalem before the Water Gate and asked Ezra to read the law (Neh 8:1–2; but cf. 8:10), it seems likely that they came from outside Jerusalem since the text has just specified that the people had "settled in their towns" (7:73). The people of Israel were again assembled (נאספו בני־ישראל) when those of Israelite descent "separated themselves from all foreigners, and stood and confessed their sins" and pledged fidelity to the law (Neh 9–10).

Ending strategically with Cyrus's declaration ("Let him go up!"; 2 Chr 36:23), the book of Chronicles enjoins the permanent relocation of Yahwists to Jerusalem. Yet pilgrimage to the city is also encouraged throughout the book, most obviously by making it an explicit and commendatory part of the reigns of Hezekiah and Josiah. Similar to the prophets, the author explicitly includes in pilgrimage festivals the people of Israel and Judah and, in one account, the nations as well. For Hezekiah's Passover in 2 Chr 30 (unparalleled in the Kings material), word of the festival in Jerusalem went to "all Israel and Judah," as well as Ephraim and Manasseh (2 Chr 30:1). Although those accepting consisted of only "a few" from Asher, Manasseh, and Zebulun, those who attended included Judahites (30:11–12) and celebrants from Ephraim and Issachar (30:18). The text also notes that the participants included resident aliens (הגרים) from Israel and Judah (30:25). The combined crowd consisted of "many people" (30:13), and the large numbers required that two thousand bulls and seventeen thousand sheep be offered and for the priests to sanctify themselves "in great numbers" (30:24).

In the account of Josiah's Passover festival (greatly expanded from Kings' summary notice; 1 Kgs 23:22–23; 2 Chr 35:1–19), pilgrims also come from both Israel and Judah, although there is no specific notice that the participants included any foreigners. The large number of animals sacrificed (over 41,000), reveals the author's desire to highlight worship at the Jerusalem temple.

The Chronicler also includes an additional religious practice related to pilgrimage, namely, the turning of the body toward the temple when praying in a different locale. Like pilgrimage, the practice emphasizes the singularity of Jerusalem for worship, and, as in the account of pilgrimage in 2 Chr 30, the practice also explicitly includes the possibility of participation by foreigners. When the book of Chronicles reiterates Solomon's prayer at the dedication of the temple, the author retains the thrice-repeated instructions to pray toward the city. First, Solomon refers to a "foreigner … [who] comes [ובא] from a distant land because of your great name … and prays toward this house [אל־הבית הזה]" (1 Kgs 8:41–42 = 2 Chr 6:32–33, where the preposition is changed to על). Then the king speaks of the time when Yhwh's people will go out in battle and "pray to Yhwh, toward the city [אל־יהוה דרך העיר] that you have chosen and the house that I have built for your name" (1 Kgs 8:44 = 2 Chr 6:34). Finally, when Yhwh's people are carried off into captivity, Solomon prays that, when they "pray to you toward their land [אליך דרך ארצם]," Yhwh will forgive them (1 Kgs 8:46–50 = 2 Chr 6:36–39, although the term אליך is missing in 2 Chr 6:38). The directions for the physical orientation of the worshiper include both Jews and Gentiles: the foreigners who are in the land (perhaps in the vicinity of the temple); warriors who have left the city; and the people who have been deported. Similar to the account of Hezekiah's Passover in 2 Chr 30, Solomon's directives for the physical manifestation of Jerusalem in worship is ethnically inclusive.

Although the historical narratives from the Persian period emphasize the holy city through pilgrimage (and, in the case of Chronicles, in the direction of prayer as well), the texts differ somewhat regarding the ethnic identity of the participants. In Ezra and Nehemiah, pilgrimage to Jerusalem includes the restored community only (with Ezra 6:21 a notable exception). Similar to the prophets, however, foreigners are included in the Chronicler's presentation of the practice (2 Chr 30), as well as the related practice of turning the body in prayer (6:32–33). There is a difference in the time frame of the practice as well: the prophets generally construe pilgrimage to Jerusalem primarily in the future, but the historical texts highlights its significance in the present life of the community via the presentation of pilgrimage in the community's history.

Psalms 120–134

The final textual evidence for pilgrimage to Jerusalem during this time is found in Pss 120–134. This cluster of texts, each of which has the superscription שיר למעלות (שיר המעלות in Ps 121), incorporates several themes that indicate and encourage pilgrimage to Jerusalem. Outside of some rabbinic and patristic interpretations, this collection is usually understood to indicate pilgrimage to Jerusalem. Some early Christian commentators such as Origen of Alexandria and Augustine of Hippo understood the title to refer to the allegorical "ascent" that the believer made to God or Christ (Crow: 4–9). Jewish tractates *Middot* and *Sukkah* interpret the superscription as a liturgical rubric, specifying where or how these psalms were to be sung. Tractate *m. Mid.* 2:5 claims that "[f]ifteen steps led up from within [the court of the Women] to the Court of the Israelites, corresponding to the fifteen Songs of Ascents in the Psalms, and upon them the Levites used to sing."[7] Likewise, *m. Suk.* 5:4 states that "countless Levites [played] on harps, lyres, cymbals and trumpets and instruments of music, on the fifteen steps leading down from the Court of the Israelites to the Court of the Women, corresponding to the Fifteen Songs of Ascents in the Psalms" (Danby: 180). According to Ibn Ezra, the superscription indicated the name of the tune to which the text was sung (noted in Keet: 4–5).

Although some scholars have understood the texts as a sort of cultic-liturgical manual used in chronological order by pilgrims at the various stages of their departure, worship in the temple, and return (Seybold; Mannati), this theory is difficult to apply to the entire collection. Ps 134 is indeed a blessing and might have been used for pilgrims while they were in the temple, yet it is more difficult to consider Ps 128 as the words of greeting that the inhabitants of Zion gave to the newly arrived pilgrims. The connection to pilgrimage in Pss 120–134 is best made via several thematic links that relate to pilgrimage throughout the ancient world (Millard: 209). After a brief discussion about the date of the collection, I will highlight four aspects of pilgrimage in the collection: the call to the shrine; an emphasis on YHWH's geographic connection to Jerusalem; the desire for agricultural and biological fertility; and the pursuit of justice.

With scholars such as Loren Crow and Mattias Millard, I date the collection to the Persian period on the basis of linguistic evidence that suggests a Late Biblical Hebrew (LBH) redaction (see also Hurvitz 1972). Evidence for this redaction includes the phrase למען לא (Ps 125:3),[8] the use of the particle

---

7. This and all following quotes from Mishnaic texts are from Danby 1933.

8. This indicator of negative purpose occurs only in exilic/postexilic texts (Ezek 14:11; 19:9; 25:10; 26:20; Zech 12:7; Ps 119:11, 80), with several semantic equivalents used in earlier texts: פן (Exod 23:33; Judg 7:2); לבלתי (Josh 23:6; Deut 17:12), למען אשר לא (Deut 20:18) and אשר לא (Gen 11:7). It also occurs in later texts outside the Hebrew Bible (Ben

שֶ instead of אֲשֶׁר (Pss 122:3, 4; 123:1, 2, 6; 129:6, 7; and 133:2, 3),[9] the plural and definite form of הַצַּדִּיקִים (Ps 125:3),[10] the noun הַסְּלִיחָה ("forgiveness," in Ps 130:4),[11] and the plene spelling of דויד (Ps 122:5).[12] Several Aramaisms in the collection may also point to a late date, including the ending of צרתה in Ps 120:1 (the Aramaic emphatic state), and the Aramaic style of the term שֵׁנָא ("sleep"), with א substituted for ה in Ps 127:2.[13] Of course, all Aramaisms are not necessarily late, since they may reflect Old Aramaic. Nonetheless, many Aramaisms may suggest a later date, during the time when Aramaic became the *lingua franca* (Hurvitz 1968). In like manner, putative northernisms in the

---

Sira 38:8; 45:26). The expression thus fulfills the three criteria of Hurvitz's list for dating linguistic elements: biblical distribution; linguistic contrast; and extrabiblical sources (Hurvitz 1995). Mark Rooker notes that Hurvitz has suggested that this phrase may appear in an Aramaic text from the seventh-century: עם לבשי שמוני למען לאחרה לתהנם אדצתי (Nerab 2:7–8; Rooker: 172–73). Although this text is similar, the parallel is not exact.

9. While I understand this to be a feature of LBH, it may also under some conditions indicate a northern provenance. According to Eduard Yechezkel Kutscher (§45), this feature is "common in the vernacular of Northern Palestine." As Dobbs-Allsopp points out (17), although the particle occurs 136 times in the Hebrew Bible, it is used in probable northern texts only six times (Judg 5:7, 7; 6:17; 7:12; 8:26; 2 Kgs 6:11). While the particle may not indicate lateness by itself, it can be a sign of lateness, especially when it is present with other grammatical and linguistic features that point to a late date. See also Seow 1996a:660–61.

10. The term exhibits the LBH preference for plural forms of terms that appear in the singular form in earlier texts. Robert Polzin points out this pattern, and as an example he cites גבורי חילים in 1 Chr 7:5, in contrast to גבורי החיל in Josh 1:14 (Polzin: 42–43; see also Dobbs-Allsopp: 14–15). In addition, the term appears with the definite article, a situation paralleled only in Qoh 8:14 and 9:1, as well as Gen 18:24, 28.

11. The term occurs in this form only in Ps 130:4 and two other late texts, Dan 9:9 and Neh 9:17. The adjective "forgiving" (סלח) appears in Ps 86:5.

12. This is an orthographic preference of LBH texts. In the corpus of Samuel-Kings, the name "David" is written 668 times with defective orthography (דוד) and only three times with plene orthography (דויד). The plene orthography is consistently used in Chronicles, Ezra, and Nehemiah, where the name occurs 271 times, all in the plene form (although note that Qoh 1:1 represents the personal name as דוד). In addition, the plene form is consistently used in 1QIsaa and 5Q51 (Rooker: 68–71; Freedman: 89–102; Andersen and Forbes: 4–9).

13. Joüon, I§7b. The other option is taking the verb as a third-א root, as with Dahood ("prosperity, peace"; Dahood 1965–70:3:223–24; cf. 1975:103–5, where he notes the parallels Syriac *šaynā'* "prosperity" and Ethiopic *sene'* "peace"). J. A. Emerton likewise posits a third-א root, with the meaning of "to be, or become high" (Emerton: 25–29, where he gives the text from *b. Šabb.* 10b, אל ישנה אדם בנו בין הבנים, "let no man exalt [show special favor to] one son above his other children." As Crow points out, this meaning is outside the theme of the psalm (67–69).

corpus (such as the use of שׁ in place of אשׁר) may alternatively be considered late markers, since southern Hebrew was probably influenced by northern Hebrew from the exilic period on.[14] Finally, Loren Crow has recognized six repeated formulae that occur throughout the collection that seem to indicate a postexilic redaction that provides cohesiveness and an emphasis on Jerusalem.[15] Of course, identifying LBH linguistic features in this collection does not necessarily indicate that the origin of the entire collection is equally late. Parts of Ps 132 predate the Chronicler, since they are incorporated into Solomon's prayer during the dedication of the temple (2 Chr 6:41–42).[16] Given this mix of linguistic features, it seems that Pss 120–134 (or parts of the texts) predate the later redaction, when a constellation of LBH features was incorporated into some of them. In the Persian period, these different texts were gathered, edited, and grouped together via repeated formulae and a matching superscription.

The Persian-period edition of the collection contains four aspects that can be related to pilgrimage. The first is the formulaic call to make a pilgrimage, consisting of the designation of the shrine and a verb of travel in the cohortative and/or imperative plural form. Such a call is scattered throughout the collection.[17] The first verse of Ps 122 reads, "I rejoiced when they said to me,

---

14. So Gary A. Rendsburg, although he does argue that there are northern elements in Pss 132 and 133, specifically the divine epithet אביר יעקב (Ps 132:2, 5), the feminine singular nominal ending on שׁנת (Ps 132:4), and a feminine singular noun with a plural ending: עדתי (Ps 132:12). In addition, Rendsburg's identification of northern elements in Ps 133 include נעים (Pss 133:1), מדותיו (Ps 133:2), a reduplicatory plural form, הררי (Ps 133:3), and the use of the particle שׁ instead of אשׁר (Ps 133:2, 3). (Rendsburg: 83–93; cf. Seow 1993).

15. The repeated formulae are: עשׂה שׁמים וארץ (121:2; 124:8; 134:3); מעתה ועד־עולם (121:8; 125:2; 131:3); יאמר־נא ישׂראל (124:1; 129:1); שׁלום על־ישׂראל (125:5; 128:6; 133:3, according to 11QPsª); יברכך יהוה מציון (128:5; 134:3); יחל ישׂראל אל־יהוה (130:7; 131:3). Crow notes that all of these phrases occur at least twice in the collection, and several appear rarely or never in the rest of the Hebrew Bible. See Crow: 129–58.

16. Other indicators of antiquity (or archaistic style) include phrases similar to Ugaritic expressions such as מעתה ועד־עולם ("for now and forever" in Pss 121:8; 125:2; 131:3)—see Aqhat 19.154 (repeated in Aqhat 19.161–62): ʿnt.brh.pʿlmh.h / ʿnt.pdr[.dr] ("Be a fugitive now and evermore / Now and to all gen[erations]"; CML, 119). Similarly, עשׂה שׁמים וארץ ("maker of heaven and earth," in Pss 124:8; 134:3) may be related to an Ugaritic expression. (Habel; followed by Crow: 42, 137–38).

17. Outside the Psalter, other calls to go on pilgrimage are found in 1 Sam 11:14, when Samuel says to the people, "Come, let us go to Gilgal [לכו ונלכה הגלגל], and we will renew there the kingship"; Isa 2:3, when the prophet sees a future time in which "many people will come and say, 'Come, let us go to the mountain of YHWH' [לכו ונעלה אל־הר־יהוה]"; and Jer 31:6, where sentinels call in Ephraim, "Arise, let us go to Zion [קומו ונעלה ציון], to YHWH our God." A related "call to worship" in the collection of Pss 120–134 closes the

'We will go to the house of YHWH!' [בית יהוה נלך]." The joy that the psalmist experienced upon hearing the call in 122:1 (שמחתי) echoes the festival legislation in Deut 16, where the people are commanded to "rejoice" (ושמחת) during the festival of Succoth (Deut 16:14). Similarly, Ps 132:7 reads, "let us enter into [God's] dwellings [נבואה למשכנותיו], let us worship toward the footstool of [his] feet."

The second aspect of pilgrimage is the claim for the unique geographic connection between Jerusalem and YHWH. This is emphasized in the texts in several ways, primarily by claiming simply that YHWH lives in the city. Like the narrative and prophetic texts, the temple is designated as the "house of YHWH" in Pss 122:1, 9 and 134:1. In addition, Ps 132 relates David's quest to provide a dwelling place for YHWH in Zion (132:1–5) and YHWH's own election of the city as a dwelling (132:13–14). The city is directly called the place where YHWH dwells: it is the deity's "place" (מקום, 132:5), YHWH's "dwelling place" (משכן, 132:5, 7), "resting place" (מנוח, 132:8, 14), and "habitation" (מושב, 132:13). The terms usually occur with a possessive suffix to indicate YHWH's possession or ownership of the place (third masculine singular in 132:7, 13 [with the preposition לו in 132:13], second masculine singular in 132:8, first common singular in 132:14 [significantly, in a direct quote by YHWH]). This theme is also picked up in Ps 122, a text that begins and ends by referring to Jerusalem as "the house of YHWH" (בית יהוה in 122:1; אלהינו בית יהוה in 122:9). This phrase, "house of YHWH," also occurs in Ps 134:1 in connection with the Zion sanctuary.

The emanation of YHWH's blessing "from Zion" (Pss 128:5; 134:3) also ties YHWH's presence to the city geographically. A similar thought is expressed in Ps 133:3, which asserts that on the mountains of Zion YHWH "ordained his blessing" (שם צוה יהוה את־הברכה).

This geographic connection of YHWH with Jerusalem is further emphasized in Ps 122 with the assertion that YHWH built the city. Verse 3 is a crux, with scholars translating that the city is well-built (de Wette: 599), compact (Perowne; Seybold), or bound firmly together (NRSV). With Rick Roy Marrs (44 n. 3), I contend that the term הבנויה may have been misread from an original בונה יה (note that the divine name יה also appears in Ps 122:4a; 130:3a). Verse 3a could be restored thus: ירושלם בונה יה "Jerusalem—her builder [is] Yah." See also Ps 147:2, where YHWH is the builder (בנה) of Jerusalem.

For all the stress that the collection places on YHWH's relation to Zion, such geographic specificity does not preclude YHWH's protection and care

---

collection: "Come, bless YHWH, all you servants of YHWH, who stand by night in the house of YHWH" (Ps 134:1–2).

of those outside the city walls. Amidst the alignment of Yʜwʜ with Jerusalem in the texts is a theme of the dissemination of the presence of the Lord. Yʜwʜ, who is enthroned in the heavens (Ps 123:1), is able to hear cries from the depths (130:1) and from those who are residing as aliens in the foreign territories of Meshech and Kedar (120:1, 5). Yʜwʜ's presence is ubiquitous: Yʜwʜ is the shade at one's right hand (121:5) and the keeper of one's going out and coming in (121:8).

The emphasis on Yʜwʜ's presence in Jerusalem is not a static or confining concept; Yʜwʜ transcends this connection and can be present outside of the city. This placement of Yʜwʜ within Jerusalem—a placement that nevertheless does not bind the divine presence to a single locale—is, of course, quite relevant to those who are on the pilgrim way and still outside the holy precincts.

In addition to the call to the shrine and an emphasis on Yʜwʜ's geographic relation to Jerusalem, the third aspect of pilgrimage in Pss 120–134 is the pursuit of justice. In the ancient world, pilgrimages were sometimes undertaken as a way to pursue justice, since centralizing the legal system to the environs of a main cult center was not unusual. There is evidence for this in association with Inanna and her temple,[18] as well as Jerusalem (Deut 17:8–9; 2 Chr 19:8–11; cf. Isa 2:3–4).[19] This same theme of judgment appears in Pss

---

18. In a Neo-Sumerian hymn to Inanna, the goddess and her house are associated with justice: "(The assembled people) come to her with…, they bring their matters before her, / Then she knows the matter, she recognizes evil, / She renders an evil judgement to the evil, she destroys the wicked, /She looks favorably upon the just, she determines a good fate for them" (translation in Reisman, lines 116–19).

19. The text records that in earlier times difficult legal cases were brought "before God" (Exod 22:9; cf. 18:15–16; 33:7), that is, to Moses or local judges. With the program of centralization, the cases were then brought to Jerusalem (אל־המקום אשר יבחר יהוה אלהיך בו) where they would be decided by the Levitical priests and the current judge (Deut 17:8–9). In the account of Jehoshaphat's reforms in 2 Chr 19, the king appointed a seat in Jerusalem for the Levites, priests, and heads of families of Israel for the judging of cases that came from the towns. Notice also that Isaiah of Jerusalem associated Jerusalem with justice in his picture of the time when people from all nations would desire to go to Jerusalem ("Come, let us go to the mountain of Yʜwʜ") so that they might be taught by Yʜwʜ. Further, in his prophecies he claims that "the law will go out from Zion, and the oracle of Yʜwʜ from Jerusalem. He will judge (שפט) over the nations and adjudicate (הוכיח) between many peoples" (Isa 2:3–4).

The tradition continued into the days of Josephus. In *Ant.* 4.218 Josephus represents Deut 17:8–9 as follows: "But if the judges do not understand how they should give judgment about the things that have been laid before them—and many such things happen to people—let them send the case up untouched to the holy city (ἀκέραιον ἀναπεμπέτωσαν τὴν δίκην εἰς τὴν ἱερὰν πόλιν), and when the chief priest and the prophet and the

120–134 as a reason for pilgrimage. In Ps 122:5 the causal כי (Dahood 1965–70:3:206; Crow: 44–45) highlights the journey of "the tribes," who went up to Jerusalem and praised Yʜᴡʜ because "the thrones of justice, the thrones of the house of David [למשפט כסאות לבית דויד]" were set up in Jerusalem (שמה). The question remains as to whether this image would make sense in Persian-era Yehud. Would pilgrims have come to Jerusalem to stand before these "thrones of justice"? Some, such as Keet and Crow, claim that 122:5 refers to a distant memory. Keet (36) claims that the Psalmist remembers preexilic Jerusalem "as a centre of justice." Similarly, Crow (47) considers the reference to the Davidic throne and "tribes of Yah" to have a "nostalgic flavor." According to Herbert Donner (86–89), 122:5 refers to "memorial places in the Temple area," where pilgrims would be guided by "local guides [who] showed them all objects of interest in Jerusalem," including the place where "thrones for judgment were placed ... in former times." In contrast to these scholars, I suggest that, since the reference to visiting Jerusalem on account of the "thrones of justice" does not specify that this refers only to past memories, it is best not to overinterpret the text.

In the Persian period, the city still functioned as a place for justice: Ezra is recorded as teaching the decrees and the judgments (משפט) in Israel (Ezra 7:10). Further, in Zech 8:16 Yʜᴡʜ promises to instruct Jerusalem to "render true and just judgments in your courts." Additionally, the term כסא was still a live metaphor to describe political power during the Persian era (Neh 3:7; Hag 2:22, 20; Zech 6:13). Thus there is evidence that the terminology of thrones was still alive and that Jerusalem continued to function as a place for justice during the Persian period.

The final theme of pilgrimage in the collection is the emphasis on fertility, something prayed for at temples throughout the ancient world. At Delphi, Kreousa is asked whether her journey to the holy site concerns "crops or children" (Dillon: 87), and such matters are related to cult centers throughout the literature of the ancient Near East, including the Hebrew Bible. In Aqhat, Dan'il pursues biological fertility by going and sleeping in a temple, after which the gods gave him a son (KTU 1.17.1.1–2.46). Other examples of visitations to a temple to cure infertility include the Hittite tradition in which male impotence is cured when a man sacrifices to a goddess and sleeps on the clothes worn during the sacrificial offering on a bed before the sacrificial altar. During his sleep, the goddess and the man have intercourse, and his dilemma

---

senate (γερουσία) have come together (συνελθόντες), and let them give judgment as to what seems fit" (translation in Pearce: 32). While the precise identity of the high court (γερουσία) and its relation to the Mosaic model of justice is a matter of debate, it is significant that Josephus's model assumes that Jerusalem was still the center of justice.

is solved (KUB 7.5 [with joins] col iv, 1-10; CTH 406). In addition, a Sumerian hymn to Nisiba claims that the goddess grants sons and that no house or city can be built without her doing (Falkenstein and von Soden: 66–67). There are many other examples of the divine cure of infertility and sickness within a sanctuary in the ancient world (Meir; Ackerman). In the Hebrew Bible, Hannah, once she was at the Shiloh temple, prayed to Yнwн that she be given a son (1 Sam 1:9–18). For the connection of agricultural fertility with the temple, see Zech 14:17, which records the belief that the amount of the fall rains will depend on whether or not the nations make a pilgrimage to Jerusalem. Note also Ezek 47, in which the prophet was shown a river that flows out from the temple, desalinizing the Dead Sea and making fish abundant (47:9).

In ways appropriate for pilgrimage texts, the theme of fertility is forcefully asserted in Pss 126, 127, and 128. In the first text, it is the fecundity of the land that is primarily in view with the request that Yнwн enact prosperity in the land just as Yнwн had done previously. The request is articulated via strategic repetition: the text begins with the historical remembrance בשוב יהוה את־שיבת ציון ("When Yнwн restored the fortunes of Zion..."). Then, after conveying what the effects of this "restoration" were ("our mouth was filled with laughter"),[20] the text uses a similar phrase to demand that the restoration continue: שובה יהוה את־שבותנו ("Restore, Yнwн, our fortunes"). Although some scholars have argued that the phrase שוב ... שבות refers to the specific return from captivity in Babylonia (Kraus: 449; Beyerlin: 8–9), and although the phrase can designate the return of property,[21] it is also used to denote agricultural abundance and fertility in texts such as Amos 9:14; Ps

---

20. The text also compares the community to חלמים after Yнwн "restored" their "fortunes." The translation of the term is difficult. Ancient versions understood the root of חלם as "be healed"; so LXX ὡς παρακεκλημένοι ("like those comforted"; cf. the Vulgate translation, *consolati*), Targum היך מדעיא דאיתסיים ("like sick ones who become healthy"). Although this sense is conceivable in a text that highlights reversal (sorrow changes to joy, tears become laughter), the term is translated by most today as "dreamers." Thus Briggs and Briggs: 455; Beyerlin; and Starbuck. I would repeat the comment of Crow (62): "the most that can be said is that in some way the word serves to indicate the joy felt by the community at God's restoration of fertility at some point in the past."

21. A line from the Sefire texts records how the territory of Tal'ayim came to belong to another through the agency of the gods, but "now, however, (the) gods have brought about the return (השבו אלהן שיבת) of my [father's ho]use [and] my father's [house has grown great] and Tal'ayim has returned (ושבת) to [PN] ... and to his offspring forever" (stela III.24–25; Dupont-Sommer and Starcky: 128, 132; Fitzmyer: 140–41, 160–61, pls. XIII, XVII). Note also the Mesha Stela lines 8–9, in which Kemosh restored property (יש[בה כמש]; P. D. Miller 1969:461–64).

85:2 (Eng. 85:1); and Jer 32:44. In Amos 9:14, Yʜᴡʜ's promise to "restore
the fortunes" of Israel occurs within a picture of a coming time when "the
mountains will drip sweet wine" and the Israelites will rebuild their cities,
plant vineyards and gardens, and consume the produce. Likewise, Ps 85:2,
draws a parallel between the time when Yʜᴡʜ "restored the fortunes of Jacob
[שבת שבות יעקב]" and when "Yʜᴡʜ was favorable to [the] land" (note that
Delitzsch [3:9–12] understands Ps 85:2–3 as referring to postexilic restoration
to the land). The text closes with a view to the future full of agricultural rich-
ness: "Yʜᴡʜ will give us what is good, and our land will yield its increase" (Ps
85:13 [85:12]). The use of שוב ... שבות to convey returned prosperity to the
land is also found in Jer 32:44. Although the restoration of refugees may be a
satisfying (re)application of the psalm, agricultural prosperity and restoration
certainly pertain to this text.

Psalm 126 is rich with agricultural images: it compares Yʜᴡʜ's coming
restoration to the wadis in the desert (Glueck: 92–94), pleads for those
who plant and reap, and ends by mentioning seed-bags and the carrying of
sheaves. While the restoration of refugees may be a satisfying (re)application
of the psalm, agricultural prosperity and restoration certainly pertain to this
text. Crow (61 n. 47) likewise argues that Ps 126 relates to agricultural fertility. He understands that the text was used in a time of "agricultural failure,"
in a time when the people hoped for "renewed agricultural prosperity" (cf.
Mowinckel: 1:223).

Psalm 128 also picks up this theme of agricultural fertility when it
promises that walking in the way of Yʜᴡʜ results in eating "the fruit of the
labor of your hands" (128:2). In addition, Pss 127 and 128 understand biological fertility as a gift from Yʜᴡʜ. Psalm 127 links Yʜᴡʜ's "building the
house" (יבנה בית) with the appearance of children and characterizes sons as
a "heritage" of Yʜᴡʜ (נחלת יהוה; 127:3). The final verse declares that special
blessings (אשרי) are upon the man whose "quiver" (אשפתו) is full of sons
(127:5). The theme of biological fertility continues in Ps 128, where verse 3
reads, "Your wife will be like a fruitful vine [גפן] within the 'private parts' of
your house."[22]

By accentuating themes that are commonly associated with pilgrimage
such as fertility and also justice and the relation of the deity with the pilgrimage site, Pss 120–134 are well-suited as pilgrimage texts. Although it is

---

22. This translation, which intends to convey the double entendre of the term ירכתים
(corners and inner thigh), comes from Crow (71–73). Crow cites Grossberg (43–44), who
relates "in the innermost parts of your house" to the concept of fruitfulness.

difficult, if not impossible, to recover whether or not they were recited at specific moments on the way, they are appropriate companions on the journey.

Conclusion

Pilgrimage is present throughout the various genres of biblical texts from the Persian period, and accounts of the practice reveal different concerns and emphases. In the prophets, pilgrimage is future-oriented and involves the community as well as the nations and their enriching wealth. In the historical narratives, pilgrimage is presented as a contemporary practice of the community (or, in the case of Chronicles, a practice from the past that has contemporary relevance), and the nations cease to be noticeably involved. The divergences between the prophets and the historical narratives are barely detectable in Pss 120-134, however, because the collection does not describe the practice of pilgrimage as much as it reflects the concerns that pilgrims manifest.

Although the textual notices of pilgrimage to Jerusalem reflect the different constructions of the authors, is it possible to determine to what extent pilgrimage was practiced by the community? That is, do the textual notices of pilgrimage reflect a vibrant pilgrimage cult, or do they reflect the wishes of the authors that Jerusalem be restored as the center of worship? According to archaeological excavation, settlement in Jerusalem was scant, limited only to the City of David (Avigad; De Groot and Ariel: 98 and figs. 28–29; Ariel, Hirschfeld, and Savir: 59–62; Shiloh: 7–9, 14, 20, 29). The archaeological record seems to confirm Neh 7:4, which specifies that the inhabitants in Jerusalem were few. Given this situation, the text's emphasis on the importance of Jerusalem via the practice of pilgrimage may have been more influenced by desire than by lived reality. According to this reading, the emphasis on pilgrimage outlined above would only represent such desire and should not be taken as factually representative.

This is not the only possible model of interpretation, however, since the significance of a cult center is not necessarily dependent on the size of its surrounding city. One might be able to disassociate the significance of a cult center from the size of its surrounding city, so that a small Jerusalem could nevertheless be the destination of a fairly large pilgrimage cult. It is indeed true that some ancient cultic centers were within thriving cities, including the cult of Jupiter in Rome and the Akropolis in Athens, which had been the site of cult and habitation since 1600 B.C.E. (Zaidman and Pantel: 97–100; Polignac). Other cult centers, however, were in uninhabited areas with few full-time residents connected to the sanctuary and whose influence and catchment-area exceeds the limits of any one population center. Cultic sites such as the oracular shrine at Delphi, the cult of Zeus at Olympia, and the shrine to Fortuna at Prinesti are examples of sacred areas that were remote from population sites and that nevertheless were frequently visited. Thus, a religious area can still be a popular pilgrimage site even if there is little evidence of related settlement.

The biblical emphasis on Jerusalem in light of the archaeological evidence for a small city is thus open to two models of interpretation: wish or reality. If it is wish, then the emphasis on pilgrimage in the Persian period is a means to encourage the faithful (including in some cases also the nations) to visit regularly and perhaps even settle in the holy center. If it is reality, then the faithful have physically placed Jerusalem at the geographic center of their religion, a placement that is borne out by their regular journeys (but not their domiciles).

Intertextuality in the Persian Period

Richard Bautch

To indicate the manner and degree to which intertextuality has entered Persian-period studies, we require a definition of the term that is sufficiently generic and straightforward. "Intertextuality is reading two or more texts together and in light of each other.... Intertextuality is not a staged process in which one first proves the parallels and then assesses the impact" (Miscall: 247). By this definition, intertextuality is a matter of texts, later texts, and the scholarly perception of a connection between them. As such intertextual studies have blossomed, many of them bring new insight into Persian-period texts.

To state that intertextuality is the connection between texts does not explain everything of how those texts relate, and the explanations of how texts connect have been various. Miscall's view that the connection between the texts is no "proven parallel" distinguishes intertextuality from traditional biblical scholarship and its efforts to establish literary dependency between texts. In the words of Jonathan Culler, "The study of intertextuality is thus not the investigation of sources and influences as traditionally conceived" (103). Patricia Tull expresses the distinction constructively: "Intertextuality is more an angle of vision on textual production and reception than an exegetical methodology, more an insight than an ideology" (2000:83) Tull likens intertextuality to insight, and it is noteworthy that she distinguishes this type of insight from ideology but not from literary theory. Theory-driven insight and intertextuality are increasingly synonymous in biblical studies, as witnessed by the diverse work of scholars such as Tull and James Charlesworth. Tull explores Isa 49–55, an exilic text, by way of Mikhail Bakhtin's dialogical concepts (Willey 1997: 2–3). Charlesworth reacts to Julia Kristeva's theory of intertextuality in setting up his analysis of another exilic text, Isa 40:3, and a text from the Hellenistic period, 1QS, the community rule of Qumran (Charlesworth: 203–4). Between the exilic and Hellenistic periods is the Persian period, whose texts are increasingly being read in terms of their intertextual dimensions.

However, the Persian period has not been dominant in the collections of intertextual studies by biblical scholars; in many ways, Persian-period texts remain underrepresented (Fewell 1992; Aichele and Phillips 1995; Marguerat and Curtis 2000). There is as yet no systematic investigation of Persian-period intertextuality, and intertextual studies that touch on the Persian period have done so with a wide variety of theoretical approaches and interests. This essay reviews the work of Donald Polaski and Christine Mitchell, who articulate a specific method of intertextuality by which they interpret biblical texts from the Persian period. The work of both scholars is directly informed by the principal theorists of intertextuality, Bakhtin and Kristeva, although not in quite the same way. Also noteworthy is Seth Sykes's article in which he reads postexilic prophets using a strategy based on Bakhtin's intertextuality. Also, I will consider studies of Persian-period literature with less direct links to intertextuality. For example, Jonathan Dyck and Brian Kelly discuss dynamics of intertextuality without forming commitments to intertextuality as a method or appealing to theorists such as Bakhtin and Kristeva. Michael Fishbane's work reflects yet another approach to intertextuality. Fishbane studies determinate textual relations in the Hebrew Bible, and using a theory of the *traditio* and *traditum* he explains instances of literary dependence.

POLASKI: INTERTEXTUAL NEGOTIATIONS IN LATE PROPHETIC TEXTS

Donald Polaski has revised his doctoral dissertation and published it under the title *Authorizing an End: The Isaiah Apocalypse and Intertextuality*. In its broad framework, the book aims to help establish the social and textual conditions that led to the rise of Jewish apocalyptic literature. Polaski focuses on prophecy and challenges the view that late prophecy merely parrots views issued in earlier prophecy. His foil through much of the book is the label of epigone or imitator applied to late prophetic texts that are assumed to be wholly imitative of precursors. Polaski rather suggests that late prophecy could be building upon or negotiating the social power of precursor texts (12). His hypothesis is that the textual authority resident in prophetic texts is not as stable as some have assumed it to be.

To build his case, Polaski engages "a more careful examination" of the nature of the connection between text and culture than that provided by Paul Hanson or Steven Cook (Polaski: 23). Because he finds the analysis of "ideology" to be problematic, Polaski focuses on the "textuality" of proto-apocalypticism (24). He analyzes textuality in terms of "texts" (the construal of a society) and "contexts" (society itself) in an attempt to demonstrate the "creativity" of the proto-apocalypticists, who in his view are not controlled by the authority of earlier texts or of other discursive structures. With these theoretical bearings, Polaski ultimately identifies a priestly group responsible for Isa 24–27 (359). In his analysis, there are hermeneutics of authority in Isa 24–27 because the apocalypse both redeploys earlier texts and controls them (364). His examples include Isa 27:9, which is said to redeploy Deuteronomic texts about a conditional covenant by ascribing them to the order of the universe. Isaiah 27:9 is said also to control texts such as Gen 28:18–22, which narrates the founding of Bethel as a cult site. When references to Jacob "setting stones" are redeployed in Isa 27:9, they become invested with additional, ironic meaning (366). The dual functions of control and redeployment are central to Polaski's use of intertextuality as a reading strategy.

Specifically, Polaski aims to define and delimit the intertextual field by describing how a text such as Isa 24–27 "participates in the textual universe" of the early Second Temple period (46), when there were current certain "rules of [textual] formation" (47). "Rules of formation" is Foucault's concept, here adapted for biblical exegesis, of "invisible" practices by which societies form texts based on power relations. Polaski also draws on the work of "new historicists," who investigate a text's active role in cultural production; the text is said to be a force involved in the material practices of the society that has produced it and other cultural forms (30). Polaski does not find helpful the concepts of author and reader as they are respectively developed by Kristeva (36) and Riffaterre (42).

In Polaski's work, the priestly group said to be responsible for Isa 24–27 is assigned no social location beyond the temple, and Polaski is wary of overstating what can be known about priests in the Persian period (20–21). His efforts at historical reconstruction, rather, focus on authoritative texts and agents of authority in restoration society. To indicate agents who may have been involved in the production of Isa 24–27, Polaski draws parallels between these writers and civic leaders in Yehud such as Ezra and Nehemiah. First, he dates Isa 24–27 to the second half of the fifth century B.C.E., thereby linking the text to the time when Ezra and Nehemiah acted in Yehud as scribe and governor, respectively. Significantly, Polaski interprets texts such Isa 25:10b–12, which indicates God's punitive action in the future, as "providing an enforcement mechanism more severe and more certain than for which Nehemiah could have wished" (197). The future prediction is required for essentially textual reasons, namely "the failure of the [postexilic] discourse's construction of reality to come to fruition." Polaski's intertextual reading of these and other verses in Isa 24–27 sustains an interest in those functions of the text whereby it points to a social and political context that the text has had a part in constructing.

Mitchell: The Chronicler as Intertextualist

Christine Mitchell wrote her dissertation, "The Ideal Ruler as Intertext in
1–2 Chronicles and the *Cyropaedia*," under the supervision of Robert Polzin,
whose three-volume study of the Deuteronomist draws significantly on the
reading strategies of Bakhtin. In her dissertation, Mitchell argues that the
Chronicler employs intertextuality to develop a literary construction of the
ideal ruler. The Chronicler, she holds, establishes criteria of the ideal ruler
through the depiction of David, which contains an intertextual or dialogical
dimension. Specifically, she notes that, although the Chronicler establishes
David's superiority to Saul through an extended contrast (1 Chr 10–12 con-
trasted by 1 Chr 13–16), David's profile as an ideal ruler comes into sharper
focus when read dialogically with 1 Samuel, a digest of Saul's shortcomings
and foibles that David nowhere exhibits (170–89). The dialogic link between 1
Chronicles and 1 Samuel also involves the contrast of David and Ahab; David
purchases the threshing floor of Onan the Jebusite for the site of the temple
in a noble fashion (1 Chr 21), whereas Ahab gains the vineyard of Naboth the
Jezreelite by treachery (1 Sam 21) (180–83).

The Chronicler's David, Mitchell adds, should also be read dialogically
with reference to Cyrus as he is presented in Xenophon's *Cyropaedia*. Both
rulers are idealized in the specific sense that they are endowed with philosophical elements that replace certain flawed elements found in depictions of
other rulers (191). In Mitchell's view, the dialogical contacts between Cyrus
and David reflect the fact that both books belong to the genre of political
philosophy, which is speculative and utopian (192). Mitchell concludes that
an ancient author's use of this particular genre helps to explain the high
degree of intertextuality in his writing, with Chronicles and the *Cyropaedia*
as prime examples.

Mitchell identifies dialogic relationships among texts by means of a complex method that is rooted in intertextuality. She defines intertextuality as "the
interrelationship of texts, including, but not limited to, the absorption, rewriting, reuse and dialogue of text with text." She identifies "the text" as "the work
which absorbs, rewrites or reuses," while "the work that is absorbed, rewritten
or reused" is "the intertext." For Mitchell, intertextuality is "a structured net-
work connecting texts and intertexts that are already associated" (58).

Mitchell's "model of dialogic intertextuality" arises from ancient authors'
writings on writing (Aristotle, Longinus, Demetrius) as well as the work
of twentieth-century theorists such as Kristeva, Riffaterre, Barth and especially Bakhtin and Lotman. Her greatest debt is to Bakhtin, whose theory of
"dialogic" she applies to both the Bible and to Chronicles. The theory of dialogic leads Mitchell to assert that Chronicles is a "composite text" with many

speech types (48) that overlap in the manner of "heteroglossia," Bakhtin's concept of language that is polyphonic due to factors such as class and geography (49). The variety of speech types, Mitchell adds, is minimized if the Chronicler's "speech plan" exerts "tight authorial control over the heteroglossia." Thus Mitchell employs Bakhtin to posit Chronicles as a dialogic work whose "basic intent and message" situates it in "one literary position" (48). It is a wonder that Bakhtin himself did not notice such striking continuities between his theories and the books of Chronicles, and Mitchell is not the first biblical scholar to "stretch" Bakhtin's views to render them serviceable in the study of biblical texts (Green 25, 186–87).

As a scholar who practices intertextuality, Mitchell identifies with the designation "traditionalist," indicating conventional literary theorists who apply aspects of intertextuality when they interpret texts (Mitchell: 24). By this definition, traditionalists are different from scholars who take a philosophical or semiotic approach to intertextuality, and traditionalists *selectively* draw on the work of theorists (Plett: 4). For example, traditionalists do not develop the revolutionary potential in theorists' work. Although Mitchell's method contains a greater degree of theoretical background than is typical of traditionalists, on the whole her identification with the traditionalists is accurate.

Mitchell's sensitivity to intertextuality leads her to identify, as would a traditional literary critic, certain "tensions" (37, 58), "ironies" (9), and even readerly "pleasures" within a work. Through intertextuality, she asserts, the "illustration" of David's fitness to rule "is even more pointed." Mitchell's reading of the biblical and classical texts echoes the New Critics whose insights reflect a deep appreciation of literature at the level of content and form.

At points Mitchell's focus on intertextuality leads her to interpretations that are essentially postmodern. Her contrast of David and Ahab invokes the language of structuralism: Ahab is the "archetypal" evil king, and he is distinguished from David through "a series of oppositions." Mitchell views the two leaders as would a structuralist critic focusing on binary oppositions embedded in the texts. Elsewhere she describes the ideal ruler in later literature, such as Chronicles and the *Cyropaedia*, as "constructed" from earlier texts (5). Mitchell here implies that certain texts may be deconstructed. Although she holds that the construction was done in a conscious manner, she concurs with John Frow that "the text's relationship to discursive authority may not reflect authorial intention." What does it reflect? Mitchell appears to recognize in texts an element of discourse that hides the systematic rules of its formation and its concrete affiliations with power (Said 1982: 216). Mitchell's clearest interaction with deconstruction occurs in her reading of Kristeva. She reports that Kristeva's model of intertextuality involves the destruction of texts, and Mitchell makes it clear that she does not adopt this element of the model. Mitchell recognizes the interpretive potential of deconstruction and other postmodern theories, but her intertextual work with Chronicles and the *Cyropaedia* centers on the modes of meaning that traditional literary critics would identify in these texts.

SYKES: BAKHTINIAN TOOLS TO STUDY THE POSTEXILIC PROPHETS

Seth Sykes bases his study of form in Haggai–Zech 8 upon concepts drawn from the literary theory of Bakhtin. Sykes adopts Bakhtin's understanding of genre as a type of utterance that is relatively stable, thematic, compositional, and stylistic (99). Citing Bakhtinian scholars, Sykes indicates that genre involves both form and ideology but is reducible to neither of these two (100). The fact that a genre provides a certain literary representation of space and time has led Bakhtin to speak of the chronotope. The chronotope is the spatial and textual context that a genre supplies for the occurrence of actions and events. Sykes adopts Bakhtin's concept of the chronotope in the following manner: created by "the synergy of form and content," the chronotope makes possible an analysis of Haggai–Zech 8 in terms of both its chronistic form and its prophetic content (103).

Sykes argues that the particular chronotope of Haggai–Zech 8 is comparable to a generic chronotope that is found in both the Babylonian chronicles and the text that served as the Deuteronomist's source for the books 1–2 Kings (108–10). Sykes claims that Haggai–Zech 8 is a "prophetic parody" of earlier chronicles; whereas the chronicles imply that a human king safeguards a capital city and keeps it prosperous, Haggai–Zech 8 indicates that the well-being of Jerusalem is dependent upon God and obedience to God's word. According to Sykes, the biblical text disputes the succession of kings, but it does privilege Haggai and Zechariah themselves as successors of the preexilic prophets (116). In short, Haggai–Zech 8 are said to contain "a theological critique of the ideological world view contained in the chronicles" (111).

If Haggai–Zech 8 critiques non-Yahwistic views of a human king, it does so in an extremely subtle manner that Sykes does not explicate. The alleged substitution of royal succession with prophetic succession is equally difficult to discern. In general, the dialogical dimension between Haggai–Zech 8 and the chronicles is not made evident, and as a result Sykes's claim that the former critiques the latter is not persuasive. Rather, parallels in literary structure are demonstrated, often with insight into form-critical issues. The article is a literary investigation that is inspired by Bakhtin and theory. Sykes's thesis, however, that Haggai–Zech 8 challenges a monarchic view of power, still requires support.

It is perhaps the case that Sykes's use of theory drawn from Bakhtin has clouded matters and kept obscure some important questions. For example, portions of Haggai–Zech 8 are royalist in nature and advocate Zerubbabel for the throne in Jerusalem (Hag 2:20–23; Zech 6:9–15). In dealing with these passages, Sykes identifies the hopes surrounding Zerubbabel as messianic (108), but his doing so is anachronistic. It is difficult to get around the fact that sections of Haggai–Zech 8 are promonarchic. As a result, Haggai–Zech 8 is an unlikely candidate for critiquing monarchy so as to offer the alternative of God as divine monarch over Jerusalem.

DYCK AND KELLY: REDACTION CRITICISM AND THE BOOKS OF CHRONICLES

Contemporary redaction criticism provides an important vista on intertextual study of the books of Chronicles. Before focusing on intertextuality, we must frame the matter in terms of a certain redactional issue. Steven McKenzie's article "The Chronicler as Redactor" surveys redaction critics such as A. Graeme Auld, who proposes that the Deuteronomistic History and Chronicles share a common source that is no longer extant. McKenzie questions the historicity of the source and otherwise critiques Auld on several points (80–87). In a response, Auld asserts that the putative source is no fabrication and may be recognized in both the Deuteronomistic History and Chronicles (Auld: 98). From the perspective of intertextuality, the question of whether the redactor responsible for Chronicles has worked from the Deuteronomistic History and/or a related source is not particularly relevant. In this scenario, rather, what draws the intertextualist's attention is the manner in which one ancient text has served as "intertext" to another.

Especially intriguing is the matter of "trace," defined as that which remains after the relationship between two texts has been obscured through an act of "exclusion, repression or marginalization" performed upon the redacted text (Beal 1992a: 24). Despite this act, the redacted text, "with its own activity as graphic trace," can draw attention to the double that is "outside" of and opposed to it (Kristeva: 53). In biblical studies, one might construe data found in the Deuteronomistic History but excluded in the Chronicler's redaction as traces that call attention to the relationship between the earlier text and its redaction. If the exclusion occurred with intent, such traces raise the prospects of identifying the redactional criteria of the Chronicler and of articulating that criteria in a way that is consistent with contemporary theory.

For an example of how redaction criticism overlaps with intertextuality and the theory of trace, we turn to the work of Jonathan Dyck. In his book *The Theocratic Ideology of the Chronicler*, Dyck employs speech-act theory to delineate the different senses of purpose that an author such as the Chronicler may have. Dyck distinguishes between what the Chronicler said (locution), what he meant or intended thereby (illocution), and what he in fact did by what he said (perlocution) (10–11). The distinctions allow Dyck, in building on work by Gerhard von Rad, to differentiate between the Chronicler's "intentions," which express theological commitment to his central idea or ideas, and "textual meanings and contextual functions," which are elements not "intended" by the Chronicler and thus not central to a reconstruction of his theology (38). Inasmuch as the "textual meanings and contextual functions" are redactional material, Dyck implies, *their potential as traces was never realized, and they remain manifest in the redacted text.*

In a similar manner, Brian Kelly suggests that the Chronicler relays from his sources certain data that are not wholly consistent with Chronistic thought but that do not contradict it outright. The data that the Chronicler includes but does not necessarily endorse are termed "critical indications" (Kelly: 161). Like Dyck's "textual meanings," these "critical indications" represent opportunities for traces that the Chronicler has declined. Kelly's example is Chronicles' account of King Solomon.

It is generally recognized that Chronicles' version of Solomon's reign omits 1 Kgs 1–2, where Solomon has three of his rivals killed and banishes a fourth, and 1 Kgs 11, which concerns Solomon's unfortunate marriages to foreign women. By and large, the Chronicler's redaction of the Solomon material is careful to excise these and other "unpleasant features" from the king's historical legacy (Noth 1987: 92). Kelly, however, points to portions of Chronicles that contain "critical indications" about the king. Solomon's forcing of hard service upon the people of the northern kingdom of Israel is reported in 2 Chr 10:4, 10–11, 14–15. Solomon is thrice associated with a heavy and unjust yoke borne by the people. Why does the Chronicler retain this data? Kelly suggests that "the Chronicler is certainly aware of Solomon's later decline and his share in the division of the kingdom, but he appears more concerned to highlight the king's obedience in the matter of temple-building and Yahweh's covenant of mercy toward his people" (161). Kelly holds that one preeminent virtue, Solomon's obedience, has changed the redactional pattern whereby the king's defects would otherwise be suppressed or traced. Although Kelly is not engaging concepts of intertextuality directly, his discussion is essentially one of traces in Chronicles with attention to special circumstances, such as Solomon's exercise of virtue, that can obviate the grounds to trace.

FISHBANE: SOURCE CRITICISM AND EZRA 9

In the work of Michael Fishbane, the investigation of intertextuality involving texts written in the Persian period and contemporary legal traditions is an extension of pentateuchal source criticism. Fishbane presupposes that Ezra's convocation in Neh 8 reflects established congregational worship in four distinct aspects, one of which is Levitical exegesis of legal traditions (113). The ceremony seems to be based on an established practice, and Fishbane suggests that the service developed during the Babylonian exile. He notes: "Certainly the custom of reading and studying the Torah under levitical guidance would have formed a sound basis for communal worship in the exile, and in the absence of sacrifices and the disinclination (in some circles at least) to recite Psalm liturgies of the Temple service (cf. Ps. 137:1–4)" (113). A proof of sorts is that the Levites in Neh 8:8 have an established exegetical procedure to facilitate worship.

The application of said exegesis is not limited to worship, and it is in this separate realm that Fishbane highlights intertextuality. Torah and its exegesis, he notes, play a role in legitimating policies toward foreigners held by the *golah* community of Ezra and Nehemiah. Ezra 9:1–10:19 comprises a sermon delivered in a liturgical context (9:1–15) and the digest of a subsequent town meeting (10:1–19) that concludes by banning intermarriage. In advocating divorce from foreign spouses, Fishbane notes, the author of Ezra 9:1–10:19 faces a challenge. There is no clear precedent in the Torah for the expulsion of foreign wives and their children, the action proposed and ratified in 10:3–5 (115). The Torah and indeed the Hebrew Bible appear both to tolerate intermarriage (Gen 41:45; Num 12:1–8; Ruth 1:4; 2 Sam 3:3) and to sanction its termination (Gen 21:10–14; Num 25:1–18); there is no unambiguous precedent for what occurs in Ezra 9–10.

To resolve the problem, Fishbane explains, the author turns to Deut 7:1–3 and exegetes the verses so as to generate a legal argument (116). The verses state that with the taking of the land, the Israelites are not to intermarry or otherwise make covenant with the seven nations whom God has dispossessed on their behalf. The prohibition of intermarriage is itself no warrant for the forced divorce of foreign spouses, but it may become so through exegesis.

The instruction of Deut 7:1–3 is recalled several times in Ezra and Nehemiah (Ezra 9:1, 11–12; Neh 13:25). One of these cases, Fishbane holds, displays the acumen of the author in question. In Ezra 9:1, four of the groups with whom Israelites may not marry (Deut 7:1–3) are listed with two foreign nations barred from entering the assembly of Yahweh (Deut 23:3–6) (116). Thus, the later sanction, exclusion, is applied to the earlier offense, intermarriage with people of the land. So that Ezra's community may fully accept the new formulation, additional support is adduced when the collective of foreign peoples (Ezra 9:1) is accused of "abominations" (9:11, 14). The term refers to the Levitical codes against impurity and abominations, which are to be punished by cutting off from the community anyone whom the land itself has not first expelled (Lev 18:26–29). Fishbane concludes that Ezra addresses the problem of precedent with "an intentional exegetical attempt to extend older pentateuchal provisions to new times" (116).

Elsewhere Fishbane provides a theoretical model that further clarifies not only his reading of the exegetical dimensions in texts such as Ezra 9 but also his understanding of intertextuality. Such exegesis starts with a received text (*traditum*) whose authority is recognized. The authority, however, requires a degree of interpretation and reapplication if it is to remain viable. Known as *traditio*, the interpretation and reapplication to later circumstances revitalizes the *traditum*, a positive effect. The *traditio*, however, also has the potential to undermine the *traditum*, and as a result Fishbane describes the matter as "paradoxical" (15). In the application of this theory, Fishbane typically understands the later text to confirm the authority of the received text, and the cases in which textual authority is undermined are relatively few.

His theory of *traditum* and *traditio* notwithstanding, Fishbane does not engage contemporary theorists of textuality and intertextuality. This is evident through Fishbane's discussion of innerbiblical exegesis, the phenomenon of ancient groups beginning with received Scripture and generating an interpretation that has also been included in the Bible (7). The Levitical exegesis of legal traditions is one example of innerbiblical exegesis. Other examples include the haggadic exegesis of legal and nonlegal traditions as well as the mantological exegesis of dreams, visions, omens, and oracles. All these practices have left "traces of inner-biblical exegesis within Scripture," Fishbane explains, adding that it is important to identify and analyze these traces (10). Analyzing traces is the essence of intertextuality as it is practiced by Fishbane. Note that Fishbane's "traces" are actual biblical verses, as opposed to "trace," defined earlier as that which remains after the relationship between two texts has been obscured through "exclusion, repression or marginalization" visited upon the redacted text. Fishbane's data may be read directly from the biblical text, and it has been observed that he "leaves less determinate textual relations in the Hebrew Bible to others who are more interested in the dynamics of reading" (Beal 1992a: 22).

CONCLUSION

Our survey of studies in Persian-period intertextuality indicates that several scholars are exploring the intertextual dimensions of texts and bringing forth insights. In some cases these insights are expressed in the concepts of contemporary literary theory; in other cases they may be rearticulated and refined through contemporary theory. Will initiatives of this type will continue? Is it likely that scholars will ask increasingly more questions of intertextuality when studying texts of the Persian period? It is not likely to the degree that intertextuality requires working with concepts that may be considered suspect in the most traditional circles of biblical studies, literary and historical criticism. At the least, these concepts from literary theory or postmodernism will attract arguments from scholars who are antithetical to these schools of thought. For example, the "trace" used in some intertextual analyses may appear to be a figment to colleagues who require that data be read directly from the biblical text. There is an ephemeral quality to concepts such as the trace, and at least some will ask if the intertextualist is not working with data that is not really there or at best advancing an argument from silence.

Challenges may discourage intertextual initiatives in the short run, but in the long run they can also help to incorporate intertextuality further into biblical studies and into investigations of the Persian period. That is to say, the rigorous and responsible incorporation of intertextuality into current modes of criticism will occur as long as biblical scholars work closely with the most determinate data in the text, namely, words and expressions. The best scholars of intertextuality will work as closely with the text as they do with the intertext and with theory. This is the approach of Polaski and Mitchell. Both render exegesis that is meaningful to the general reader as well as the specialist. They demonstrate that theory has its place and as well its limits. Directly or indirectly, theory can be a source of valuable insight, as witnessed by current studies of the Persian period. For this period's scholarship, however, the ultimate roles of theory and of intertextuality in particular are yet to be glimpsed. The coming decades of biblical studies may prove to be quite revealing in this regard.

WHAT MEAN THESE STONES?
INSCRIPTIONS, TEXTUALITY AND POWER
IN PERSIA AND YEHUD*

Donald C. Polaski

It is reasonably clear that, by the end of the Achaemenid period, the residents of Yehud possessed a text, something quite similar to the Torah, which they were coming to understand as authoritative (Grabbe 2001: 113). It remains unclear how this particular text became invested with authority. Recently the notion that the Torah received official authorization from the Persian Empire has enjoyed a revival (Frei). Other scholars, notably Philip Davies, have claimed that "canonizing" is essentially a scribal phenomenon, and, as such, "canonizing" served as a strategy of legitimization of a particular social class: an "immigrant elite" (Davies 1998: 106).

It is not my intent to adjudicate between these views. In fact, these positions both make the rather large assumption that texts are a natural means of encoding authority. But there is no requirement that societies even develop writing, much less view the results of writing as somehow authoritative. In my view, a better way to approach the canonizing dynamic is to ask a different question: Why does *textuality itself* become authoritative in this period and at this place? Why does scribal activity on noneconomic, largely nonadministrative texts become worthy of significant social investment? Whatever else canonizing in early Judaism may have been, it was certainly embedded in the discourse of the Achaemenid period. Examining that discourse, as it generated material social practices, should illuminate some of the social reasons behind the elite of Yehud adopting texts as an authoritative medium.

---

* Earlier versions of this paper were presented to the Social-Scientific Studies of the Second Temple Period Section at the Annual Meeting of the Society of Biblical Literature (Denver, November 2001) and to the Christianity and Judaism in Antiquity Colloquium of the Department of Religious Studies, University of Virginia.

I will use the Behistun Inscription as an entry point into Achaemenid discourse about writing and power. The Behistun relief, cut into a prominent mountain face along a major thoroughfare in what is now western Iran, visually represents Darius standing on top of the would-be king, Smerdis. While other vanquished monarchs file in to acknowledge his power, Darius raises an arm in praise of his god, Ahura Mazda. On panels around this iconography, Darius's account of the successful conquest of his rivals appears, written in Elamite, Babylonian, and Old Persian.[1] These inscriptions claim that Darius ordered the account to be widely distributed throughout the empire; a papyrus copy of the inscription found at Elephantine and two fragments of the inscription found in Babylon confirm this.

The function of the relief is fairly obvious: to persuade at least part of the public of Darius's legitimate claim to the throne, not completely established at the time of its construction. So we could view this text as an expression of royal authority looking to buttress itself, using the portable mode of writing on papyrus as well as the imposing mode of inscription. In that analysis, textuality is authoritative only in a derivative sense: specific texts matter because kings say they do.

The Behistun Inscription, however, is a much more curious event in textuality than that analysis allows. First, the carefully worked inscription is visible, yet not legible, from the base of the cliff. Something is written, but a person either at the base of the cliff (60 m below) or at a closer observation point (20 m below) cannot read it (Schmitt 1991: 17). Second, getting close enough to read the inscription is almost impossible. Darius directed the destruction of all means of access to the inscription after its completion, leaving only a narrow ledge directly under the relief. Darius did so in order to prevent any alteration of the inscription (Schmitt 1991: 22–23).

This frankly odd circumstance can hardly be accidental; the inscription is not a mere afterthought written in too small a "font size." The space for writing was carefully smoothed to provide the best surface possible. There is still evidence of the guiding lines the inscribers used to make sure their lines of text were spaced evenly. Henry Rawlinson, who was the first modern to view the inscription closely, was positively effusive in his praise for the inscribers' care: "for extent, for beauty of execution, for uniformity and correctness, [the inscriptions] are perhaps unequalled in the world" (Rawlinson: 193).

When Darius had the iconography expanded to include a final vanquished monarch, part of the Elamite inscription had to be erased. That

---

1. For the *editio princeps* of the Old Persian version, as well as an English translation and introduction, see Schmitt 1991.

inscription was then "meticulously copied" to another part of the display (Schmitt 1991: 17), and the Old Persian inscription, which seems to be the final one inscribed, represents the first use of Old Persian cuneiform (Gershevitch: 114). It is clear that the inscription itself was of great importance to the project and the project of great importance to the empire. But why would Darius have gone to the trouble of writing an inscription no one could read?

Most scholars do not seem very exercised over this problem, rarely mentioning the inscription's "visible yet illegible" status. Rüdiger Schmitt at least suggests a rationale: "the texts seem to have been intended to impress by their very existence, in an almost magical way" (1991: 19). While an appeal to magic here may be a way of dismissing the question as unanswerable, I want to examine the supposed magic of this text. After all, "magic" does at least give us a clue that we are in a world involving power, display, and obfuscation.

I believe that the Behistun Inscription valorizes copying as an essential social practice, a practice of power. At first this claim would not seem to be obvious, as the relationship between "original" and "copy" here is rather convoluted. Darius probably dictated the "original" text in Old Persian, and scribes immediately translated it into Elamite, as Old Persian script did not yet exist. This Elamite translation was apparently "to be preserved as the model for all later versions" (Schmitt 1990: 302) and was the first inscription placed on the mountainside. After Old Persian script had been developed at Darius's order, an Old Persian version was added to the display. This version was a translation of the Elamite, yet it appears, in Darius's view, to be the standard version. In the Old Persian Behistun Inscription itself, Darius emphasizes that the Old Persian version is "original":

> Proclaims Darius the king: By the favour of Auramazdā this (is) in the form of writing, which I have made, besides in Aryan [Old Persian]. Both on clay tablets and on parchment it has been placed. Besides, I also made the signature; besides, I made the lineage. And it was written down and was read aloud before me. Afterwards I have sent this form of writing everywhere into the countries. The people strove (to use it). (Schmitt 1991: §70)

So the question of the relationship of "original" to "copy" is, in this instance, quite perplexing. There were two "permanent" originals: the Elamite in the Persian archives; and the Old Persian at the cliff at Behistun. But of the two simultaneous existing "originals," the later translated and edited Old Persian "original" seems to have been the authoritative text, the "real" original, the one emphasized as more permanent. The Behistun Inscription foregrounds the utter inviolability of the original as well as its utter unavailability. All we can ever know are copies; all we can ever know is the craft of the scribe. Authoritative textuality means authoritative copying.

But Behistun does not simply represent an exercise in scribal power, of scribes using textual authority as a "magical" device. The utter unavailability of the inscription cuts both ways. A thought experiment will demonstrate this. We can picture a scribe sitting at the base of the mountain on which the Behistun Inscription is written. This scribe lives a few generations after the inscription was completed, and we can imagine him copying (for whatever reason) the Behistun Inscription from a scroll he has in his possession. By this act of recopying a "missing" original, the scribe is showing the authority of copies. But this scribe can also see the text on the mountain and cannot realize that it is the very same text he is currently copying. The knowledge of the content of the illegible text on the mountain has been lost, so the Behistun Inscription is an authoritative yet in a sense uncopyable text. The text is obviously of political import, yet it exists in a realm unreachable even by the scribe.

The Behistun Inscription invites us to look in texts from Yehud for other such complicated events in the history of textuality. In my view, three texts in Joshua stand in some relation to the kind of textuality displayed in the Behistun Inscription: the covenant at Shechem in Josh 24; the controversy with the Transjordanian tribes in Josh 22; and the celebration on Mount Ebal, located in the MT at the end of Josh 8. These texts, which may plausibly be dated to the early Achaemenid period, are typically understood to demonstrate the authority of Deuteronomy. They are thus supposedly part of a discourse that affirms the authority of a particular text, which was itself the core of a forming canon. These texts could easily be seen as an episode in the canonizing process, but, like Behistun, they may disclose a more complicated understanding of textuality.

JOSHUA 24

Joshua 24:1–28 is impossible to date with any certainty. The cultic use of Shechem in this passage is an important crux: Why would the Deuteronomistic Historians include a story that assumed worship outside Jerusalem (cf. Deut 11:29–32; 27:1–26)? Many scholars thus understand the passage as reflecting pre-Deuteronomistic tradition (see the survey of views in Anbar: 7–22). Ernest Nicholson claims that an exilic origin commends itself, since Shechem was known during that period "as a place of pious Yahwistic groups" (1986: 161). John Van Seters suggests that an exilic author (the Yahwist) used Shechem as the setting simply because of its known role in early Israelite history, while intending "to give a new meaning to the sacred stone under the oak in the sanctuary at Shechem" (1984: 152).

In my view, that granting of a new meaning could easily be located in the Achaemenid period. One could read Deut 12 and 27 together to legitimate Samaria/Shechem, but Josh 24 (as well as 8:30–35) casts worship there into the past. In a very real way, Josh 24 buttresses the authority of Deuteronomy in the face of current Samarian practice. Rather than simply say worship in Shechem was illegitimate (the implication of Gen 35:2–4, which has Jacob bury the teraphim in Shechem), Joshua makes Deuteronomy's allowance of it exceptional, conjuring it up as a historiographic note. The implication is that now Yhwh has moved on to Jerusalem, and so should we. Rather than a pre-Deuteronomistic survival, Josh 24 is a post-Deuteronomistic polemic.

Joshua 24 presents the establishment (or reestablishment) of a covenant between Yhwh and Israel at Shechem. Most of the chapter deals with Joshua's claim that the people are incapable of following Yhwh, a sentiment they deny vociferously no less than four times. Only after hearing this fourfold assurance will Joshua "make a covenant" with them, a covenant also described as a "statute and ordinance" (*ḥoq ûmišpāṭ*, 24:25). This covenant making involves writing and rocks:

> Joshua wrote these words in the book of the law of God; and he took a large stone, and set it up there under the oak in the sanctuary of the Lord. Joshua said to all the people, "See, this stone shall be a witness [*lĕʿēdāh*] against us; for it has heard all the words of the Lord that he spoke to us; therefore it shall be a witness [*lĕʿēdāh*] against you, if you deal falsely with your God. (Josh 24:26–27)

This story presents the covenant as a textual event. Joshua writes a statute and ordinance, terms that frequently stand for written covenant agreements in general and Deuteronomy itself in particular. Indeed, "these words" (*haddĕbārîm hāʾelleh*) that Joshua writes nicely echo the beginning of Deuteronomy itself: "these are the words" (*ʾelleh haddĕbārîm*; 1:1). The meaning appears clear: the written object is the official and authoritative record of the agreement, and, one may suppose, it would be stored at the sanctuary.

But these written words vanish once written. Joshua does not place the text in the sanctuary; he sets up a large stone there. It is the blank stone, not the written text, that will serve as an authoritative witness for the covenant participants. The blank stone, as a permanent, public feature, relieves the narrative's oft-repeated anxiety about the people's lack of ability to obey. The rock will serve as a "touchstone" for the people scattered to their inheritances in the next verse. The stone has "heard" the words of Yhwh, in a sense absorbing them. The "words of the Lord" may thus be said to have become a part of the stone. So the blank stone has become an illegible yet visible text, drawing the attention of the reader away from the written yet invisible book.

JOSHUA 22

Joshua 22 also features stones, stones that will make up a controversial altar. The text clearly engages fraught questions of identity and practice outside the land that were important in the Achaemenid period. Anthony F. Campbell and Mark A. O'Brien claim that "there is a strong likelihood that the traditions dealing with the east-of-the-Jordan tribes have been incorporated quite late" and suggest that Ezra's construction of an altar may have served to stimulate "fear of exclusion across the river" (Campbell and O'Brien: 157; cf. Vink: 73–77). While this may be correct, one need not accept the account of Ezra as historically accurate to understand that Josh 22 relates to issues that would naturally arise with the continuation of the Diaspora after 515 B.C.E. Indeed, the eastern "anxiety" may be the creation of a Jerusalem elite anxious to demonstrate its centrality post-515 B.C.E.

The story begins as Joshua dismisses the Transjordanian tribes with a blessing that invokes Moses no less than three times and is fully Deuteronomic in style (22:5). Despite this thorough discussion of obedience to Deuteronomic strictures, the Transjordanian tribes soon stop on their way home and build an altar at the edge of the land, an altar literally "large for seeing" (gādôl lĕmar'eh, 22:10). This action sets off a violent reaction from the other tribes. They claim the building of the altar abandons the belief in only one place of sacrifice (22:19) and thus threatens the whole nation's relationship with YHWH. This would result in divine violence against the whole nation (22:18, 20), so it was expedient to liquidate this threat as soon as possible: "When the people of Israel heard of it [the building of the altar], the whole assembly of the Israelites gathered at Shiloh, to make war against them [the Transjordanian tribes]" (22:12).

The Transjordanian tribes make what seems at first glance an exceptionally odd defense. They assert that they did not build the altar for sacrifice but to be a witness, an 'ēd (22:27, 28, 34) just like the blank stone in Josh 24. The altar would demonstrate their perpetual membership in YHWH's people despite their residence beyond the Jordan. In fact, this new altar even demonstrates their loyalty to the one altar at the cultic center:

> Far be it from us that we should rebel against the LORD, and turn away this day from following the LORD by building an altar for burnt offering, grain offering, or sacrifice, other than the altar of the LORD our God that stands before his tabernacle. (22:29)

The rest of Israel accepts this odd argument, and peace returns.

It is tempting to dismiss, or at least challenge, the Transjordanian tribes' argument as clever excuse-making: "The entire explanation seems contrived and the denials are suspiciously passionate. The explanation itself borders on the implausible" (Hawk: 127). But the story takes their argument seriously and at face value. Altars are the major characters in this story, and the story assumes that the altar at the central cult site is central to national identity. As Richard Nelson puts it, "[This story] must have persuaded generations of readers to hold fast to national unity in spite of geographic separation and the dangers of diverse viewpoints. The unity of Yahweh's people is founded not on geographic proximity, but on shared faith and fidelity in worship" (Nelson 1997: 251). But behind this rhetoric of national unity lies a set of assumptions about copying.

The Transjordanian altar serves its supposed purpose only insofar as it replicates the central altar. It must be seen as a reminder of another altar; perhaps its great size helps here. The Transjordanian tribes claim that they may copy the central or "original" altar in order to prove loyalty to it, thus privileging the original. But this privileged original cannot really be fully copied; the "copied" altar cannot and will not function as an altar. This relationship between the privileged original and the sufficient yet somehow not-quite-complete copy makes perfect sense in a scribal "economy" of circulating texts.

The story of the Transjordanian altar validates the copy only as derivative. The Transjordanians conjure the scene of their descendents demanding a visual inspection, using the imperative of *rā'āh* where *hinnēh* would have served (22:28). That they describe the altar using the same root (*gādôl lĕmar'eh*, 22:10) indicates that the altar was in some sense designed for inspection, built to be seen by future delegations from Jerusalem. In addition, the word for "copy" here is not the common word *mišneh* (see Josh 8:32) but *tabnît*, a word that indicates the pattern, sometimes written, by which something is to be built (see especially 1 Chr 28, where the *tabnît* for the temple is said to represent "writing from the hand of the Lord" [28:19], and 2 Kgs 16:10, where the *tabnît* in question is a pattern for an altar). So the Transjordanian tribes demand the westerners see how well their altar replicates the (written?) pattern of the original, while also seeing that it is not a perfect copy (it never has been used).

With this expectation, the Transjordanian tribes validate copying as essential to national identity. It is, after all, the prospect of future inspection of this copy by people from the central shrine that guarantees the future of the Transjordanian tribes within Israel (22:28). By conjuring up this future inspection, the story also validates those who inspect the copy, those who authorize the copy on behalf of the original. So what looks at first to be a brewing battle over sacred space becomes a quick agreement regarding copyright and fair use.

Joshua 8

The book of Joshua's focus on stones and our present focus on texts come together again in Josh 8:30–35, almost certainly a late, structuring addition to Joshua, a prime spot to mine for an ideology of textuality. The fact that this passage is located in different places in different text traditions indicates it probably came into the book of Joshua as a late (if not indeed the latest) addition. The question remains of the historical origin of the passage before its addition to Joshua. Many scholars rely on the parallels between Joshua and Josiah for assistance here (Nelson 1981: 531–40). Sweeney relies on this parallel to claim that 8:30–35 were the product of a redaction "designed to establish the analogy between Joshua and Josiah" (135). Further, the association of 8:30–35 with the conquest of Ai, located near Bethel, "facilitates critique" of Bethel. Thus 8:30–35 may be seen as an explanation of the fall of the northern kingdom (they disobeyed the commands Yhwh gave them through Joshua) as well as a warning to Josiah: if you observe Torah like Joshua, you will be secured.

But if critique of the northern kingdom, especially its cultic apparatus, was in view, why is 8:30–35 not set at Bethel? I think the echoes and parallels that Sweeney and Nelson discern are real, but they would rather serve to remind an Achaemenid period reader that proper worship at Shechem/Samaria was a failure (after all, 8:30–35 is located in the MT and LXX between two "failures": the sin of Achan and the trickery of the Gibeonites). Hence worship there is sealed in the past and is now inappropriate. In addition, Josiah is echoed in order to echo his destruction of northern sites. The point is not only that Josiah, like Joshua, followed Torah, but that he also (like Joshua) successfully controlled the region. The analogy does not mean that Josh 8:30–35 comes from the Josianic period. The Josiah placed into analogous relation with Joshua is the later, mythologized Josiah: the Torah-observant subjugator of the north, a figure used to discuss present (Achaemenid-era) tensions with Samaria.

This story in Joshua 8 concerns texts. In this relatively brief account of the ceremony on Mount Ebal, we see Joshua following commands "written in the book of the law of Moses" (8:31), and indeed that book is quoted. Joshua then copies the "law of Moses" onto stones, perhaps from a copy he himself had already made: "And there, in the presence of the Israelites, Joshua wrote on the stones a copy of the law of Moses, which he had written" (8:32). Finally, Joshua reads "all the words of this law" (8:34). The story carefully relates that this reading was "according to all that is written in the book of the law" and "there was not a word of all that Moses commanded that Joshua did not read before all the assembly of Israel" (8:34–35). This textual focus leads me to think that, rather than viewing Joshua here as a royal figure leading a covenant renewal, as Nelson has it (Nelson 1981), we should see Joshua here at least as much as a scribe carrying on the work of writing and public reading. Joshua here is as much Ezra as he is Josiah (Vink: 77–80).

Beyond its general focus on texts, this story concerns one text in particular: Deut 27. In that chapter Moses and the elders direct the Israelites to set up large stones on Mount Ebal "on the day that you cross over the Jordan" (27:2). They are then to cover the stones with plaster and "write on them all the words of this law" (27:3). After this, they are to build an altar of unhewn stones and make sacrifices on it. Finally, Israel is to divide, with one half going to Mount Gerizim and one half staying on Mount Ebal, in order to hear the recitation of curses and blessings by the Levites (27:11–14). The parallels here are striking, leading one commentator to claim that in Josh 8 "the nation carefully pauses … to build an altar and read the law at Shechem in obedience to Deuteronomy" (Nelson 1997: 6).

Yet within these parallels lie numerous discrepancies about writing, where the book of Joshua muddies the fairly clear statements of Deuteronomy. There are three main discrepancies between Joshua and Deuteronomy that I wish to address: (1) they differ concerning when the act of writing should occur; (2) they differ concerning where and on what writing should be done; and (3) they differ concerning what should be written.

When Should Writing Occur?

The ceremony in Josh 8 does not take place on the day the people cross the river, as Deut 27 explicitly enjoins. The ceremony in Joshua occurs only after Israel secures the central highlands. Instead, Joshua mentions a different heap of stones erected on the day of the crossing, a heap that is not thought of as an altar (Josh 4). This problem between the texts has long engaged exegetes. 4QJosh[a] places the Mount Ebal story earlier in the narrative of Joshua, making it fulfill the commands of Deuteronomy. Likewise, the Talmud (*b. Sotah* 32a) recounts the Israelites crossing the Jordan and celebrating on Ebal on the same day. However, both MT and LXX locate this story after the first day in the land had long passed.

Given this chronological problem, how are we to understand Joshua's supposed obedience to the authoritative text, Deuteronomy? Joshua violates Deut 27's clear commands. Richard Nelson wishes to describe the Deuteronomistic authors of Joshua as providing in their hero Joshua "a parenetic model, for he himself is scrupulously obeying the very law that he is proclaiming" (1997: 120). But to do so, Nelson must explain the chronology. He does so by introducing an authority other than Deuteronomy:

> Although Deuteronomy commands that the Ebal/Gerizim events happen
> on the very day of the Jordan crossing (Deut 27:2), the pre-deuteronomistic
> structure inherited by the Deuteronomistic History permitted nothing more
> than an erection of stones at that stage in the narrative (chap. 4). (1997:
> 117–18).

So while the Deuteronomistic Historians wished to present Joshua as perfectly obedient to Deuteronomy, modeling their own view of obedience to
that text, a previously existing tradition forced them to present Joshua as literally not fulfilling Deuteronomy.

Nelson simply takes the unresolvable tension between Deut 27 and Josh
8 and displaces it into a chronological sequence. But even that cannot save
the authority of Deuteronomy here. In Nelson's historical argument, it bows
before pre-Deuteronomic traditions. While I am not certain about Nelson's
particular construal of Israelite traditions, I would claim that his analysis
points to the difficulties of assuming certain texts were authoritative at certain times. In my view, the synchronic picture in Josh 8 shows that Joshua's
relationship to the very scroll he will copy is more an active negotiation than
a passive submission.

WHERE SHOULD WRITING BE DONE?

Deuteronomy 27 instructs that stones be erected first, stones on which Israel
will write the law. Only later are they to build an altar, apparently separate
from the stones. Joshua begins by building an altar, only later writing on
stones, and the relationship between the stones and the altar is uncertain:
"they offered on it [the altar] burnt offerings to the Lord, and sacrificed offerings of well-being. And there, in the presence of the Israelites, Joshua wrote
on the stones a copy of the law of Moses" (8:31b–32). So, while Deuteronomy is clear as to where the writing will take place, Joshua leaves the location
unclear: Is the altar written on? Or are the stones like the stones in Deuteronomy? Both options are worth pursuing, as the text remains unclear.

Many scholars claim that the stones here cannot be part of the altar,
solving the difficulty by claiming that the author assumed the details of the
Deuteronomy account would have been common knowledge among his readers: "it is more likely that the writer simply assumed that readers are perfectly
familiar with the cited text and will understand that the stones of v. 32 are
different from the stones of v. 31" (Nelson 1997: 119). But such a move also
points to the insufficiency of the book of Joshua's replication of Deut 27's
command. The narrator here produces an unclear copy, which sets the reader
off in search of an original for a clear verdict.

It appears more likely that Joshua actually writes on the altar. In that case, the altar serves two purposes. First, it actually functions as an altar, unlike the altar built by the Transjordanian tribes. But, second, the altar literally becomes a text, something to be read. So, similar to the Transjordanians' altar, this altar's significance really lies in its being seen, in its being read. And, in fact, it is the reading of this altar that dominates the narration here, rather than sacrifices upon this altar. While in Deut 27 the sacrifices are to be consumed amidst rejoicing, Joshua does not pause to enjoy a meal before passing directly to the main concern: writing.

WHAT SHOULD BE WRITTEN?

While it is not certain what stones Joshua writes on, it is equally unclear what it is that Joshua writes upon them. Deuteronomy is at least consistent: the writing is to include "all the words of this law" (27:3, 8), although one could dispute what text is thereby intended. Joshua writes a copy of the "law of Moses" (8:32) but then reads "all the words of the law," which is immediately qualified as "blessings and curses" (8:34). But the next sentence removes this limitation: "There was not a word of all that Moses commanded that Joshua did not read before all the assembly of Israel" (8:35).

So what did Joshua write and read? Suggestions abound: perhaps the Decalogue; perhaps Deuteronomy; perhaps the 613 mitzvoth from the Torah; perhaps the whole Torah, "all the words" (*m. Sotah* 7:5). This very uncertainty points to the acts of writing and reading being seen as important, so important that the precise content does not matter.

The narration of the scene in Joshua underlines this view and can be made clearer by comparing Joshua's presentation to another account of the reading of the law. In Neh 8 Ezra reads the law for several hours to an attentive crowd. Other scribes offer a translation or explication of this public reading. The account in Nehemiah emphasizes the importance of the people understanding the content of the reading (8:3, 8, 12, 13), but the people also respond to the text as text, rising to their feet when Ezra opens the text (8:5).

Joshua's reading resembles Ezra's: both are public readings of what could be the same text. But unlike Ezra's reading, Joshua's reading is prefaced by Joshua's writing. In front of the gathered people of all Israel, Joshua first writes. In Ezra's case, the scribes keep the people well informed. But here we see "all Israel," almost entirely illiterate, watching Joshua write, with no help in understanding. "All Israel" cannot read and, in fact, will need Joshua to read to them. They cannot read along, apprehending the content of the law, as Joshua slowly copies whatever text he is copying. All they can do is watch the scribe at work, while the text itself is illegible.

Joshua 8:30–35 expresses an ideology of textuality. First, it textualizes the altar, inviting us to understand the location of cultic transaction, the seat of priestly power, and center of national identity as a text, an object in writing. Second, it refers to other texts, but not simply to follow their directions. The story transforms Deuteronomy's commands, problematizing simple notions of the replication of texts and undermining claims for authority of particular texts. Third, it refers to other texts, but with a lack of concern about the texts' precise content. Instead, it focuses on the act of writing itself as decisive.

Conclusion

I believe that the passages from Joshua assert textuality itself as an authoritative social practice. In doing so, they are at home in the Persian context, in which writing was one of many contested points in the circulation of power. As we have seen with the Behistun Inscription, textuality as a social practice not only undergirded scribal pursuits by valorizing copying but also in some sense resisted being absorbed by scribal interests. Behistun also re-presents the person of the emperor as text, making his voice both unalterable and capable of being heard throughout the empire.

We see similar moves in Joshua. Each in its own way, the stories from Joshua show a marked concern for textuality as a practice in some sense separable from the content of the texts under discussion. And the practice of textuality is related positively to concerns over national identity and the proper function of the altar, key themes for the Achaemenid period. The book of Joshua does not ape Persian power; Joshua absorbs and redeploys it, advising unity around not so much a text as textuality itself.

Scholars, Witches, Ideologues, and What the Text Said: Ezra 9–10 and Its Interpretation

David Janzen

Ezra 9–10 narrates the story of the Persian-period community's mandating of a divorce and expulsion of all foreign women from its midst. In his commentary on the book the nineteenth-century scholar Friedrich W. Schultz provided no explanation as to why this community undertook such a drastic action. The presence of foreign women, he wrote, threatened Israel's existence (Schultz: 99). The biblical author surely would have agreed with this assessment. However, Schultz does not go further and attempt to provide a reason for the community's action, to explain why it believed these women to be such a danger. Some readers might hope for more from a commentator, particularly an attempt to explain why such women would have been considered a threat, an attempt to illuminate the rationale behind the action that the text relates. Perhaps we should not be too hard on Schultz, however, for if he is less than forthcoming on this issue it may be because the text of Ezra 9–10 seems equally so. This story of the divorce and expulsion of foreign women from the community's midst appears to give no rationale for the apparent danger lurking in these *personae non gratae*—or at least no rationale immediately obvious to the modern reader. There are, as a result, a number of scholarly attempts to explain the community's action. Three basic types of explanations in particular can be identified: the divorces and expulsion were mandated because (1) the community was attempting to prevent widespread apostasy caused by these foreign women; (2) the community was hoping clearly to define its ethnic identity; and (3) there were economic and/or political factors that would benefit some or all of the community should these women be forced to leave.[1]

---

1. It is only fair to add that some scholars have provided explanations that do not fall neatly into any of these categories and to note that I have taken the liberty of thus demarcating the bounds of the discussion for ease of presentation.

Part of this essay will examine these various explanations and will ask how fully they can account for what is going on in the story of Ezra 9–10. Because the result of this inquiry suggests that not all of the details of the story nor all of the evidence has been accounted for, I will go on to suggest that anthropological theory, notably that of Mary Douglas, can be employed to produce a helpful basis for understanding the community's motivation in expelling the foreign women. Relying on her work and that of the sociologist of religion Richard Fenn, I will argue that an explanation that takes into account the community's social boundaries and contemporary theory on the social creation of witches may prove more helpful in understanding Ezra 9–10 than explanations that rely solely on apostasy, ethnic purity, or *Realpolitik*. A short investigation into the argument of the text itself will be used to provide support for this assertion. Finally, I want to address the notion of ideology as it has been used or not used—at least implicitly—by some of the more recent interpreters of the text. Two questions will be at the forefront here: Did the editor of Ezra 9–10 hide the community's *real* motives for the expulsion of the foreign women behind an ideological veil of piety, and do we employ an appropriate understanding of ideology when we limit the rationale for this expulsion to a social action solely in reasons of economic and political expediency? When it comes to answering these questions, I will argue, anthropological theory can again save the day and point us toward a helpful understanding of ideology and ideological motivation.

So that I do not mislead readers, I should point out as a final introductory comment that I do not pursue the results of the anthropological groundwork that I lay here. That is, having drawn on the work of Douglas and Fenn that suggests that communities with particular types of social boundaries will actively search out witches whom they can then expel or exterminate, I do not go on to demonstrate that the Persian-period community centered around Jerusalem had such boundaries (for a presentation of that argument, see Janzen 2002). Here I wish only to show that scholarly approaches to finding a rationale for the expulsion of the foreign women narrated in Ezra 9–10 do not adequately deal with the explanation provided by the narration itself. The story in question provides an explanation, I will argue, but it is one that has been overlooked by scholarship. Specifically, the text does not charge the women with any crime but regards them as sources of impurity. This is precisely the language that we would expect to hear from communities with the types of social boundaries that sends them looking for witches to kill or expel. In this essay that conclusion is as far as I go before turning to address the importance of various understandings of ideology in scholarly attempts to reproduce a rationale for the expulsion of the women.

1. Scholars

1.1. Apostasy

Few scholars still argue that the divorces and expulsions of Ezra 9–10 resulted from a concern that foreign women were spreading apostasy through the community, but it is a frequent enough claim in commentaries produced until recently. Given the frequent prophetic polemic against foreign worship, it is an understandable place for scholars to turn as they search out a rationale for the community's action. It is also not one without foundation in Ezra 9–10. As noted by Ernst Bertheau, the story opens with the leaders of the community approaching Ezra to tell him that the community had not separated itself "from the peoples of the lands with[2] their abominations, from the Canaanites, the Hittites, the Perizzites, the Jebusites, the Ammonites, the Moabites, the Egyptians, and the Amorites" (9:1). The eight ethnicities listed here include five of the seven from a similar list in Deut 7:1–6, where Israel is commanded not to intermarry in the land, since that would "turn aside your children from after [Yhwh], so that they will serve other gods" (Deut 7:4; Bertheau: 109). In fact, as Ezra responds to these charges in his prayer of 9:6–15, he appears to appeal to Torah when he says,

> What shall we say, O our God, after this? For we have abandoned your commandments that you commanded in the hand of your servants the prophets, saying, "The land that you are about to enter to possess is a polluted land with the pollution of the peoples of the lands with their abominations that they have filled from end to end in their impurity. So now do not give your daughters to their sons and their daughters do not take for your sons." (9:10–12)

Mark Throntveit, whose commentary appeared more than a century later than Bertheau's, agrees with the latter's assessment of the list of peoples in Ezra 9 and its connection to the law of Deut 7. He suggests that Ezra could also have been drawing upon a similar law in Exod 34:11–16, which also prohibited

---

2. MT reads כתועבתיהם here, but the preposition makes little sense. In every other biblical occurrence of the phrase כתובעבה תובעבה or ככל תובעבה or the like, the preposition functions to indicate a simile with another phrase including a verb, usually עשׂה. So, for example, Deut 18:9: ההם לא תלמד לעשׂות כתועבתם הגוים "you will not learn to act like the abominations of those nations." To read the preposition here in Ezra 9:1 as original, we would expect to see some action on the part of Israel that is like an abominable action that the nations do. That is how like phrases are always used in the Hebrew Bible. Since this is not the case, I have emended to -ב, following בתועבתיהם in a similar phrase in the MT of 9:11.

intermarriage lest it lead to apostasy (Throntveit: 51). It is true, writes David
Clines, that the laws of Exod 34 and Deut 7 are never actually quoted in Ezra 9,
and it is equally true that Exodus and Deuteronomy prohibit marriage only to
non-Israelite Palestinians. This is certainly not the case in Ezra 9, he admits, yet
to Ezra this discrepancy would have been "a mere technicality," for Ezra's application of the law was within the spirit of the pentateuchal provisions (Clines:
116–17). This was a community decision, and the group as a whole determined
the meaning of the laws for their own time (133).[3]

1.2. Ethnic Purity

Wilhelm Rudolph would not agree with the line of reasoning followed later
by Clines. The Torah does not prohibit marriage with foreigners in general,
he argued, only with non-Israelite Palestinians in particular, and we can find
a number of biblical examples of Israelites marrying foreigners (Rudolph
1949:87). If Ezra was concerned about purity of religion within the community, he was equally concerned with racial purity, and it was this, in Rudolph's
view, that led to the expulsion of the foreign women (89). Hugh Williamson
also acknowledges that, if the similarities between Ezra 9–10 and the pentateuchal laws of intermarriage are striking, they are not exact. He specifically
notes that, while the laws of Exodus and Deuteronomy specify apostasy as
the rationale for prohibiting miscegenation, this explanation is entirely missing in Ezra 9–10. He concludes that the Persian-period community needed a
"distinctive self-identity" and that it misinterpreted the laws of the Pentateuch
(which were really concerned with apostasy) as dealing with matters of race
(Williamson 1985:160–61).

Peter Ackroyd suggests a solution that includes both apostasy and ethnic
purity. He believes that, if purity of religion was the primary motivating
factor behind the expulsion, it manifested itself in a desire for racial purity.
That is, he argues that the whole point of the expulsion was to achieve "the
preservation of the life and faith of the community" and that the community moved toward this goal by aiming for "fitness at the centre" in regard
to priests. Instead of appealing to the laws of Exod 34 and Deut 7, Ackroyd
notes that Lev 21:7 indicates that priests were held to stricter standards of
marriage partners (Ackroyd 1973:261–63; however, I would point out that
Lev 21:7 does not deal with ethnicity). C. F. Keil, on the other hand, does not

---

3. Another modern scholar writing in a major commentary series who agrees with
this assessment is Jacob Myers. Although he does not explicitly comment on a reuse of
laws in the Pentateuch by the Persian-period community, he states that the expulsions
resulted from the danger of "compromise and idolatry" (Myers: 77).

see religious purity as entering into the matter at all. As he understands the situation, the text alludes only to separation from the peoples and makes no claims to thereby prevent apostasy. In fact, he states that such connections with the surrounding ethnicities would have been harder to break had there been no flagrant idolatry to point to as a rationale (Keil: 135–36).

A reading of Ezra 9–10 closer to that of Ackroyd's is Daniel Smith-Christopher's, who points out that the text speaks of the marriages in question both along national/ethnic lines (in the list of nations in 9:1) and along religious ones (such as in the reference to the community as "the holy seed" in 9:2; Smith-Christopher 1994:247). What is really at stake, however, is an ethnic matter. Using studies of other cultures, he shows that males from disadvantaged communities will often marry above their social status and that their own communities will legislate against such actions when it becomes concerned about its own identity. This, he argues, is what happened in the Persian-period community: Ezra 9–10 witnesses to "an attempt at inward consolidation of a threatened minority." Further, since we know that the community consisted only of those who could trace their ancestry to returned exiles, the expulsions may well have resulted from a debate over who should really be considered a community member (1994:249–57).

1.3. TWO RESPONSES

It should be clear already that even within the same category there are varieties of explanations. Since this is even more the case when we get to the third category of explanation, some of those will demand individual responses. Thus, before I move there I will respond with two general comments to the first two categories of explanation. The first response could also apply to the third category, and it is this: Ezra 9–10 does not offer any of the scholarly explanations as a rationale for the expulsion of the foreign women. Perhaps Schultz was being more true to the text than any scholar we have thus far surveyed, for he found no explanation for the expulsion in the story and so reported none. There is, it is true, a reference to "commandments" in 9:10–12, and I think that a strong case can be made that these verses at least allude to Deut 7:1–6. The list of nations in Ezra 9:1 closely resembles that of Deut 7:1. The use of a phrase such as אתם באים לרשתה הארץ אשר, "the land which you are about to enter to possess," in 9:10–12 sounds remarkably like the language of Deuteronomy, as does a reference to foreign things as תועבה "an abomination."[4] When the prayer of Ezra mentions "commandments" in

---

4. It is important to point out in this regard that תועבה in the Deuteronomic Code,

9:10–12, the author probably had Deut 7:1–6 in mind, if in fact he or she did mean to allude to one law specifically. (It is unclear why the text refers to these commandments as having been given by "your servants, the prophets" [9:11], however.) The fact remains, however, that Ezra 9–10 never actually indicates that apostasy is the basic rationale for the expulsions. Unlike Deut 7:4, it does not state that intermarriage will "turn aside your children from after [YHWH], so that they will serve other gods," nor does it say that because of intermarriage the foreign women "will cause your sons to prostitute after their gods," as Exod 34:16 does. The only part of the law in Deuteronomy to which the text alludes is the part that forbids foreign marriage, not the part that provides a rationale for this proscription. All the scholarly rationales surveyed so far, as well as the ones that we are about to survey, thus supply a rationale in the face of this apparent lacuna. They all presume that Ezra 9–10 has omitted or obscured the rationale for the community's actions.

The second response—and this specifically to the explanations of the first two categories, apostasy and ethnic purity—concerns 10:18–44, the list of the men in the community who had married foreign women. It is short. In MT, the list contains 111 names, while LXX contains 109–112 names (it is possible that in some cases it has two names for the same person), and 1 Esdras 101 or 102.[5] Did the community truly believe that such a small number of women would become the cause of mass apostasy or that a mere handful of foreign-ers would drastically threaten ethnic identity? Because it seems unlikely, a number of scholars have argued that list must be incomplete. Frank Michaeli, for example, states that Ezra 9–10 makes the situation sound far too serious to really believe that there were so few intermarriages (Michaeli: 306). An expla-nation followed by a number of scholars (most of whom we examine in the next category) is that the list contains the names only of those in the upper economic and political strata of the community. Jon Berquist (1995a:118) and Kurt Galling (1954:215) argue that only the economic elite within the com-munity were involved in intermarriage, or at least that those responsible for compiling this list were concerned only with intermarriages among the rich. Rudolph states that, while poor and rich alike intermarried, the Chronicler (the author of Ezra-Nehemiah, in his opinion) did not wish to reveal the full

---

as well in other biblical writings, can refer to the worship of foreign deities, but to many other things as well. It is clear, for example, that in Deut 12:31 and 20:18 the term refers to worship practices that the Israelites are not to imitate, while in 14:3 it refers to unclean animals, in 22:5 it refers to the transvestitism, and in 25:13–16 it refers to the practice of using false weights in order to defraud a customer. The presence of this word alone in Ezra 9:1, 11, 14 cannot be used to imply that apostasy is the threat the text condemns.

5. For these numbers, see Myers: 87; Michaeli: 306.

extent of this divisive problem and so included only the names of the wealthy (Rudolph: 97). Joseph Blenkinsopp concludes that the list contains only the names of those who actually divorced. While the matter of the intermarriages appears to be an explosive one within the community, the list is short because the plan to divorce and expel these women was not fully carried out (Blenkinsopp 1988:197–98).

What all of these scholars realize is that the list of names in Ezra 10 appears far too small to explain the great danger to the community that the story as a whole presents. Yet there is no textual-critical evidence to suggest that this list is incomplete. Ezra 10:17–18 makes it clear that this is a list of "all men who had caused foreign women to dwell [within the community]," not simply a list of the wealthy who had done so or simply a list of those who had complied with the demand to divorce. If Berquist and Galling are right in their assertions that it was only the wealthy who intermarried (or that the community concerned itself only with the wealthy who did so because of particular economic and political reasons), then the length of the list should be no surprise. Here, however, I mean only to address the explanations of the first two categories, where no one has made such an assertion.

These two responses do not make such the explanations surveyed in categories one and two impossible, but they do make them unlikely candidates for the community's rationale for the expulsion. If one cannot explain why the text does not supply the rationale that one supplies for it, and if one cannot explain why the list included by the text seems far smaller than the problem portrayed in the text, then some further explanation is warranted.

1.4. ECONOMIC AND POLITICAL ISSUES

1.4.1. Land and Wealth

Both Harold Washington and Joseph Blenkinsopp link the aversion to the נכריות נשים "foreign women" in Ezra 9–10 to warnings against the אשה נכריה "strange woman" of Prov 1–9. Washington argues that the fear of the strange woman in Proverbs reflects the attempts in the Persian-period temple community to force foreigners from its midst. In the case of the divorces and expulsion of the foreign women in Ezra 9–10, he writes, the community was trying to keep control of its land. Marriage to foreign women became a problem because women in ancient Israel were eligible to inherit land, and thus the property of men who had intermarried could be alienated (Washington 1994a:230–35). Blenkinsopp focuses less on the connection with the "strange woman" of Proverbs (see Blenkinsopp 1991:467–68), and while he believes that the divorces of foreign women mentioned in Neh 6:18–19 and 13:28–29 were "doubtless" in order to promote the political and economic interests of the community, he is less certain that this was also the case in Ezra 9–10 (1991:472). Tamara Eskenazi appears more certain and states that the divorces and expulsion were enacted for fear of foreign women inheriting property (Eskenazi: 35). Berquist believes that the true interest was not land alone but wealth in general. Marrying inside of one's class, he points out, would help to centralize the elite's control over land and wealth. By proscribing marriage outside of one's class, the wealthy are able to make sure that their children have connections only to other families of wealth (Berquist 1995a:118–19). His argument, then, is that the community was not really interested in dissolving foreign marriages but in making sure that the wealthy married only the wealthy.

One of the key ingredients to these arguments—a matter that is explicit in the writings of Washington and Blenkinsopp—is the fact that Num 27:1–11 and 36:1–12 specify that women in Israel can inherit property and wealth from their fathers if they have no brothers (see Washington 1994a:235; Blenkinsopp 1991:470). This is especially the case since Ezra 9–10 concerns not a divorce of foreigners (or the poor) in general but of women only. Had the community's fear of losing control of land truly been uppermost, the community would have legislated not only against marrying foreign women but also against allowing Yehudite women with inheritances to marry foreign men. The presence or absence of foreign *women* would not have been an issue. The case of the daughters of Zelophehad in Numbers concerns only daughters inheriting from their fathers, not wives inheriting from their husbands.

The only oddity—at least from the standpoint of its cultural neighbors—in the inheritance laws of ancient Israel was that daughters could inherit if they had no brothers. But nowhere in this region do we find that wives could inherit from their husbands.[6] The Code of Hammurabi (CH) 171, for example, specifically states that, should a husband predecease his wife, she may live from the usufruct of whatever her husband has given to her but prohibits her from selling it, since "her estate belongs to her sons." CH 172 mandates that a widow's sons must provide for her if her husband has failed to do so. If she refuses to accept this arrangement, then her dowry must be returned to her. That is, she maintains ownership *only* of what she has brought into her marriage and nothing of her husband's property. Moreover, CH 172–173 state that even in this case her sons will share her dowry when she dies. The same scenario is found in the Middle Assyrian Laws (MAL). MAL 25 states that, when

---

6. There is a case, however, from later in Persian Egypt. Miphtahiah inherited the home of her first husband in the Elephantine documents (Yoder: 53).

a husband predeceases his wife and the couple has produced no sons, the husband's brothers, not his wife, will inherit his property. So it is that MAL 46 demands that sons must provide for their widowed mother, a necessity as she does not inherit the property of her dead husband. In a much later period this custom remains, for Neo-Babylonian Law 12 states that a widow receives only her dowry and marriage gift upon the death of her husband, which is to say that any property that she did not bring to the relationship falls to the sons. It seems clear that this custom, visible in over eleven hundred years of Mesopotamian law codes, was operative among the Israelites as well. A second century c.e. Aramaic marriage contract from Murabba'at, for example, states that "if I go to that house (i.e., of death) bef[ore you, you will live] and be nourished from [my possessions] all the days (at) their house, (the house) o[f our son]s, the house of [your] widow[hood, until your] death" (*Mur 21 ar* 14–16). Precisely the same arrangement is present in two other marriage contracts from Murabba'at that also date to the first half of the second century c.e. (*Mur 115 gk* 10–12; *Mur 116 gk* 8–12).

If the community's concern was to protect its land from poorly devised marriages, a mass divorce of foreign women would hardly have been its response, since the foreign wives would not have been eligible to inherit their husband's land. A more likely course of action would have been to forbid women from within the community (women who were eligible by pentateuchal law to inherit if they had no brothers) to marry foreign men. In fact, male members of the community who married foreign women could have received land as part of the dowry and so have increased the community's holdings. All that this divorce of foreign women would have accomplished was a communal *loss* of land. As Raymond Westbrook has demonstrated, Old Babylonian laws and marriage contracts distinguished between divorce with and without grounds. If a man could not prove legal grounds for divorce in court, he was forced to repay the dowry to his ex-wife, in addition to a fine. Moreover, if the couple had sons, the women received all of her estranged husband's property so that the children, who would reside with her, could receive a decent inheritance (Westbrook: 71–75). While the biblical and epigraphical record are almost entirely silent on this issue, postbiblical evidence shows that the same practice was current in Israel.[7] As no acceptable legal

---

7. The Babylonian laws and marriage contracts often specifically spell out what amounts to grounds for divorce on the part of the husband or wife. CH 141 states that, if a woman neglects her husband's household because she is attending to her own affairs, and if the husband can prove this in court, *ukānūši* "they will judge her" and allow the husband to divorce without payment even of the dowry. This is an example of grounds for divorce. An instance of a judgment for determining grounds is found in CT 45 86, where a

grounds are provided for the divorces in Ezra 9–10, we can only assume that the women would have been provided with their dowries and that those with children would also have received their husbands' land, thereby *decreasing* the community's landholdings.

1.4.2. Persian Influence

There are other scholarly explanations of the community's rationale for the expulsion of the foreign women that hinge upon Persian involvement. Blenkinsopp notes that the Achaemenids employed endogamy in order to preserve patrimony. He is quick to point out that this is not to imply that the Persians would have approved of the tactic of mass divorce followed in Ezra 9–10, but he does at least hold it up as one possible impetus behind this movement (1991:472–73). On the other hand, Smith-Christopher argues that the Persians could have supported the intermarriage of leaders of the Jerusalem community with leaders of the surrounding groups and so have been partly responsible for the situation that the community attempts to correct in Ezra 9–10. He notes that Herodotus 5.32 records an account of a foreign king attempting to marry into the Persian aristocracy. He also points to an account in Arrian's *Anabasis* wherein Alexander arranges marriages for himself and his officers with Persian women, an act that Arrian believed was an imitation

---

court finds the husband's evidence lacking and orders in regard to his estranged wife that he *muššilši* "make her equal," or repay her dowry. One of the worst offenses is adultery, and CH 129 stipulates that the husband can demand the death of his wife if he so desires (resulting, naturally, in no monetary payment on his part). The payment on the part of the husband appears to have been only a dowry (and sometimes a fine) if the couple has no sons (so CH 138), but the Code of Eshnunna 59 states that if the couple has children the husband must surrender all of his property. This is assumedly because, as the marriage contracts VAS 18 114 and PBS 8/2 107 make clear, the one who has been divorced retains custody of the children (see Westbrook: 85–86).

The best evidence for such a practice in Israel comes from the Mishnah and Talmud, and while this material is postbiblical it seems logical that the practice was one that Israel shared with its neighbors from a much earlier time. *M. Giṭ.* 9:10 discusses the acceptable grounds for divorce, while *m. Ket.* 7:6 and *b. Giṭ* 90a–b state that there are actions on the part of the woman that give her husband no choice but to divorce her. While it appears to have been normal practice for the dowry to be returned to the woman upon her divorce (so *m. Mak.* 1:1; *m. 'Arak.* 6:1–2), *m. Ket.* 7:6 states that women who disobey Jewish law and custom must be divorced without the return of dowry. All of this sounds just like the Babylonian practice of discerning grounds for divorce that do not demand the return of the dowry. Just as in Babylonia, a Jewish man who divorced his wife had to prove that he had grounds to do so, and if he could not he was forced to repay the dowry (*m. Soṭ* 6:1–2).

of Persian custom (7.4.4–7; 7.6.2–5; see Smith-Christopher 1994:261–64). Blenkinsopp and Smith-Christopher thus use a similar point (the Persians intermarried) in order to come to two different conclusions: Blenkinsopp arguing that the Persians may have encouraged the local leadership in Yehud to marry amongst itself (influence that could have led to the expulsion); and Smith-Christopher arguing that the Persians may have encouraged the local leadership in Yehud to marry outside of its own group in the first place.

The difficulty with either line of argument, however, is that, while it may be true that Zoroastrianism sanctioned the marriage of close relatives,[8] there is no evidence that the Persians *encouraged* this practice among the provincial leadership, even for reasons of political expediency rather than cultural habit. Kenneth Hoglund argues that the Persians attempted to keep particular ethnic groups separated into clearly defined units in the interests of ameliorating the flow of taxes into imperial coffers (1991:65–68). In the specific case of the community in Yehud, he concludes, "[m]embership in the assembly was contingent on one's ethnic identity as a 'Yehudian' or 'Jew.' Loss of such ethnic distinction carried with it the possible diminution of collective privileges or property and subsequent impoverishment of the assembly" (1991:67). The community, he argues, had a stake in clearly delineating its ethnic boundaries in order to receive Persian sponsorship. However, Hoglund's argument lacks evidence that would show such a requirement of ethnic purity to be imperial policy. Hoglund does mention an account in Herodotus of a deported ethnic group (apparently) remaining together for some time, and he makes mention of four of the Persepolis Fortification tablets that refer to rations being given to work groups indicated by ethnicity. All that this tells us, however, is that in one case a deported group remained together and that in some cases the Persians dispensed rations to work groups that they designated by national origin. We do not see an empire-wide program to promote intermarriage.

2. What the Text Says

Thus far I have found some sort of fault with all of the proffered explanations and have said, moreover, that all of them presume that Ezra 9–10 obscures or omits the community's rationale for the expulsion. That the author would do so seems odd, for the text certainly portrays the community's situation and the danger of these women's presence as dire, yet appears to offer little in the way of *why* they are dangerous. Indeed, one of the glaring peculiarities of the

---

8. Blenkinsopp (1988) points to two studies that make this point: Herrenschmidt: 53–67; Schwartz: 655–56.

text is that the women are charged with no crime or even with the danger of
committing a crime. I have noted that Ezra 9 bears some reflection of Deuteronomic language and that it is possible that here the author is thinking of
Deut 7:1–6, a law that prohibits intermarriage with Canaanites lest they turn
Israel to apostasy. Yet I also noted that Ezra 9 omits Deuteronomy's rationale
for proscribing such marriages. So is it really true that the text provides no
reason at all for the expulsion of these women?

If the women themselves are charged with nothing, it is the men in the
community who have married them who are indicted. The charge is specifically that these men have caused foreign women to dwell within the
community (the text uses the hiphil of ישׁב), that they have failed to separate
themselves from the surrounding peoples (the text uses the niphal of בדל).
Thus, when the issue is introduced in 9:1, the text states that the Israelites,
including the priests and Levites, had not נבדלו "separated themselves" from
the peoples of the lands, since (זר הקדשׁ) "the holy seed" had "mixed itself"
with them (9:2). After Ezra's prayer of 9:6–15, which emphasizes the danger
of intermarriage to the continued existence of the community, Shechaniah
acknowledges the community's guilt, since, he says, נשׁב נשׁים נכריות "we
have caused foreign women to dwell (here)" (10:2). The hiphil of ישׁב is also
used in reference to the community's actions in 10:10, 12, 14, and 17. While it
is often translated as "married" rather than "cause to dwell," the usual Hebrew
verbs for associated with marriage (נשׂא, נתן, and חתן) are used in 9:1, 12, 14;
10:44. The sense of this verb in this *binyan* is somewhat different, especially as
nowhere else could ישׁב in the hiphil refer to marriage. It is easiest to take it
at face value: the men have been charged with causing foreign women to live
in a place where they should not. After (perhaps) citing or at least alluding to
Deut 7:1–6 in Ezra 9:10–14 (Deut 7:3 also uses the verbs נתן and חתן to refer
to foreign marriages), the story in Ezra goes on to get at the root of the problem and from then on consistently uses the hiphil of ישׁב until 10:44. That is,
the text alludes to a law forbidding intermarriage and uses the verbs found
there that are commonly associated with marriage, but in the mind of the
author the real problem is foreign women being in a place where they should
not be. The solution must be a separation of the men of the community from
these women and their peoples, precisely the solution that opens the story in
9:1 and that Ezra orders in 10:11, both cases using the niphal of בדל.

Should this not be done, the text indicates, the danger to community
could be total. In his prayer of 9:6–15, Ezra states that Israel had betrayed
God from earliest times, yet God had graciously allowed a remnant to remain
במקם קדשׁו "in his holy place" (9:8). This recent abandonment of God's commandments (the apparent allusion to Deut 7:1–6) could result in a complete
destruction of the remnant (9:14). Is the problem merely the fact that the

community has broken a divine commandment? Or is there something especially dangerous about breaking this commandment in particular? I believe
that the author has left us his or her answer to this question in the text and
that the original readers would have been able to discern the answer in it.
Remember that the community has been described as זרע הקדש "the holy
seed" (9:2) that dwells במקם קדשו "in his (i.e., God's) holy place" (9:8) and
that it has been charged with illegally causing foreign women to dwell in this
place. Why does the author specifically mention locale as a problem and not
turn, as Deut 7:1–6 (and Exod 34:11–16) do, to claiming that intermarriage
will lead to apostasy? Because that is not really the issue in the author's eyes.
What is at issue is the nature of these foreign women (?): they are polluting
(נדה) women who have polluted the land with their impurity (טמאה; 9:11).

The import of these descriptions of the community as holy and the
nations (and their women) as polluting and impure would not have been
lost on the original readers. Leviticus 15:31, following a series of laws dealing with the impurity of bodily discharges, states that "you will separate[9]
the Israelites from their impurity [מטמאתם], and they will not die in their
impurity by making impure my tabernacle that is in your midst." The real
difficulty foreseen in this imperative concerning nocturnal emissions and
the like is not impurity per se, since Lev 15 as a whole deals with impurities
of bodily discharges that an individual cannot prevent. What is necessary is
that others take steps to avoid coming into contact with this טמאה and that
proper cleansing rituals be carried out at the appointed times. If this does
not happen, then impurity will be brought into contact with the tabernacle—
God's holy place[10]—and death will result. The same point is made in Lev 22:3,
where the Aaronides are warned that "anyone among your descendants who
approaches the holy things [קדשים] that the Israelites have made holy for
Yhwh while his impurity [טמאתו] is upon him, that one will be cut off from
before me." Leviticus 22:1–7 in general warns that any priest who has been in
contact with the contagious טמאה is forbidden to approach the קדשים.

In the Priestly writing נדה is used almost exclusively to refer to menstruation (so especially Lev 15:19–30). Here נדה is something that is טמאה,
as the phrase טמאת נדתה "the impurity of her pollution/menstruation"

---

9. Reading והזרתם with MT, *Targ. Pseudo-Jonathan*, and *Targ. Onqelos*, not והזהרתם
with the Samaritan Pentateuch, the Syriac, and LXX. The latter reading ("you will warn
the Israelites from their impurity") makes little sense in the context. As Jacob Milgrom
points out (945), there hardly seems to be a reason to warn people from impurities that
are unavoidable.

10. In P, the tabernacle becomes קדש "holy" when Moses anoints it immediately after
its construction (Exod 40:9).

of 15:26 indicates. The word appears to function in the same way in Ezek 18:6 and 22:10 (and in the latter verse we again find the phrase טמאת הנדה "the impurity of the pollution/menstruation"). As a kind of טמאה, נדה is something contagious. A "righteous" person does not approach a אשה נדה "menstruating/polluting woman" (Ezek 18:6), for those who touch what a menstruating woman has touched are impure until the end of the day and must purify themselves (Lev 15:19–24). This is because "all that the impure person [הטמא] touches will be impure [יטמא], and the one who touches *that* will be impure until evening" (Num 19:22).

The difficulty with the foreign women in Ezra 9–10, the author explains, is not that they are criminals, actors responsible for particular crimes, such as apostasy. The story, while alluding to a law that forbids intermarriage because the foreigners will actively induce foreign worship, deliberately avoids providing that Deuteronomic rationale for the proscription. The difficulty that this narrative sees with foreign women is their nature: they are sources of pollution, ontologically opposite of "the holy seed" in the "holy place." This is why separation (בדל) is important. As Jacob Milgrom points out, in the Bible "[t]he source of holiness [קדש] is assigned to God alone. Holiness is the extension of his nature; it is the agency of his will" (Milgrom: 730). "There can be no doubt," he continues, "that the antonym of *qādôš* 'holy' is *tāmē'* 'impure'" (Milgrom: 731). Jan Joosten draws upon Milgrom's study of קדש and טמא as opposites in his own examination of Lev 10:10, which orders the Aaronides ובין הטהור להבדיל בין הקדש ובין החל ובין הטמא "to separate between the holy and the common and between the impure and the pure." Like Milgrom, Joosten concludes that what is חל "common" may be טמא "impure" or טהור "pure" and that what is pure may be קדש "holy" or common but that the holy and impure are "absolutely incompatible" (Joosten: 124). Specifically, as we have seen, those who have been contaminated by the impure, even unwittingly, and who come into contact with the holy could suffer death. This is the worldview that undergirds Ezra 9–10 and that gives rise to the solution involving separation. When Ezra states that the collision of the impure peoples with the holy seed in the holy place could lead to the utter destruction of the remnant, he merely extrapolates from the sentiment of Lev 15:31.

3. WITCHES

The text, in short, states that the danger lies with the foreign women who are in a state of נדה and טמאה and that the guilt lies with those who brought them into contact with the holy community in its holy place. The warnings regarding impurity in the legislation of the Torah make it clear that the law sometimes deals with such high degrees of impurity by death. So Ezra 9–10 does, in fact, provide us with a rationale for the community's action. The frustrating thing about this rationale, however, is that it makes little sense to us. Does the author of the text truly believe this explanation? Or is he or she merely using the religious language of the time in order to hide the true reason for the expulsion beneath a pious veneer, attempting to advance an ideology that the first readers of the text would swallow in place of the real reason for the expulsion? I want to argue that this explanation can make sense to us when we rely upon the aid of anthropological theory. How ideology functions is something that I will return to in the next section. For the present I want to draw upon the work of Mary Douglas and Richard Fenn, who have independently shown that the language of impurity is precisely the type of vocabulary we would expect to hear from societies with a strong group identity (i.e., they can easily identify themselves in distinction from other societies) but that are concerned that their ethical codes are not being followed. Such societies, they demonstrate, will tend to identify a group of people as impure and exclude them from the society, precisely the case in Ezra 9–10. Following their lead, I will argue that the rationale for the expulsion in Ezra 9–10 sounds just like the type of justification one would expect to hear from a society with strong group identity but weakening adherence to social morality. As I mentioned in the introduction, I shall not attempt to demonstrate that the community was such a society (since I have done that elsewhere), merely that the argument of Ezra 9–10 leads us to the path laid out by Douglas and Fenn as a way out of the current scholarly dilemma that locates an explanation for the expulsion outside of the text itself.

If we grant the supposition that terms and concepts are whatever a society agrees they are, then it is simple to grasp Douglas's point that what is dirty or impure is a social construct and differs from society to society. Naturally, for the notion of impurity to be helpful as defining a concept with different social manifestations, these manifestations must have some overlap. For Douglas, this commonality between societies regarding the concept of impurity is the universal understanding of dirt as chaotic, the opposite of order. Dirt is something that in any society one cleans up, since its presence is universally considered to be offensive (Douglas 1966:35–41).[11] To move beyond

---

11. "Where there is dirt there is system. Dirt is the by-product of a systematic ordering and classification of matter, in so far as ordering involves rejecting inappropriate elements. This idea of dirt takes us straight into the field of symbolism and promises a link-up with more obviously symbolic systems of purity.

"We can recognize in our own notions of dirt that we are using a kind of omnibus compendium which includes all the rejected elements of ordered systems. It is a relative

this very general point, what does it mean to refer to animals or menstruation as impure in the manner of the biblical law codes? Douglas's analysis of these codes' picture of impurity accords with her analysis of impurity in other cultures: what is impure is chaotic and outside of the social order and worldview; it is something that endangers and thus does not belong.

If the Hebrew Bible's conception of holiness is that it is the extension of God's nature and the agency of God's will, as Milgrom claims, it can also be described as "order, not confusion," "unity, integrity, perfection of the individual and of the kind" (Douglas 1966:55). In her analysis of the list of animals in Lev 11 and Deut 14 that are טמא "impure"—the opposite of קדש "holy"—Douglas concludes that the proscribed animals are those that do not conform to the recognized characteristics and habits of the Israelites' usual food. Since cloven-hoofed, cud-chewing ungulates are the standard livestock raised by pastoralists, those animals that did not conform to this pattern were considered impure—they failed to conform to the known and expected order. The passages say the same about four-legged animals that fly, animals without fins and scales that swim, and so on (1966:55–58). One can see, then, how certain types of behavior could be labeled as impure. Ezekiel 22:1–16, for example, condemns the sins of Israel, including the shedding of innocent blood, the failure to honor parents, the extortion of aliens, and refers to all of this as טמאתך "your impurity" (22:15). Behavior that does not conform to the social order of morality is impure; it is a manifestation of chaos, for widespread disregard of the social order will lead to the collapse of the society. In the Bible, such behavior is thus the opposite of the holy, the opposite of God's will.

As I have already noted, however, the author of Ezra 9–10 does not charge the foreign women with any crime and does not look at their behavior as the cause of their impurity. The text does not regard the women as agents at all, only as sources of impurity. It is their ontological status and not their actions that are at stake. Only the men who caused them to live where they should not are charged. Why is the men's antisocial behavior not termed impure? To answer this we must turn to anthropology.

Fenn writes that societies with *strong external* boundaries are those that can clearly differentiate themselves from others, less likely to be "polluted" by foreign influences. Societies that have *weak internal* boundaries are ones where there is a relatively greater degree of individual freedom, where social roles and hierarchy are not as tightly defined as in others, where individual

---

idea. Shoes are not dirty in themselves, but it is dirty to place them on the dining-table; food is not dirty in itself, but it is dirty to leave cooking utensils in the bedroom.... In short, our pollution behaviour is the reaction which condemns any object or idea likely to confuse or contradict cherished classifications" (Douglas 1966:36–37).

identity is not rigidly prescribed from birth to death (Fenn: 29–30). Douglas refers to these societies with strong external and weak internal boundaries as ones with high group and low grid (1973:82–92). Both scholars claim that, when the internal system of social norms in such societies grows weak and the community becomes anxious that the group as a whole may collapse, it will begin a hunt for the impure, often focused on impure women, described in many cultures as witches. Those branded as witches will not always be those who have caused the internal integration in the society to weaken.

Why will this kind of society take this kind of action? Let us for the moment set aside the question of external boundaries and look at a society with *strong internal* boundaries, or high grid. In such groups social roles and demands are rigidly defined. There is a clear and strictly enforced moral code. There is no doubt what children owe their parents, what students owe their teachers, what community leaders owe their constituents, what citizens owe their country, and so on. In societies with weak internal boundaries, however, social norms are ill-defined in relation to the community with a strictly enforced moral code, and individuals have more freedom to act as they choose, more freedom to give allegiance to unorthodox sources of leadership, wisdom, healing, and so on. Persons in authority, for example, may not always receive the loyalty, money, or honor that they believe they are owed (Fenn: 31; Douglas 1973:83–86). Such societies, then, are competitive, because people have to compete for the rewards and benefits that they are not guaranteed as a matter of course. In such societies it is a simpler thing to lose out on the recompense one believes one has coming. Where there is such social ambiguity, writes Douglas, where there is less of a rigid sense of payments and actions that must be followed by everyone, then there is competition, and loss becomes the fault of the rival. Doing the right thing with integrity does not mean that one will always receive one's reward. Competition for reward is thus fierce, and there is less confidence in justice, either human or divine (Douglas 1973:91). Evil in such societies generally corresponds to a fear of witchcraft, for in a society where proper reward is no sure thing there is no worse crime than using illicit means to take what was really owed to one's rival. This illicit means of intervention in the social order to benefit oneself or harm one's rival is what Douglas means by witchcraft (1973: 136–39).

In such societies that still retain strong *external* boundaries, the main task of rituals will be "to remove disruptive and unwanted influences from the social order" (Fenn: 33). When it is clear that foreign influences have not entered by means of a full-scale invasion or pollution from outside sources—a society with strong external boundaries does not, by definition, fear such things[12]—then social deviancy that extends beyond the norms sanctioned by a society with low internal integration will be understood as caused by foreigners masquerading as natives—witches, as Douglas calls them. The group's wrath will fall on those who have allowed such foreigners and their evil to infiltrate the society, and rituals of cleansing, expulsion of spies, and the redrawing of boundaries preoccupy such communities (Douglas 1973:169). These rituals will attempt to recapture the allegiance of those who appeal to unusual sources for their behavior and allegiance. "These are rituals of purification, in which the burdens and debts, the pollution and dangers threatening the society from within are eliminated" (Fenn: 33). Fenn writes that there may or may not be a scapegoat involved in such rituals; the use of a scapegoat is a convenient but not a necessary part of such attempts to purify the society of deviancy (Fenn: 55). He notes also that it is simply easier for a society with these types of boundaries and experiencing this kind of social deviancy to blame these destructive desires and actions on foreigners rather than on community members (142). Hence the creation of witches: as Douglas notes, they are described in terms that portray them as the opposite of human (Douglas 1973:139); they are the ultimate outsiders, the people whom the community has designated as the foreign influence that has crept inside the strong external boundaries in an attempt to destroy the society. They are the antisociety. How much more clever their subterfuge must seem when they can actually marry community members!

When such societies have come to the conclusion that social deviancy runs high, even by the standards of a society with weak internal integration, they begin to engage in actions of purification. We should hardly be surprised, then, to see such a society looking for foreigners, those who might be responsible for the fear of social collapse that is widely felt. Such witches need not necessarily be charged with a crime, nor need they necessarily have even acted in any way that is particularly foreign; the need for purification can simply be a knee-jerk reaction that occurs when deviation from the social norm is thought to run too high. The rite of purification has the added benefit of forcing the community to bow to the social order—a massive request in the case of the hundred or so men in Yehud who were asked to give up their wives and children. In this action the primacy of the community to demand

---

12. "When a society becomes less tightly integrated, its people become the bearers of outside influences. Individuals assimilate, as in the case of colonials who adopt the manners and ideas of their colonial masters, or Jews who found themselves at home in pre-fascist Germany. Without losing control of its [external] boundaries, a society can nonetheless have a population that is discovering new temptations and horizons, not only in work but in love, in politics and in play" (Fenn: 131).

particular actions from its members is acknowledged. The language employed in Ezra 9–10 is precisely what we would expect to hear from a community with strong external and weak internal boundaries that anxiously believes social deviancy is growing out of control: it wants to purify itself from the dangerous impurity of outside groups. It acted the way it did and supplied the explanation it did because it was the type of society that high levels of social deviancy will cause to act that way.

As I have demonstrated elsewhere, the community had well-defined external boundaries. Even by the fifth century, more than one hundred years after the exile, the community surrounding Jerusalem referred to itself in Ezra-Nehemiah as בני הגולה "the children of the exile." It produced writings such as Chronicles and Ezra-Nehemiah that prominently displayed genealogies so that members of the community could authenticate their positions within the group by appeal to descent from the exiles. This was also a group, I have shown, that was exposed to a wide range of foreign cultures. Trade was high throughout Persian-period Palestine and brought to Yehud foreign traders, along with their customs and religion. The Persians established small garrisons throughout the region to protect the roads and thereby brought foreign soldiers to the area. While it was a clearly defined group, it was one where outside sources were available so that the habitual forms of morality could be called into question. This was a society ripe for a witch-hunt.

4. Ideologues

"Ideology" and "ideologue" are terms that are often used pejoratively; Clifford Geertz points to the former as frequently indicating "radical intellectual depravity" (197). As I surveyed the scholarly opinions of the community's rationale for the expulsion of the foreign women, I did not mention the various scholars' opinions of ideology specifically, although I did note that many of them assume that the true rationale had been omitted or obscured by the author of Ezra 9–10. In my own attempt to locate a rationale I questioned whether the author has simply employed this explanation as a cover for the true one. I will return to that question here in the context of asking what ideology is and does and whether it is something that acts as a mask to hide an actor's true politico-economic motives, a function of ideology that could be said to have been utilized by some of the scholars surveyed above.

Geertz refers to the view that ideology is "a mask and a weapon" that advances particular political and economic agendas by institutionalizing a party's or class's view of reality both as the "interest theory" of ideology and, less kindly, as "superficial utilitarianism" (Geertz: 201–2). The difficulty with this view of ideology, writes Geertz, is that it fails to explain how it is that ideology manages to convince people. How is it that ideology may be employed to convince others? How does it tap into "systems of interacting symbols, ... patterns of interworking meanings" (207)? Note a similar sentiment expressed by Douglas:

> Money can only perform its role of intensifying economic interaction if the public has faith in it. If faith in it is shaken, the currency is useless. So too with ritual; its symbols can only have effect so long as they command confidence. In this sense all money, false or true, depends on a confidence trick. The test of money is whether it is acceptable or not. There is no false money except by contrast with another currency which has more total acceptability. So primitive ritual is like good money, not false money, as long as it commands respect. (Douglas 1966: 70–71).

Replace "(primitive) ritual" with "ideology," and one sees the crux of Geertz's problem. For ideology to function it has to make sense to those it is trying to convince. Ideology in this sense works as something that explains, not obscures. If it is to convince and move others to action, it must tap into the interacting symbols and interworking meanings by which those others organize their lives. It has to explain to them, in terms that are meaningful to them, why they should think and act in particular ways. To return to the instance of Ezra 9–10, the description of the foreign women as dangerous impurities that must be purged if the community is to survive will only be accepted if the community is willing to accept it—if it is a community with the types of social boundaries that I have described. A society that does not feel any need for a purification ritual will not willingly engage in one.

Marx's writings certainly contributed to the notion that ideology is a sort of "ethereal medium which veils the hard reality of material production" (Thompson: 16). Yet as José Guilherme Merquior points out, strengthening Geertz's argument, ideology cannot be tied to the worldview of a particular social class. Class ideologies cannot be total, if only because they need to employ a common code, tap into a common set of interacting symbols that addresses other classes. The difficulty with the interest theory, he writes, is not only its "crude utilitarian psychology" but also its failure to account for the acceptance of the beliefs ideology advances by groups that do not benefit from them. Merquior claims that, while Marx argued that ideology is "a socially determined occultation of the actual motives of class behavior," it in fact must be an unconscious belief held by everyone, or else it simply will not function (Merquior: 3–12). It has to make clear, not obscure. If the metaphor of ideology is to work—if someone is going to make the claim that foreign wives are an impure substance whose presence endangers society, for example, or that the labor act proposed by a rival party in Congress will, in effect, reintroduce slavery—then it must be able to bind the discordant meanings that it places together in the metaphor into a single framework by means of symbols. The success of ideological tropes depends not just on their rhetoric but also on the fact that the meanings they "spark against one another" are socially rooted (Geertz: 210–11). Because human thought is primarily a cultural matter, metaphors must be able to tap into the public basis of thought (213–14).

"How Lonely Sits the City":
Identity and the Creation of History

Christine Mitchell

How lonely sits the city
    once full of people!
She has become like a widow,
    once great among the nations!
Once a princess among the provinces,
    she has become a vassal. (Lam 1:1)

What led to the development of the literary genre of historiography in postexilic Yehud? Where were the roots of the genre of historiography? Once developed, how was historiography used? These questions are rarely asked in biblical studies, or their answers are unproblematized: the existence of genre is a given; development and transformation of genre has to do with *Sitz im Leben*, specifically preexilic. Although naïve presentations of the so-called Succession Narrative in 2 Samuel as "an eye-witness account" are now mercifully rare, the discussion of the reasons for the development of historiography has not moved much past earlier discussions. Historiography as a genre and as a practice has remained a given. Even Marc Zvi Brettler (1995) and Baruch Halpern (1988), who have recently written finely argued books on biblical historiography, do not write about the origins of the historiographic impulse. In this essay, therefore, I will discuss the development of the genre of historiography in the Persian period. In order to do so, I will first outline my understanding of historiography as a genre, an understanding grounding in the work of Mikhail Bakhtin. I will then use two approaches, which I will synthesize in order to make a third.

The first approach will be inspired from the rabbinic practice of midrash.[1] Midrash has a typical form that can be roughly described as follows: a verse

---

1. Midrash can be defined in many different ways, but I am taking my definition from Renée Bloch's classic article: midrash is the noun form of the Hebrew root *drš* "to search."

of Scripture is quoted, and a dialogue ensues between various rabbis on the meaning of the verse. It is a dialogue of commentary, expansion and replete with intertextuality. As part of the midrashic process, other parts of the Hebrew Bible are used in order to illuminate the verse under examination. I quoted the first verse of Lamentations at the beginning of this paper, and presently I will perform something akin to midrash in order to elucidate meaning from this verse. As with midrash, we might end up somewhere very different from where we started, or we might end up back exactly where we started.

The second approach will be comparative in nature. Here I will look at the development of historiography in the Greek world and try to answer some of the questions I posed at the beginning: What caused historiography to develop in the Greek world? How did it develop? How was it used? Then I will combine the results of this analysis with the results from my first section. This will allow me to answer the questions with respect to the development of biblical historiography.

Genre

The issue of genre is complicated, because it is so nebulous a term. The idea of genre is as old as thinking about literature: Aristotle began the *Poetics* by stating that he wanted to consider poetry (*poiēsis*) in general and its genres or forms (*eidos*; 47a1). In *The Problems of Dostoevsky's Poetics*, Mikhail Bakhtin described literary genre as containing "the most stable, 'eternal' tendencies in literature's development," yet a genre is "reborn and renewed at every new stage in the development of literature and in every individual work of a given genre" (1984:106). In "The Problem of Speech Genres," where he discussed the speech genres of utterances (ranging from the sentence to the full-length text), he noted that speech genres are heterogeneous in the extreme and that their diversity is linked to the diversity of the human experience (1986:60–61). Thus, speech genres can be seen as an ever-shifting array of speech types. Bakhtin divided speech genres into primary (simple) and secondary (complex) speech genres; the complex speech genres such as novels absorb primary speech genres such as letters (61–62). However, most important for our pur-

---

In its classic sense, therefore, midrash is "a seeking." However, it came to mean a specific kind of seeking, "something written for the purpose of interpreting the Bible ... always in rapport with Scripture, in the sense of searching, trying to understand the meaning and content of the biblical text in order to reveal ... the meaning of Scripture" (Bloch: 31). According to Bloch, there are several fundamental characteristics of midrash: its point of departure is the Bible (Tanak); it is homiletic; it is attentive to the text; and it adapts the text to the present, either as commentary (haggadah) or as law (halakah) (31–33).

poses is Bakhtin's assertion that "style is inseparably related to the utterance and to typical forms of utterances" (63): there is an "organic, inseparable link between style and genre.... each sphere has and applies its own genres that correspond to its own specific conditions" (64). He also stated, "Where there is style there is genre. The transfer of style from one genre to another not only alters the way a style sounds, under conditions of a genre unnatural to it, but also violates or renews the given genre" (66). Finally, Bakhtin also suggested that an individual's speech is adapted for a specific genre; it takes the form of the genre, and if speech genres did not exist, communication would be almost impossible (78–79). We rely on stylistic markers in order to determine genre, which makes communication possible. Genre is thus linked to form as well as theme. Contrary to this view, Meir Sternberg (30) has claimed that one cannot tell the difference between fiction and history by formal characteristics alone; they can be distinguished only by their purpose. Sternberg's understanding of genre is the understanding implicitly shared by most scholars of the Bible: How else can we understand scholars who see Genesis as legend and Kings as historiography? Ultimately, if a Bakhtinian understanding of genre is realistic, there must be formal markers to distinguish these two genres. If there are no such markers, then we have to consider the possibility that for the ancients, both Genesis and Kings belonged to the same genre.

Of course, there are reasons why scholars do not want Genesis and Kings to be examples of the same genre. The most important is due to a confusion between the literary genre of historiography and the idea of history as "what really happened." Sara Japhet notes that the obvious is often lost sight of: narrative is not necessarily fiction; literary works should be studied in their own genre; and historiography is a literary genre. She also implies that fact and fiction is not a useful dichotomy in biblical historiography (1991:188). We want the events narrated in a work of historiography to be true. This understanding of historiography as something true is based on Aristotle's definition of history in the *Poetics*. He separated out history from poetry as a genre, then defined history as the genre that "relates actual events" and poetry as the genre that relates "the kind of events that might occur." He went on to suggest that poetry is "more philosophical and more elevated than history" (51a36–51b8). However, Aristotle did not describe how one would know the difference between history and poetry, thus leaving the door open for those like Sternberg who see no formal differences. In the context of biblical literature, Marc Zvi Brettler has defined history as "a narrative that presents a past" (12) and has opposed it to ideology, which he defines as a type of sets of beliefs (14). He does not use the term *literature*; instead, he uses *ideology*, suggesting that, just because a text has literary features, that does not mean it is literature (17).

Glen Bowersock does not explicitly define the terms "fiction" and "history" in his *Fiction as History* but implies that history is what really happened and fiction is what did not. However, he does go on to show how, later in the classical period, Roman authors such as Lucian "trie[d] to pull down the distinction between fiction that we accept as fiction and fiction that is presented as a record of real events" (5–6). Although Herodotus had described his work as "researches," by the first century B.C.E. the term *historia* meant plot, "the received account of the past that reached back into mythical times without a break" (7–8). Creating fiction through the rewriting of history (the reuse of plot as Aristotle described such reuse) was important in ancient times (12). Sternberg describes the usual opposition between history and fiction but then describes both history-writing and fiction-writing as discourses: one claims to be factual, and the other claims the "freedom of invention" (25). I would suggest that, although for us it is unclear as to the genre of ancient texts, for the ancients it might have been perfectly clear (see Bakhtin 1986:98). Thus, at this point we shall assume that there is a typical historiographical style and that Genesis through 2 Kings belongs to it.

MIDRASH

So let us begin with the first line of the first verse of Lamentations: *ʾêkâ yāsĕbâ bādād hāʿîr rabbātî ʿam* "How lonely sits the city once full of people!" The city sits alone. This city is Jerusalem, as the rest of Lam 1 makes clear. We may assume that, since the city of Jerusalem represents Judah, therefore Judah sits alone. It is the use of the word *bādād* "alone" that gives us our first link, to Jeremiah.

Jeremiah 15 is a dialogue between God and Judah concerning Judah's impending destruction. Jeremiah says, "I have not sat in the company of merrymakers, nor have I rejoiced; with your hand upon me I have sat alone [*bādād*], for you have filled me with anger" (15:17). Jeremiah insists that the nation has already held itself apart from the other nations because of its belief in YHWH. The complaint is futile. God has already decided to destroy Judah and has expressed it by making use of the personification of Jerusalem: "For who will pity you, O Jerusalem, and who will console you, and who will turn aside to wish you well?" (15:5). So although it is the city that sits alone in Lamentations, it is really the nation, in accord with a prophetic convention of identifying city with nation. The nation Judah is alone, its people scattered, its identity destroyed. This may remind the reader of Isaiah, who says, "For the fortified city is alone [*bādād*], an abandoned and forsaken place, like the desert" (27:10). However, Isaiah is also looking forward to the day when the empty city is again filled with people, when Judah is again gathered into Jerusalem; thus, in 27:13 we read: "[T]hose who were lost in the land of Assyria and those who were driven out to the land of Egypt will come and worship YHWH on the holy mountain of Jerusalem."

We have just linked Lam 1:1 to prophetic literature. The prophets see Judah (or Israel), as personified by Jerusalem, to be alone. Not only do they foretell this loneliness and destruction; they also seem to get some kind of vicarious pleasure out of it: YHWH has finally fulfilled his promise to destroy the people who had disobeyed him for so long (see Jer 32, 52; most of Ezek 1–24; Mic 1, though cf. Beal 1994 on the identity of the speaker in Mic 1:8–9). Lamentations mourns the destruction of the city, mourns the loneliness of its isolation, and calls for the pity that Jeremiah says will not come. However, by this midrashic linking of Lamentations with Isaiah, we can also see that there is hope for the future: the city is alone for now, but it will again be filled with people.

As far as form goes, the second and third lines of Lam 1:1 augment the first; they repeat the idea of the abandoned city, not in the plain language of the first line but in metaphorical language. The second line, *hāyětâ kě'almānâ rabbātî baggôyim* "How like a widow she has become, once great among the nations," uses the familial image of the husband and wife, whereas the third line, which I will come to presently, uses the metaphor of political organization.

The importance of the husband-wife image can be made clear when we look at the Song of Songs, as exemplified by this verse: "You are beautiful, my dearest, as Tirzah, lovely as Jerusalem, formidable as armies bearing banners" (6:4). In the rabbinic tradition, the erotic love poetry of the Song of Songs was accepted into the canon of Jewish scriptures because of the allegorical understanding of the two lovers as YHWH and Israel. If we look at this verse with this understanding, then YHWH is telling Judah that she is as beautiful as her city Jerusalem. This verse also has the intriguing second half that describes the lover Jerusalem as "formidable as (armies bearing) banners," an image that unfortunately does not have the same force in translation as in the Hebrew.[2] This image has a nice double meaning when we tie it to the situation here: a formidable enemy has conquered Judah, but Judah could rise again as a formidable army herself.

The imagery of Jerusalem/Judah as a widow can be found also in Hosea, where the relationship between Israel and YHWH is often expressed as husband and wife: "And on that day, so says YHWH, she will call me 'My husband,'

---

2. See Long for a contrary view on the meaning of this phrase; he suggests it should be translated "Overwhelming like the[se] sights" of Tirzah and Jerusalem (708). However, he also notes that the terminology here is linked with the "fearsome Neo-Babylonians" (706).

and she will not call me 'My Baal' again" (2:18). Once Israel has repented, she will take her rightful place as the bride of Yнwн. This verse also holds another link; in this scenario reported by Hosea, Israel repents of her abandonment of Yнwн and does so by calling Yнwн by his name alone, not by the name of the gods of the nations around her. Yнwн is Israel's husband, not Israel's Baal. Yet at the same time Jerusalem is his widow. How can Yнwн be dead, so that Jerusalem can be like a widow? The key here may be found in Lam 5:20, where it is clear that Yнwн has abandoned Jerusalem, and therefore the children (i.e., the inhabitants of Jerusalem) are orphans (Renkema: 121). The singular position of Yнwн is made clear, echoing the loneliness of the city Jerusalem. This verse also helps us explain why the image of the widow is juxtaposed with the former position of Judah/Jerusalem as great among the nations. We would call this a mixed metaphor, but the mixing of the metaphor is apt when we consider that the husband of Judah, Yнwн, has forsaken her for now, while the gods of the other nations around her seem to be enjoying their wedded bliss. The theme of loneliness, which was first stated in the first line, is now expressed as a sort of theological loneliness; Judah is alone without her God, unlike her enemies.

The third line of Lam 1:1 makes the transition to theological loneliness clear. It is a political metaphor: śārātî bammĕdînôt hāyĕtâ lāmas "Once a princess among the provinces, she has become a vassal." The inclusion of śārātî "princess" introduces a term used elsewhere as part of a message of hope. The word śārâ "princess" only occurs a few other times in the Hebrew Bible, and one of those occurrences is in Isaiah: "And kings shall be your foster fathers, and their princesses shall be your nurses; they will prostrate themselves before you and lick the dust from your feet, and you will know that I am Yнwн" (49:23). Again, a message of hope: the former princess Jerusalem will be attended by the princesses of the nations around her. However, it is the word mĕdînâ "province," that is really interesting here. This word, which refers to an administrative district, is used almost exclusively in the books of Esther, Daniel, Ezra, and Nehemiah, as follows: "And the king declared a holiday in the provinces, and he gave gifts like a king" (Esth 2:18). This is the Persian king that is referred to, and the four aforementioned books are books that deal with the position of Judah once Persian rule has come, after the destruction of Jerusalem. The word "province" makes no sense here unless it reflects on Yehud's present reality as a vassal-province: Jerusalem could not be a "princess among the provinces" unless the rule of empire has already come. This image therefore shows how Jerusalem's former position of centrality has already come to be a position of marginality.

The image of marginality is further confirmed by an examination of the word mas "vassal." Regarding vassals, Deuteronomy says, "And if they declare peace to you and open their gates to you, all the people found in the city will become vassals to you" (20:11). This passage refers to the vassals that Israel created as she entered the Promised Land, and Lamentations reflects that Jerusalem/Judah has become a vassal just as Israel had marginalized the nations it had conquered. Her shame in becoming a vassal is linked to her shame in being abandoned by her husband/protector, having abandoned her covenant with her protector YHWH (Olyan: 215–17).

I would summarize the argument I have constructed above as follows: Lam 1:1 asks a question: Now that we in Yehud are not central, but marginal, and our God has forsaken us for now, and we are lonely, what do we do? We are also confident that God will remember us, but we now exist in a new reality. How do we make sense of this reality? This is not only a literary device but a question that would have resonated throughout the society. I would then make a suggestion as to the solution to the question posed in Lamentations: the great so-called "historical" narrative of Genesis through 2 Kings is the answer to the question of how Yehud should construct itself. In doing this reading, I am reading against the order of the biblical books, and I am also reading against the traditional dating of those books. However, reading against the canonical and chronological order of these books, as I have just done, gives us a different way to see their relationship. One can be seen as the response to the other: the two bodies of text (Lamentations and the Genesis–2 Kings) are in dialogue, not separated and irrelevant to each other. Brian Peckham (1–12) has argued along similar lines in *History and Prophecy*, suggesting that the historical and prophetic bodies of literature grew together, albeit in the preexilic period. Similarly, Philip Davies has suggested (somewhat tongue in cheek) that the various genres of biblical literature emerged out of various "colleges" located in postexilic Yehud and that the dialogue between the genres arose out of the competing agendas of these colleges (1995:116–17; cf. Berquist 1995). I will return to Peckham's and Davies's arguments below.

I would like to finish my midrash by looking at how the historical books answer the question posed by Lamentations. In Lamentations, loneliness is not a desirable characteristic, nor is it a desirable characteristic in the prophets I linked to Lamentations. The only good thing about loneliness is that it will end. The city will be filled again, and YHWH will remember Israel. However, the great historical narrative transforms loneliness and isolation: it becomes a highly desirable characteristic. What about "Hear Israel, YHWH our God one YHWH" (Deut. 6:4)? This is a wonderfully polyvalent phrase in Hebrew, in that it is entirely without verbs after the initial command to hear. It can therefore be understood in several ways: "Hear, O Israel, YHWH our God is one YHWH," as I have given in the text, or "Hear O Israel, YHWH is our God, YHWH is one," or "Hear O Israel, YHWH is our God, one YHWH," or even "Hear O Israel, YHWH is our God, YHWH alone." No matter where the emphasis is placed in the phrase, however, the singularity of YHWH is apparent. YHWH is alone. Not only is YHWH alone; this is a good way for YHWH to be. Isolation becomes the defining characteristic of Israel's God.

YHWH then takes his isolation and imposes it on Israel. This selection of Israel as YHWH's chosen people is a pervading theme of the great history of Genesis–2 Kings, and it may be summarized in YHWH's command, "You will be holy, for I am holy" (Lev 11:45). What does this holiness mean? The root *qdš* means to be separate or sacred (see Daly 1966:51–53). Israel is to be as isolated as her God. Now, loneliness, *bādād*, becomes a good characteristic, as in Deut 33:28: "And Israel settles down in safety, alone [*bādād*] is Jacob's abode." So Jerusalem's loneliness as expressed in Lam 1:1 becomes her defining characteristic. I would like to put this in terms with which we might be more familiar: the great history of Genesis–2 Kings arose as a response to the destruction of Israel's defining symbol, Jerusalem, and as a response to Persian imperialism. Israel's loneliness became a way of coping with the new reality.

COMPARISON/CONTEXT

It is important to remember that historiography as a genre does not seem to be known to the author(s) of the main narrative of Genesis–2 Kings. The author of the so-called Primary History was a literary pioneer. We might therefore say that this narrative takes the form that later writers recognized as historiography. This would be an interesting argument in itself; however, there is another great narrative work from the same time period that later writers also recognized as historiography. That, of course, is Herodotus's *History*. Like the biblical author, Herodotus did not know the genre of historiography, and it is his description of his work, *historiē* (1.1), which means "inquiry," that has given us the word "history." Both the biblical author and Herodotus pioneered a narrative genre that told about the past events of their peoples. Herodotus set his work against the backdrop of the great conflict between the Greeks and the Persians, while the biblical author set his work against the backdrop of Israel's conflicts with all of the nations it came into contact with. Both works are heavily influenced by the power of God in human affairs. Both works can be seen as framing history as a tragedy (see Nielsen). And both works can be seen as identity-forming exercises.

How did historiography develop in the Greek world? Both John Van Seters and Simon Hornblower have described the development of Greek historiography in some detail; here I will only summarize. There were several factors or features that combined to form historiography as a genre. First, there was the influence of the epic; it is a truism that Herodotus's work was a prose epic, telling a story of massive scope and consequence. T. James Luce points out (3) that the themes of war and descriptions of foreign lands, prominent in the Homeric epics, are also prominent in the histories. Second, there was the influence of drama, specifically tragedy; it is equally a truism that Herodotus's work was a tragedy in the Sophoclean mode. Third, there was the impact of the logographers of the sixth and fifth centuries: authors of lists and descriptions of all kinds, who also began to write local histories. The origins of this form of writing are also difficult to determine (Luce: 11). However, the works done by these authors—genealogies, ethnographies, annals, and chronologies—were all incorporated into the historiographic impulse (Fornara: 4–29). Fourth, there was the influence of the pre-Socratic philosophers, which led to the emergence of rationalism and the separation of myth/legend from fact (although questions of truth and fiction are best left aside here). Fifth, the Persian Wars were crucial to the formation of Greek self-identity, by defining Greek identity over against the Persian "other" (Hall: 44–45). Finally, in his study of the Near Eastern antecedents to historiography, Marc Van de Mieroop suggests that Greek literary historiography arose as a result of a breakdown in oral and visual historical transmission, when there was a panic about the preservation of historical memory (84–85). Historiography, then, is a genre developed in a mature literary tradition, and it is a genre that not every literary tradition has necessarily developed (80–81). Yet the vast majority of biblical scholars would probably agree that the historiography of Genesis–2 Kings (or portions thereof) was the first literary genre to develop in the biblical tradition. Even John Van Seters, in his trenchant criticism of previous works on the development of biblical historiography (1983:209–48), in a book that is more often read than actually used, does not escape this assumption. Philip Davies's heuristic device of scribal colleges all working together to develop literary traditions in Yehud (discussed above) does not help us, since it does not allow us to see the development of genres.

When we turn to the factors that led to the development of historiography in the biblical tradition, it is much harder to find clear evidence. Although Herodotus is the first historian in the Greek tradition whose work has come to us intact, we know from other ancient sources something about his predecessors. We have examples of the epic tradition and examples of the tragic tradition; we can see how these other genres influenced the development of historiography. In studying the biblical tradition, we must rely almost wholly on the Bible itself, and, more importantly, we must deal with how the texts are dated and understood by scholars. Although Davies's heuristic device may be flawed for understanding the development of genres, his dating for the texts (Persian-period products) is more helpful (see 1998:115). Van Seters had the right idea when he argued that biblical historiography developed out of the combination of chronologies, inscriptions, and annals/chronicles (1993:356–57); this corresponds to the logographers' works in the Greek tradition. However, because he was working from a preexilic date for the biblical tradition, he could come up with no other influence than a vague notion that historiography was the ideal vehicle for presenting an authoritative tradition. If we work with a postexilic date for the biblical tradition, then we have a clear incentive for the development of biblical historiography.

There was another factor that led to the development of historiography in the Greek world—the Persian Empire—and this factor is directly relevant to our understanding of the development of historiography in Persian-period Yehud. From the mid-sixth to the mid-fourth centuries B.C.E. the Persian Empire was the greatest power the world had ever seen. We should remember that Herodotus was from Halicarnassus, an Ionian Greek city on the western edge of the Persian Empire (some of his logographer predecessors, such as Hecataeus, were also Ionian). We should also remember that Herodotus's work was about the great conflict between the Greeks and the Persians. If we turn to the situation in Yehud, Jerusalem was on the southern edge of the Persian Empire, one of the last outposts before Egypt, which was not always under Persian control. Arnaldo Momigliano argued repeatedly for the need to consider the Persian context when studying the origins of historiography in both the Greek and Judean contexts. He suggested that it was a "generic influence of Oriental institutions and literary traditions" that led to the development of Greek and Judean historiography (1990:12; cf. 1977:25–33). He went on to suggest that the Greeks and Judeans had a similar reaction to the annalistic tradition of the Persians and their predecessors, developing a historical tradition pertaining to the community and not to the royal leadership. This tradition of historiography was a reaction against Persian imperialism, occurring as societies began to focus inward on the community, rather than outward internationally (1990:16–17).

However, what I would argue is that the genre of historiography arose simply because the Persian Empire was so vast. Before the era of the vast empires, there was a national symbol that would unite a particular group, and that symbol was local and based on the land. Thus Jerusalem could be a symbol for the people who lived in the land called Judah (or Israel). Jonathan Hall has suggested that an ethnic group is distinguished from other groups "by virtue of association with a specific territory and a shared myth of descent" (32). The coming of the great empires destroyed those local symbols. What arose as a response to that destruction was a loyalty to an ethnic group instead of the former loyalty to place, although the ethnic group itself might have a loyalty to place. One way to cement that loyalty was to write the great national history. E. Theodore Mullen Jr. has suggested that the

Deuteronomic History was written in the context of exile as an exercise of identity maintenance and that the Deuteronomist believed that adherence to the principles in the Deuteronomic History would lead to Israel (Judah) being given back its land (283, 285). It is also important to remember that the Persians were not cultural imperialists. They did not force adherence to their religious symbols. The space was there for ethnic groups to promulgate their own history, and the narrative genre of historiography arose to fill that space.[3] This literature offered identity to "people deprived of their familiar structures of state," regardless of whether this literature was fact or fiction (Weeks: 155). This literature also was an identity-forming exercise by opposing the group's culture and history to the strange and foreign one of the Persians (see Hall: 44; Hartog).

However, if we return to the development of biblical historiography, we have not moved beyond Van Seters's factors with the Persian factor added in. These explanatory factors were not enough to account for Herodotus's history, so why should they be enough for the biblical history? Here is where the midrash I performed above makes its reappearance. I said above that the biblical history answers the question posed by Lam 1:1, but we also saw that the question of identity implicit in 1:1 is amplified by the prophetic corpus. I would argue that the prophetic corpus contributed to the development of historiography much as Attic tragedy contributed to Herodotus. Here is where Peckham's work becomes useful, if we adjust it slightly. Peckham sees the development of the historical traditions in much the same way as source and redaction critics have seen it, relying on our old friends J, E, D, and P, combined in some later period. He calls J an epic, but it would only be a *prose* epic and thus not directly comparable to the Greek epic tradition, to which he does compare it (88). However, if we see Genesis–2 Kings as having been written to include material from other sources (as Herodotus wrote his work), and are not too concerned with the shape of those sources, then suddenly Peckham's work becomes invaluable, if we adjust his dating slightly: Isaiah is the earliest biblical book, followed by the other prophets in reasonably quick succession. Of course, Isaiah would know some of the traditions that would materialize in Genesis–2 Kings (Peckham: 134), just as the Attic tragedians knew the myths and legends of their culture. The themes taken up in the prophetic corpus influenced the development of historiography, just as the themes of tragedy

---

3. Stuart Weeks has come to similar conclusions by a different route: he suggests that postexilic Judaism's concept of Israel and its emphasis on the authority of written texts for the constitution of Israel was unusual in the ancient world and that these two features were possibly related (154–55).

influenced Herodotus. Showing these themes and their development in the
historiographical corpus is a matter best left for another place.

The example of Herodotus and his predecessors also can help us in terms
of time frame. It has been commonly supposed that a great deal of time was
needed between the writing of the various parts of the biblical corpus in order
to explain the differences in ideology between them. However, we should
remember that about one century passed from the time of the beginnings of
Attic tragedy to the time of Herodotus. Within another century, philosophy
and full-blown historiography had arrived and prospered. Drawing on the
Attic-Ionic model, then, it would not be unreasonable for us to assume that
the literary production of the bulk of the Hebrew Bible took place within a
span of two hundred years. In the Greek world, books like Herodotus became
"canonical" very quickly, and it would not be unreasonable for us to hypoth-
esize that the same happened in Persian-period Yehud.

Concluding Remarks

I am not claiming in this paper that Lamentations and the prophetic voices I
linked to it represent a preexilic or exilic ideology or ideologies. Although I
have argued that historiography arose in the Persian period as a reaction to
an earlier literary tradition, I am not arguing that the earlier tradition was
preexilic. My notes about the dating and time frame of these texts (above)
should make this clear. The work of Bakhtin (1984; 1981) should alert us to
the possibility of multiple ideological voices emerging from the biblical text.
The ideology of the loneliness of Yhwh and Israel that emerged from my
midrash should be seen as coming from the Persian-period context, but so
too should the ideology that loneliness was an evil to be avoided.

Historiography arose as a postcolonial form of writing, that is, as a way of
writing shaped by cultural experience of and resistance to imperialism. These
histories also had a subversive effect. The effects of works such as Herodotus's
History and the biblical narrative of Genesis–2 Kings were not immediately
apparent. However, it can hardly be coincidence that a hundred years after
Herodotus, the scholars accompanying Alexander the Great on his conquest
of the Persian empire took Herodotus's work along with them and compared their own observations with his. It can also hardly be a coincidence
that the author of 1 Maccabees, about 250 years later than the biblical history,
describes the Jewish liberator Judas Maccabee in terms drawn directly from
the great history (e.g., 1 Macc 9:21, 73). The genre of historiography became a
powerfully subversive tool in the hands of those who would overthrow their
imperialist masters.

Eventually, of course, the genre of historiography was taken over by the
imperialists themselves. Those writers who were part of the large empires of

Alexander and Rome found that this narrative genre of historiography was excellent for defending the existence of the empire. By establishing an empire or emperor's "historical" right to rule, a Roman historian could show that empire or emperor's right to rule in the present day. Such a historian could also show the superiority of the Roman empire (or British or American) over any other forms of rule available. It is ironic, I think, that this identity-forming narrative genre of marginal peoples became the identity-crushing genre of later Western tradition. And all of this from, "How lonely sits the city once full of people."

"A World under Control": Isaiah 60 and the Apadana Reliefs from Persepolis[*]

Brent A. Strawn

Official Persian art was designed for widespread dissemination and message conveyance, just as the official decrees were.... [T]he overarching message is one of a world under control.... The pervasive image of imperial domain and social hierarchy stresses cooperative—even joyous—service and the virtues of blamelessness. (Root 1992:446)

1. Introduction

Isaiah 56–66 (Third or Trito-Isaiah) is typically assigned to the Persian period. Unfortunately, however, scholarship on these chapters has been much divided. The disagreements are many and complex, involving, among other things, different opinions on historical- and source-critical analyses. Following Duhm's ground-breaking work (1968, orig. 1892; see Clements 1983:62–66), subsequent scholarship, while generally agreeing that a Trito-Isaiah of some sort exists, has disagreed on two major points: (1) whether Trito-Isaiah is really a unified composition stemming from one hand; and (2) whether all of Trito-Isaiah dates from the mid-fifth century, shortly before Ezra and Nehemiah, as Duhm had proposed.

The general consensus has been negative on both counts. Consequently, proposals for the historical and social location of the prophet have quite literally run the full gamut of options. Fortunately, however, these options are still

---

* I would like to thank John W. Wright, who first suggested that a look at Isa 60 and the artistic material from Persepolis might be fruitful. My thanks also go to Bill T. Arnold, Jon L. Berquist, Othmar Keel, J. J. M. Roberts, and C. L. Seow, each of whom read and commented on earlier drafts of this paper. A version of the essay was delivered in the Literature and History of the Persian Period Group at the Annual Meeting of the Society of Biblical Literature, November 2000, Nashville, Tennessee.

relatively finite. They can be reduced, in the main, to three possibilities. Trito-Isaiah either: (1) dates to the mid-fifth century (so, e.g., Duhm and others); (2) dates to the late-sixth century (so, e.g., Elliger and others); or (3) dates to both; that is, it is a document composed of multiple chronological layers (so, e.g., Volz; Westermann; and others). It is safe to say that most recent scholars have favored the third option and have broken these chapters up accordingly, assigning them to different hands and periods. The majority opinion has been that Trito-Isaiah is *not* a unified document but does, in fact, stem from different hands and from completely different (and perhaps even antagonistic) communities. With this said, it becomes possible, if not likely, that the materials date to more than one period (Wanke: 170; for alternative understandings of textual differences, see Berquist 1995b:37). The work of Paul Volz (see Seitz 1992:502) represents one of the most extreme examples of *adversus* Duhm scholarship, assigning the various oracles to centuries as disparate as the seventh to the third.

As Volz's work demonstrates, the results of diachronic analyses have varied widely; they cannot be summarized here. More recent work has advanced still other and quite different understandings of Trito-Isaiah and its relationship to the rest of the book of Isaiah both in redactional and canonical ways.[1] Two general points of agreement ought to be stressed, however. First, despite large and small disagreements, there is still a wide consensus that the vast majority, if not the entirety, of Trito-Isaiah dates to the Persian period. As Lester L. Grabbe has pointed out, given the many differences over the details surrounding Trito-Isaiah, "so minimal an agreement as this is both surprising and significant, which makes the use of this part of Isaiah to illustrate the early period following the return less controversial" (1992:47). A second general point of agreement is that most scholars agree that Isa 60–62 is the "nucleus" around which the rest of the collection conglomerated (Westermann: 296–308, esp. 304; P. A. Smith: 204–7; de Moor: 342–45). This nucleus is often said to be similar to, perhaps even dependent on, Deutero-Isaiah, especially in theological emphases (e.g., the stress on salvation).[2] If so,

---

1. For diachronic analyses, see Seitz 1992:501–7; Soggin: 393–97; Eissfeldt: 341–46; Sellin and Fohrer: 385–88; Blenkinsopp 1996:212–22; Koch 1982:152–59; Childs: 311–38; Westermann: 295–308; Grabbe 1992:46–49; Berquist 1995a:73–79; Schramm: 11–52; Driver: 230–46; P. A. Smith. On redactional approaches, see, e.g., Steck 1986a; 1991: *passim*, note the chart on 278–79; Beuken 1989; 1990:67. For canonical approaches, see Childs: 325–38; Brueggemann 1984:889–907; 1992:252–69; Seitz 1992:502–6; 1996:219–40.

2. See, e.g., Koch 1982:153; Blenkinsopp 1996:216 on the school or disciple-like relationship between Deutero-Isaiah and Trito-Isaiah. For citations or allusions in Trito-Isaiah to Deutero-Isaiah, see also Wanke: 170 n. 4; Zimmerli 1950:110–22; 1963:217–33.

perhaps Isa 60–62 ought to be dated similarly, around 520 B.C.E.[3] Of course, not all scholars would accept such a dating, and it might be challenged on a number of counts (see, e.g., Driver: 246 on the work of Cheyne).

Whatever the case, despite these two points of agreement, it is nevertheless apparent that the historical and linguistic arguments regarding Trito-Isaiah are at something of an impasse. A way forward, furthermore, does not seem to be forthcoming. As Christopher R. Seitz has pointed out, any potential solution to the dilemma of Trito-Isaiah's sociohistorical location must invariably have recourse to "a larger reconstruction of postexilic life, utilizing the internally contradictory and by no means perspicuous historical sources of Chronicles, Ezra-Nehemiah, Malachi, Haggai, and Zechariah" (1992:503). This is to say that appealing to other biblical material is no less problematic, with scholarship no less divided, than is the case with Trito-Isaiah proper. It seems both necessary and attractive, then, to look for additional, *external* data that might provide a way around or beyond this impasse without doing violence to the valuable insights gained by previous scholarship: historical, literary, and otherwise.[4] Artistic *realia* provide such information and are of special interest, not only because they offer a resource that is still in its infancy in biblical research (see Keel 1997), but also due to the presence of fairly recent discoveries and scholarly syntheses of Achaemenid art (especially Root 1979; see also Briant 2002:165–254; Frei and Koch). For reasons that will become readily apparent, I begin with Persepolis and the Apadana reliefs found there.

2. The Apadana Reliefs from Persepolis

It can be suggested that the ultimate goal of both the architecture and the decoration of Persepolis was to present to the world the concept of a *Pax Persica*—a harmonious, peaceful empire ruled by a king who contained within his person and his office the welfare of the empire. (Young: 236)

Cyrus located his capital at Pasargadae despite the fact that centers of Persian power and royalty were already present at Ecbatana, Babylon, and Susa.

---

3. So, e.g., Wanke: 170. P. A. Smith (204–5) puts the later of his two Trito-Isaiahs around 515, which would make the author responsible for Isa 60:1–63:6 (Smith's "nucleus") still earlier.

4. In my judgment, this is often the problem with more recent approaches. While these are often highly insightful and provide additional critical tools for the interpretive endeavor, they often too easily and effectively eliminate the insights painstakingly gained by previous generations of scholarship.

Darius I, in turn, decided to build a new capital, choosing a site not far from
Pasargadae. There he built Persepolis (modern-day Takht-i Jamshid). Figure
1 shows the plan of the city, which in the early period had only one main
entrance (stairway L on fig. 1 at the northwest corner). According to Young
(236), the platform, cistern, drainage system, central part of the Apadana,[5]
and several sections of the Treasury building (structure B) were begun and
completed by Darius himself (522–486 B.C.E.). Construction on the site probably began shortly after his reign began, perhaps around 520 (so Young: 236)
or upon his return from Egypt in 518 B.C.E. (so Root 1989:33–50). Xerxes
(486–465) subsequently expanded and finished much of the work at Persepolis, adding, for instance, Gatehouse K, which he called the "Gate of All
Nations."[6] Xerxes also built a new palace (structure F) as well as the Harem
(structure C) and the Tripylon (structure E), to name a few of his endeavors.
Later rulers continued construction, but this was little more "than the completion, or the enlargement, of the building plans laid down by Darius and
modified by Xerxes" (Young: 236).

Of primary concern for the present study is the Apadana (structure J on
fig. 1) and the reliefs preserved upon it. Figure 2 shows the plan of the Apadana.
As is the case with Persepolis as a whole, there is some uncertainty with regard
to the precise date(s) when the Apadana was planned, executed, and finished.
In light of Xerxes' inscriptions (XPb and XPg), it would seem that he is the one
who completed the structure, but Erich F. Schmidt argued that the trilingual
foundation inscription found at each corner of the Apadana (DPh) demonstrates that the structure was planned and construction begun under Darius I
(Schmidt 1953:70; cf. Root 1979:90). The inscription reads as follows:

---

5. Old Persian *apadāna*; lit: "palace" or "hall of pillars" (see Olmstead: 162; Kent:
168). None of the Persepolis inscriptions refer to the structure as an Apadana, but see
Schmidt 1953:70 for the term in inscriptions referring to very similar (or identical) build-
ings elsewhere (Susa, Ecbatana, and perhaps also Babylon and Pasargadae). The Persian
term occurs as a loanword in Dan 11:45: אָהֳלֵי אַפַּדְנוֹ ("the tents of his Apadana"; NRSV:
"his palatial tents").

6. Cf. inscription XPa (= Xerxes Persepolis inscription a), lines 11–17: "Saith Xerxes
the King: By the favor of Ahuramazda, this Colonnade of All Lands I built. Much other
good (construction) was built within this (city) Persepolis, which I built and which my
father built. Whatever good construction is seen, all that by the favor of Ahuramazda we
built" (translation of this and all other Old Persian inscriptions cited in this study are taken
from Kent, here 148). It is possible that Xerxes named the gateway after the Apadana reliefs
with their depictions of representatives from the far reaches of the Persian Empire. If so,
this is another reason to believe that the north facade, at least, was planned and begun—if
not completed—before Xerxes' construction of his gateway and thus probably during the
time of Darius I (see further below).

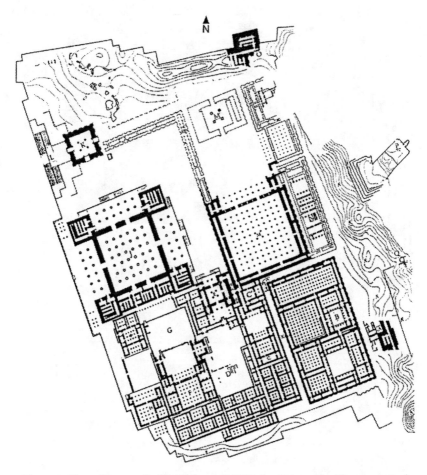

Figure 1. Plan of Persepolis (Frankfort 1996:352 fig. 414, used with permission).

> Darius the Great King, King of Kings, King of countries, son of Hystaspes, an Achaemenian. Saith Darius the King: This is the kingdom which I hold, from the Scythians who are beyond Sogdiana, thence unto Ethiopia; from Sind, thence unto Sardis—which Ahuramazda the greatest of the gods bestowed upon me. Me may Ahuramazda protect, and my royal house. (DPh; Kent: 137; cf. Schmidt 1953:70)

In light of the fact that this inscription does not allude to Darius's conquests against the European Scythians (ca. 513 B.C.E.?), it may be safe to conclude that "at least the substructure of the building had been completed prior to this time and that the construction of the walls—in which the foundation records were

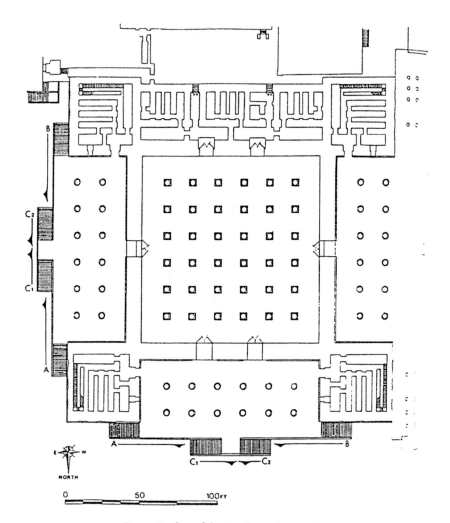

Figure 2. Plan of the Apadana, Persepolis
(after Root 1985: illus. 2; Root 1979:87 fig. 10).

imbedded—had been started" (Schmidt 1953:70; cf. Root 1989:34, who dates
DPh 519–510 B.C.E.).

Fortunately, the issue of the exact chronology can be set aside temporar-
ily, for it is the *program* of the reliefs that is of ultimate import here. They are
found on the north and east sides of the Apadana (see fig. 3 for a reconstruction of the north facade). Both sides are virtually identical (with only minor
differences), appearing in mirror opposite (see Dandamayev and Lukonin:

Figure 3. Reconstruction of the north facade of the Apadana, Persepolis (Root 1979: fig. 11 adapted from Krefter 1971 by Cynthia Susmilch, used with permission; cf. Amiet 1980:574–75).

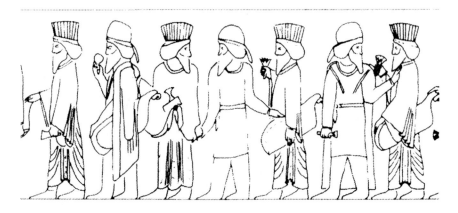

Figure 4. Detail of Persian troops from the east side of the Apadana, Persepolis
(after Roaf 1983:104 fig. 111; cf. Root 1979: pl. 22).

260).[7] The reliefs span nearly 300 feet. In panel A (see fig. 2 and fig. 3 left
side), Persian nobles, horses, chariots, attendants, and guards process toward
the center (C_1 and C_2). A detail of this larger procession scene from the east
side is found in figure 4. Earlier interpretations took these figures to be a
mixture of Persians and Medes, but further analysis has revealed that all of
the figures are Persian; the altered presentations represent courtly and military attire. Panel B (see fig. 2 and fig. 3 right side) shows delegations bearing
tribute—also processing toward the center—each led by a Persian marshal or
usher. These groups are arranged according to ethnicity and are depicted with
enough detail that scholars have been able to identify the various locales and
ethnic groups depicted (see, e.g., Schmidt 1953:85–90; 1970:145–58; H. Koch
1993:93–116; 1992:93–123, esp. 114–23; Walser; cf. also Roaf 1974:73–160). A
detail of one such group (delegation 11: the Saka Tigraxauda or Pointed-Hat
Scythians), again from the east side, can be found on figure 5. Both panels
then, A and B, move inward toward panel C (see figs. 2–3), with the effect
being that the latter becomes the focal point of the scene. Margaret Cool Root
(1979:88) and Ann Britt Tilia (125–208, esp. 191–208; cf. already Schmidt
1953:168) have argued that the present central panel, which is still *in situ*,
was not the original. That panel, which depicts two groups of Persian soldiers
facing one another with an empty space between them (fig. 6), is a replacement. Presumably the empty space between the soldiers was to be inscribed

7. Since the east side was covered with debris following Alexander's destruction, it has
been better preserved than the exposed, weather-beaten north.

Figure 5. Detail of tribute procession from the east side of the Apadana, Persepolis (after Walser 1966: Falttafel 2; cf. Root 1979: pl. 24).

Figure 6. Replacement central panel of the Apadana, Persepolis (drawing by Ulrike Zurkinden; cf. Porada 1969:154–55 fig. 83; Frei and Koch 1996:161 Abb. 2).

with a building inscription, although this conclusion is not certain, and the inscription was never executed. Whatever the case, Tilia and Root have argued that the original central panel was, in all actuality, part of what is now known as the "Treasury Reliefs," since they were discovered in the building by that name (B on fig. 1). Apparently the original panel was removed from the Apadana proper at some point, for some reason—perhaps for safekeeping.[8] This "original" central piece (fig. 7) is much better suited to the theme of panels A and B, as it depicts the enthroned king receiving a Persian official (note the dress) who may be understood as announcing the arrival of the

8. See Root 1979:94 for a discussion. She argues that the switch took place after the time of Xerxes, concurring with Tilia that, if the present central panel were in place with its central empty space available, there would have been no reason for Xerxes to squeeze his building inscription (XPb) onto the two wing panels.

Figure 7. Original central panel of the Apadana (north facade), Persepolis
(after Roaf 1983:115 fig. 122; cf. Frei and Koch 1996:162 Abb. 2a).

various groups in panels A and B, particularly B (Root 1979:282). Which-
ever panel was originally present in C, it is critical to note that on the frame
directly above it is a frieze (visible in fig. 6) depicting the winged sun-disk
(Klaus Koch in Frei and Koch: 161). In the Achaemenid context, of course,
that disk must be interpreted as a symbol for Ahuramazda (Lecoq: 301–25
and pls. XXVIII–LII).[9] The exact details of the original central panel are thus
not of primary import; in either case the procession of tribute and dignitaries
moves toward the center, where the winged sun-disk is highlighted. Even so,
it is significant to note that, in the case of the original Treasury relief panel,

---

9. See further below on the winged sun-disk in Mesopotamian art and for challenges
to Lecoq's interpretation by Shahbazi (1974; 1980) and Calmeyer, along with Lecoq's
rebuttal. In support of Lecoq's view one might note the exact similarity between the upper
register of the central panel of the Apadana reliefs and the upper part of the central section
of the western stairway facade of the palace of Xerxes (directly above XPd, which—notably—praises Ahuramazda in lines 1–6; see Schmidt 1953: pl. 160; Moscati, Tilia, and
Citeroni: pls. 87–88). Note the human-headed, winged lion touching the tree to the right
of the central sun-disk figure and the vegetable motifs. The only significant difference
between the two reliefs is that the winged sun-disk on the palace of Xerxes has the torso of
a human figure rising out of the disk and is thus similar to the depiction of Ahuramazda
at Behistun or Naksh-i Rustam. In light of these similarities, it is altogether probable that
the winged sun-disk without elevated human figure on the central panel of the Apadana is
also to be understood as a representation of Ahuramazda.

the sun-disk would be immediately over the king's head (see fig. 3; H. Koch 1992:100 Abb. 49).[10]

The overall force of these reliefs is quite impressive, especially when it is remembered that this would be the first sight a visitor would see upon entering Persepolis via stairway L and then through Xerxes' "Gate of All Nations" (see the reconstruction in H. Koch 1992:135 Abb. 93). Furthermore, the program of the reliefs is such that the eye, whether it begins with the impressive rows of Persian troops (the "Immortals") or the seemingly endless groups of tribute bearers, invariably moves toward the central panel. There, in the Treasury relief, the observer comes to the king and his reception of the official. However, the eye does not stop there. Although to this point it has been moving mostly horizontally, given the horizontal rows of panels A and B that face and move toward the center, it now reaches the clash of these two movements. Representing the A side is the king with the crown prince and other officials. Representing the B side (or both) is the official who announces the arrival of the processions. The A side clearly dominates, as the king is placed in the middle of the scene and his servants surround the official who faces him. Furthermore, the king and the prince are depicted larger than any of the other figures. For this reason, among others, it is clear that the Persian side (A) is and will be the victor of this encounter. The orientation of the figures in the central panel, moreover, is on the vertical axis. Thus, when the two horizontal movements meet, the energy and eye move upward. As they do, the eye encounters the winged sun-disk representing Ahuramazda. The king and his god, then, are the focal point of this massive, most impressive facade.[11]

Obviously, such art would have had a significant impact on its observers. Moreover, that the Apadana reliefs are so beautifully executed on such a grand scale and are strategically placed as they are would seem to constitute still further proof that they were intended to disseminate a particular mes-

---

10. The reconstruction in fig. 3 contains a fuller depiction of Ahuramazda (i.e., the winged sun-disk with a human torso rising from its midst) in the middle of the Apadana structure as part of the roof ornamentation (see uppermost register). While this reconstruction is attractive and possible on the basis of similar depictions of Ahuramazda elsewhere in Persepolis, I know of no proof that such was the case.

11. The phrase "and his god" is an addition that serves to correct Root's conclusion (1979:282) that "the entire facade is, then, a grandiose unified composition which focuses upon the figure of the king." Of course, in Persian imperial propaganda, no less than other Near Eastern types, there is a good bit of connection between the king and his god(s). See further Ahn (*passim*, esp. 195: "Die Reziprozität der beiden komplementären Vorstellungen 'Gottkönigtum' und 'Königtum Gottes' wird also auch durch das Beispiel des achämenidischen Iran zumindest implizite bestätigt") and more below (also Root 1979:170).

sage. One aspect of that message, to be sure, was the power and extent of the empire. Such a message was not restricted to the Apadana reliefs nor even to Persian iconography, for that matter. Other examples are found in the inscription and reliefs from Darius's tomb at Naksh-i Rustam. There Darius boasts of the peoples he subjugated:

> By the favor of Ahuramazda these are the countries which I seized outside of Persia; I ruled over them; they bore tribute to me; what was said to them by me, that they did; my law—that held them firm; Media, Elam, Parthia, Aria, Bactria, Sogdiana, Chorasmia, Drangiana, Arachosia, Sattagydia, Gandara, Sind, Amyrian Scythians, Scythians with pointed caps, Babylonia, Assyria, Arabia, Egypt, Armenia, Cappadocia, Sardis, Ionia, Scythians who are across the sea, Skudra, petasos-wearing Ionians, Libyans, Ethiopians, men of Maka, Carians.... If now thou shalt think "How many are the countries which King Darius held?" look at the sculptures (of those) who bear the throne, then shalt thou know, then shall it become known to thee: the spear of a Persian man has gone forth far; then shall it become known to thee: a Persian man has delivered battle far indeed from Persia. (DNa, lines 15–47; Kent: 138; cf. DPh [see above] and DPe [see Kent: 135], associated with the Apadana and the palace, respectively; cf. Root 1979:45)

The "sculptures" of which Darius speaks are found in the related reliefs that depict the king borne aloft by two rows of subjugated people (cf. fig. 8 from Persepolis; Root 1979: pls. XII–XIII).[12] These throne-carriers are portrayed in the "Atlas pose," in that they bear the entire weight of the king effortlessly on the thumb and index finger (Root 1979:147–61 and pl. XLI [two genies bearing Ahuramazda in the same fashion]; Frei and Koch: 188 Abb. 14; 192: Abb. 15). Root has argued that the use of this pose in Achaemenid art "represents ... deliberate selection ... precisely because of the iconographical impact it ... conveyed.... [T]hese formal aspects seem calculated to enhance the *aura of dignity and effortless, one might also say joyous, cooperation* with which these subject peoples are imbued" (1979:153, emphasis added). It is, as Root goes on to say, *a visual incarnation of the textual promise of Darius*: "The man who cooperates, him according to his cooperative action, him thus do I reward" (DNb, lines 16ff.; Kent: 140).

---

12. The same motif is found at the tomb of Xerxes (Root 1979: pl. XIV) as well as on the south and north doorjambs of the eastern doorway of the main hall (see Schmidt 1953: pls. 77–81; 1970:159–60). See further Ahn: 272–77; Schmidt 1970:161–63. See also Roaf 1974 and Stronach 1974:61–72 for the statue of Darius from Susa that depicts rows of subjugated peoples. In short, the motif is well-known in Persian iconography.

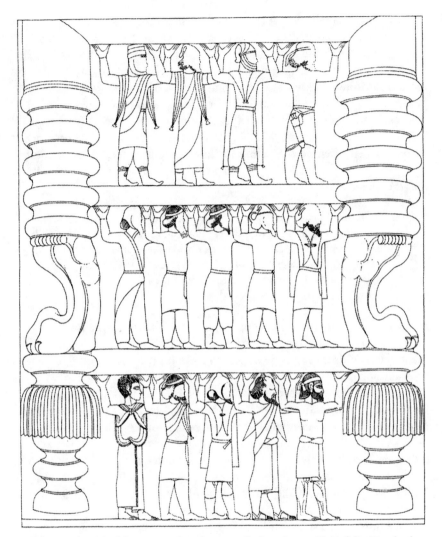

Figure 8. Detail of throne-carriers from south door (west side) of the Hundred
Column Hall, Persepolis (after Walser 1966:62 Abb. 5;
cf. Frei and Koch 1996:176 Abb. 10; Keel 1997:351 fig. 476a).

As an aside, it should be noted that such statements are not merely empty
rhetoric. Darius was telling the truth about the extent and prowess of his
empire. To cite but one example, which will prove important to the further
discussion, it is clear that Darius imported both materials and artisans from
all over the empire (perhaps most notably Ionia) in the work at Persepolis
(Collon 1995:177).

The Apadana reliefs, in turn, provide further motivation for such "joyous cooperation," largely because the presentation seems to portray the Persians as semidivine, with the king as fully—perhaps even supremely—divine. This can be demonstrated by comparing figure 9, a detail of one of the Persian marshals leading a representative of one of the delegations by the hand, with figures 10–11, showing two much earlier (Ur III) seals depicting the so-called "presentation scene." In this latter type, a human supplicant (often a royal) is led by the hand (see Root 1979:267–72), by a minor deity into the presence of a supreme deity. Behind the supplicant another figure intercedes. The similarity of figure 9 to figures 10–11 is rather striking and would seem to indicate that the Apadana relief

> reflects a *conscious selection* of the antique theme of the presentation scene as an eloquent way of rendering the type of relationship between king and vassal states which the Achaemenids wished to have expressed.... *there can be no doubt that the designers of the Apadana facade were aware* of the aura of religiosity and pious trepidation implicit in the presentation scene as a type. (Root 1979:270, emphasis added; see further 277)

If this is correct, the Persians adopted this well-known theme for their own imperial purposes. In so doing, the bringing of tribute was "transformed by the Achaemenids into a scene of pious reverence though a conscious sculptural allusion to age-old Mesopotamian and Egyptian motifs of the petitioner's introduction into the presence of an awe-inspiring divinity" (Root 1979:284). Hence, on analogy with the presentation scenes, the delegations become petitioners introduced by Persian officials who have themselves become the minor deities representing the human supplicant to the supreme deity. The Persian monarch, in turn, becomes identified with the latter, perhaps in some sort of symbiotic relationship with Ahuramazda (see Koch in Frei and Koch; Ahn; Root 1979:170; Gnoli: 167).[13] The propagandistic message of the reliefs is thus obvious: the observer is motivated to cooperate and serve the monarch/deity just like those on panel B (and A). The quicker this cooperation and service, the better!

This is but a brief overview of the Apadana program (see further Root 1979:129–311), but it is sufficient to demonstrate the power and ability

---

13. The iconographical combination/identification of the king as a deity/with the deity Ahuramazda makes the relative size, prominence, and depiction of the sun-disk (or a fuller depiction of Ahuramazda; see fig. 3 top) as the focal point of the facade less critical. Indeed, in light of the iconographical (semi-)divinization of the king, perhaps we should be surprised by the inclusion of the sun-disk in the first place.

Figure 9. Detail of tribute procession/"presentation" from the east side of the
Apadana, Persepolis (drawing by Ulrike Zurkinden; cf. Root 1979: pl. 23).

Figure 10. Presentation scene from Mesopotamia (Ur III; ca. 2050)
(after Keel 1997:199 fig. 272; cf. Collon 1987: fig. 532).

Figure 11. Presentation scene from Mesopotamia (Ur III; ca. 2050-1950)
(after Keel 1997:310 fig. 414).

of Achaemenid art to encapsulate the imperial propaganda of the Persian Empire. Many other examples could be added, but to conclude, the following comment by Young must serve as representative of most scholarly assessments of Achaemenid art:

> Characteristic of these reliefs [from Persepolis] is that they are entirely *unhistorical*; they tell no developing story, as did many reliefs of the Assyrians and the Egyptians. Instead they give a *static picture* of something that is already done, that already exists, that is accomplished (tribute brought, monsters slain, fire honored, dignitaries received). More important, the king is everywhere and is the focus, in one way or another, of almost all the reliefs. Yet this king is not an individual; there are no portraits of Darius, Xerxes, or Artaxerxes. *Instead they project a dynastic image of the glory and concept of kingship, rather than a realistic depiction of a particular king.* Thus the whole of even a complex composition such as the great reliefs on the stairways of the Apadana present *a planned, spiritual, abstract, and almost cosmic composition of static totality.* (Young: 236, emphasis added)

3. ISAIAH 60

To summarize to this point: the subject matter of Achaemenid art in general and the Apadana reliefs in particular is rife with the religio-political ideology and propaganda of the Persian Empire. The force of the whole produces, as Dominique Collon, has put it, "an impression of immutable power" (1995:179). Such a message would have well served the interests of the empire and would have made a significant impact on its constituent entities. This was an empire that would endure; theirs was a law that was not to be broken—that was, still further, *impossible* to break (see Dan 6:8 and DNa: "what was said to them by me, that they did; my law—that held them firm" [Kent: 138]). In short, then, the visual art of the Achaemenids—and the Apadana of Persepolis is but one example of such—helped to enforce and reinforce the notion of the *pax Persica*. The Persian world was stable; it was a "world under control" (Root 1992:446), and the satrapies, at least the wise ones, knew this. It is thus not surprising to find reflexes of this sort of ideology not only in art but also in texts from the Persian era, as, for example, in the royal inscriptions already discussed. What *is* surprising is to locate such a reflex in Trito-Isaiah, given the typical interpretation of this material. Be that as it may, Isa 60 comes immediately to mind and bears striking resemblance to the subject matter of the Apadana reliefs.

There are a number of marked similarities between this chapter and the motifs present on the Apadana. To begin with, one notes that the addressee in Isa 60, a personified Jerusalem, is a capital city (of sorts), not unlike Persepolis. Admittedly, this is a rather minor point of comparison, but further, and more significant, parallels are not difficult to locate. The solar imagery of Isa 60:1–3 and 19–20 is perhaps the most obvious of these.

> [1] Rise! Shine! For your light has come,
>   and the glory of Yahweh has dawned over you.
> [2] For behold the darkness will cover the land,
>   deep darkness the peoples;
> but over you Yahweh will dawn,
>   over you his glory will be seen.
> [3] The nations will come to your light,
>   kings to the brightness of your dawn.
>
> [19] The sun will no longer be your daylight,
>   neither for your light will the moon shine,[14]
> but Yahweh will be your eternal light,
>   your God (will be) your beauty.
> [20] Your sun will no longer go (down),
>   neither will your moon be withdrawn,
> Because Yahweh will be your eternal light,
>   the days of your mourning will be over. (My translation)

Here Yahweh is described as "light" (אור; 60:1, 3) and as "eternal light" (לאור עולם; 60:19, 20). This may, on its own, be enough to evoke astral connections (see, e.g., Gen 1:16), though it must be admitted that light imagery is quite common in the Hebrew Bible and elsewhere (e.g., Isa 2:5; 10:17; Ps 27:1; Mic 7:8; M. S. Smith 1990; 2002: 148–59; Langer: 156–204).[15] Be that as it may, the language here is specified as *particularly solar* by use of the root זרח, a verb that is characteristically used, not of God, but of the rising of the sun.[16] Outside Isa 60 it is used of Yahweh only in the early Deut 33:2 (cf. Hos 6:3;

---

14. 1QIsaᵃ adds בלילה; cf. LXX (τὴν νύκτα) and the Targum. However, one might argue, on the basis of Jer 31:35 and Ps 121:6, that the MT of Isa 60:19 is actually the *lectio difficilior* (see Langer: 16).

15. Cf. also Hebrew and other Semitic personal names (PNs) constructed with אור and Akkadian names with the element *-nūrī*.

16. See Gen 32:32 (Eng 32:31); Exod 22:2; Judg 9:33; 2 Sam 23:4 (of a just ruler); 2 Kgs 3:22; Jonah 4:8; Nah 3:17; Job 9:7; Ps 104:22 (see *DCH* 3:138); 112:4 (of those who fear Yahweh); Qoh 1:5 (2x). The only other instance, 2 Chr 26:19 (of the appearance of leprosy), is of a different sort and seems to be a singular case, unless Hos 7:9 is emended from זרק to זרח (see *DCH* 3:138). This emendation is probably unwarranted. Other possible emendations include references to the righteous in Prov 13:9 (ישׂמח to יזרח; so J.

further Hab 3:4, 10–11).[17] In light of the Apadana reliefs, the application of such imagery to Yahweh strikes one as altogether apropos for the Persian period and is reminiscent of Ahuramazda depicted as the winged sun-disk— the ultimate focal point of the Apadana program. There, of course, the winged sun-disk shines over the central panel. It is at this point that the prevalence of the preposition על, used with respect to position and in connection to sun/ dawn imagery in Isa 60, takes on increased significance (עליך: 60:1, 2 [2x]; see K. Koch 1985:158).[18] Still further, it is not only Yahweh who is depicted in this fashion. The glory of Yahweh (60:1: כבוד יהוה; 60:2: כבודו) also "has dawned over you" or "will be seen over you." This, too, may evoke the winged sun-disk of Persian iconography, if A. Shapur Shahbazi and Peter Calmeyer are correct in their interpretation of the winged disk as a representation of Xvarnah ("glory, splendor" or the like) (see Shahbazi 1974:135–44; 1980:119– 47; Calmeyer 1979:347–65; Boyce 1992:124–25).

Although Shahbazi and Calmeyer's view seems unlikely (see Lecoq: 301–25, esp. 325; cf. Root 1979:169–76), further solar imagery that may be inspired by Persian iconography is found in other texts from Trito-Isaiah, perhaps with reference to Yahweh. One notes, for example, Isa 58:10: "if you give your food to the hungry and satisfy the soul of the afflicted, then your light [אורך] will rise [זרח] in the darkness and your gloom will be as (bright as) noon."[19] This passage is quite similar to 60:1, which puts אורך in parallel with כבוד יהוה. Isaiah 60:19–20 has similar force. In those verses there is a contrast between the physical sun and "your sun," which may be understood as Yahweh. Finally, one might note the presence of this imagery in other texts stemming from the Persian period, such as Mal 3:20 (Eng 4:2): "But the sun of righteousness will dawn on those of you who fear my name, with healing in its wings" (see Hill 1981; 1983; 1998; note also Gaster: 2:689–91). Compare also Ps 84:12 (Eng 84:11), attributed to the Korahites (Hutton: 100–101): "For Yahweh my God is a sun [שמש] and shield; Yahweh gives grace and glory [וכבוד]. He does not withhold goodness from those who walk perfectly." At

---

Fichtner in *BHS*) and Ps 97:11 (זרע to זרח; so NRSV with one Hebrew manuscript, the LXX [ἀνέτειλεν], the Syriac, and Jerome).

17. Note God's power over the sun in Job 9:7 (perhaps also Ps 104:22, if the verb is emended to the H stem). For *zrḥ* at Kuntillet ʿAjrud, see below. Note that the segho-late noun זרח is a *hapax legomenon* found only in Isa 60:3. *DCH* 3:138 posits another occurrence at Isa 53:10, if the text is emended which again seems unwarranted and unnecessary.

18. Apart from these three references, עליך occurs only at 59:21; 60:5; 62:5.

19. Another text that deserves attention is Isa 59:9, esp. if Westermann is right in his theory that Isa 59 is a lament quoted by Trito-Isaiah only to refute or answer it in Isa 60.

this point a comparison to the emphasis on blamelessness found in official Persian art (see Root 1992:446) may be particularly apt.

However, given the ubiquity of solar imagery in the Hebrew Bible and throughout the ancient Near East, further evidence must be cited if one wishes to argue that the imagery in Isa 60 is distinctively *Persian*. Thankfully, such evidence is not difficult to locate. One prominent item is the procession of foreigners with tribute in both Isa 60 and the Apadana. The general impression is similar, and many of the details are exact. Isaiah 60:6 mentions a multitude of camels (שׁפעת גמלים); at least five are intact on the Apadana (see fig. 12). The listing of various locales in Isa 60 (Midian, Ephah, Sheba, Kedar, Nebaioth, Tarshish, Lebanon) recalls the delegations of distinct ethnicities in the Apadana reliefs as well as the catalogues in Persian royal inscriptions (e.g., DNa, above; in DSf, Lebanon is named as the source for construction timber; see Kent: 144; Frankfort: 409 n. 43). That "foreigners" (בני־נכר, 60:10)[20] will build up Jerusalem's walls finds a parallel in actual Persian practices in the construction of Persepolis (Collon 1995:177). The reference to the coastlands and ships (60:9) could parallel groups from the empire, specifically the Ionians and the Scythians across the sea (cf. DNa; Xerxes' "Gate of All Nations"). What is perhaps most significant, however, is that this tribute procession (60:4–7, 9, 11, 13)—like that found at Persepolis—is *unforced*.

This last observation is critical. The main motifs highlighted thus far are not particularly new nor unique to the Persian Empire. One can find earlier examples of these in both text and iconography. From a textual point of view, there can be little doubt that Isa 60 belongs to the broader theophanic tradition of the Hebrew Bible (see Jeremias; Hiebert: 505–11; Nötscher; Scriba; Schnutenhaus: 1–22, esp. 9; Cross: 147–94). Iconographically, solar imagery—especially as encapsulated in the winged sun-disk—is extremely well-attested, found in Egypt and Mesopotamia as early as the second millennium B.C.E., if not before (see, e.g., Keel 1997:27–28; Mendenhall: 32–66; Mayer-Opificius; Pering). Solar imagery, not to mention solar worship, is also a well-known phenomenon in textual sources throughout the history of religions (Eliade: 124–53, also 38–123; Gaster: 2:689–91) and also in the Hebrew Bible (Stähli; Taylor; M. S. Smith 1990:29–39; 2002:148–59; Keel and Uehlinger 1994b). These antecedents, textual and iconographical, must be explored and dis-

---

20. That the foreigners are not explicitly catalogued in Isa 60:10, in contrast to the Apadana and the royal inscriptions, need not be seen as problematic because, as Root points out, "it was … a non-specific concept of foreigners willingly bearing gifts which was considered the essence of the Apadana relief system, at least by later generations of Achaemenid planners" (1979:279).

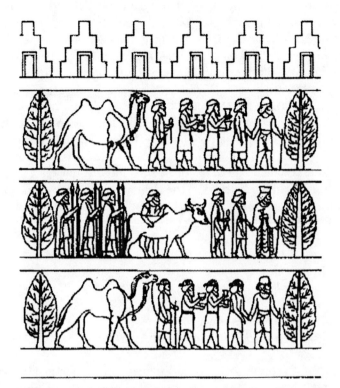

Figure 12. Detail of camels from tribute procession, Persepolis
(after Walser 1966: Falttafel 2; cf. Sarre 1925: Abb. 26).

cussed if a case is to be made that the imagery of Isa 60 is inherently Persian
in origin or orientation.

TEXTS

Light (אור) is a rather common motif in depictions of the divine in the
ancient Semitic world (Langer). It is also a typical element in Semitic
theophoric names. There is nothing inherent, therefore, in such imagery that
would assign it exclusively to the Persian period. Similar is זרח: it is attested
in the PN Zeraḥ (probably an abbreviated theophoric name; cf. the Akkadian
PN Zarḫi-ilu), which would seem to belong to periods prior to the Persian
(e.g., Gen 38:30; 46:12; Num 26:30; Josh 7:1; 18:24; 22:20) and to peoples
other than Israelites (e.g., Gen 36:33//1 Chr 1:44; 2 Chr 14:8). This PN is
also attested on a bulla (seal 562) from Tell Beit Mirsim dating to the late
seventh or early sixth centuries B.C.E. (G. I. Davies: 195; *DCH* 3:138), which

reads *hnnyhw zrḥ*, "(Belonging to) Hananyāh (son of) Zeraḥ." Similar is the evidence for the full theophoric PNs זרחיה and יזרחיה. While these names show up in Ezra's lineage (1 Chr 5:32; 6:36; Ezra 7:4) and for persons from the Persian period (Ezra 8:4; Neh 12:42), at least one of them also occurs on a seal from the ninth century that apparently belonged to one Zeraḥiah the Rabbathite (*zrḥyw hrbt*; *DCH* 1:139; but see Tigay: 51; cf. also Taylor: 282–83; and Silverman for אור and זרח in PNs at Elephantine). In sum, then, there is nothing in the particular light or dawn language of Isa 60 that confines it exclusively to a Persian provenance, but neither does it exclude such a horizon.

The same could be said of the theophany motifs. Apart from Isa 60:1–2 the verb זרח with Yahweh occurs in the Hebrew Bible only in Deut 33, hardly a Persian text. Moreover, it also appears in the broken context of a plaster inscription from Kuntillet ʿAjrud, probably dating to the first half of the eighth century:

...]*wbzrḥ.ʾl.br*[...
...]*wymsn hrm wydkn gbnm*[...
...]*wšdš ʿly*[...
...]*lbrk bʿl bym mlḥ*[*mh*]
...]*lšm ʾl bym mlḥ*[*mh*] (Meshel: 107; cf. *DCH* 3:138; G. I. Davies: 82)

Unfortunately, the preservation of this inscription is poor, making an overall interpretation inexact. Further, several consonants, including one on the crucial (for our purposes) word *bzrḥ*, seem to be damaged and are thus somewhat uncertain.[21] Even so, the general sense of the text is clear insofar as it is "obviously a piece of an ancient theophany describing the revelation of God in language echoing the OT" (Meshel: 107). This instance of a theophany employing the word זרח, not to mention Deut 33:2, may well give one pause, then, when connecting its use in Isa 60 to Persian thematics. Perhaps the Isaianic text is a theophany entirely similar to earlier examples. If so, the portrayal of God as "light" or as a dawn "dawning" on Jerusalem would be stock theophanic language and have nothing whatsoever to do with Persia or Persepolis.

At first such a possibility seems quite compelling. Apart from the solar language, several other elements found in Isa 60 can be traced to other (and earlier) theophany texts. One notes, for example, that a concern for the "name" of God is present in Isa 60:9 and in the plaster inscription from Kun-

---

21. I thank C. L. Seow and Andrew G. Vaughn for discussions of the text.

tillet 'Ajrud (*lšm*). Darkness (חשׁך), deep darkness (ערפל), and thick cloud (עב) are also common to theophanies (e.g., Exod 19:9; 20:18; Deut 4:11; 5:19–20; Judg 5:4; 2 Sam 22:10, 12 = Ps 18:10, 12).

However, this is not the whole story. While the similarities between Isa 60 and other, earlier texts are significant—and I do not wish to challenge the generic identification of Isa 60 as a theophany of sorts—notable differences from those same texts are also apparent and equally as important. Among these differences is the tribute procession. While several theophanies seem to have similar processions (e.g., Ps 68; Judg 5; 2 Sam 22 = Ps 18), the bringing of tribute is not a dominant theme in them. The largest difference between Isa 60 and the earlier theophanic tradition, however, is that the latter tends to be dominated by the violent imagery associated with the coming of the Divine Warrior (see P. D. Miller 1973). These theophanies generally discuss the upheaval and withering of nature along with references to war, battle, enemies, and the like. This is, however, *exactly not the case* with Isa 60. Compared to other Divine Warrior texts, there is almost a total lack of militaristic imagery in Isa 60. Yahweh does not come in a storm (Hiebert: 508–9; cf. Taylor: 235–36);[22] while there is certainly darkness and thick cloud in Isa 60, Yahweh dawns on Jerusalem almost as the calm *after* the storm, as it were. Neither is there a description of Yahweh destroying his enemies (contrast Isa 60:9 with Ps 48:7). Tribute comes, to be sure, but it is apparently voluntarily and willingly brought. It is not forced by Yahweh or brought out of fear or intimidation by a subjugated and dejected foe.[23]

In would seem, therefore, that while Isa 60 clearly describes a theophany, it is nevertheless a different kind of theophany than that typically encountered in the Hebrew Bible. While the narratives of Exod 19 and 34 also contain what might be termed nonviolent theophanies, the poetic material tends toward violent storm theophanies with the Divine Warrior wreaking havoc on his foes (e.g., Exod 15; Deut 33; Judg 5; Mic 1; Hab 3; Ps 68). *This is patently not at work in Isa 60.* None of those other theophanic texts, furthermore, seem to

22. Ringgren (141) posits that the context of Deut 33:2 "suggests a comparison to thunder and lightning rather than to the sun." If correct, Deut 33, while still describing a theophany, can be treated independently of Isa 60.

23. The possible exceptions to this may be Isa 60:12 and 14. These verses, however, with their awkward meter and their content, both of which seem out of place in the context of this chapter, may be later additions (Clements 1997:451–52; Steck 1991:58–61; cf. the commentators and the apparatus in *BHS* and *BHK*). This is esp. true of v. 12 (see Steck 1986a). Even if original, however, their brevity does not compare with the violence so prevalent in the other Divine Warrior texts. In any event, one should note that the bringing of tribute in Isa 60 *precedes* vv. 12 and 14.

contain the main elements (in both presence and tenor) that are present in *both* Isa 60 and the Apadana reliefs. Therefore, while selected motifs from Isa 60 may have textual antecedents, *the overall constellation of motifs is not found in any of these textual ancestors.* They are found, however, at Persepolis.

ICONOGRAPHY

I would argue that the same judgment holds true of possible iconographical antecedents. But to discuss all of the antecedents for the imagery found in Persian art—even just that found on the Apadana—would be to survey the history of ancient Near Eastern and Egyptian art, if not the entire Mediterranean. This is because the Achaemenids purposefully used the iconographical vocabulary of earlier periods and peoples, especially the Neo-Assyrian, and also because they employed artisans from all corners of the empire in the construction of their monuments. It is not surprising, then, to find the winged sun-disk in Egyptian and Neo-Assyrian contexts. Nor is it surprising to find tribute processions depicted on earlier art from Mesopotamia and Egypt. Such antecedents have been discussed at length by Root (1979) and others; a full discussion lies outside the scope of this study. Even so, it is instructive to examine an earlier monument that contains most, if not all, of the motifs common to both Isa 60 and the Apadana: the ninth-century Black Obelisk of Shalmaneser III (fig. 13; for recent studies, see Keel and Uehlinger 1994a; Uehlinger 2001:50–57).

This obelisk, some six and a half feet tall, depicts on its program of twenty panels the reception of tribute by Shalmaneser III. Each panel is accompanied by an inscription that describes the scene. Five different sets of tribute are indicated: (1) from Sua, the Gilzanite; (2) from Iaua (Jehu), son of Omri; (3) from the land of Musri; (4) from Marduk-apal-uṣur of Suhi; and (5) from Karparunda, of Hattina. In two of these panels the king himself encounters, respectively, Sua and Jehu, who bow before him directly underneath a winged sun-disk and an eight-pointed star, probably a symbol for Inanna/Ištar (Black and Green: 169–70). What is important here is the presence of tribute processions (including four camels) and solar imagery in a monument that predates the Apadana by several hundred years. Could the Black Obelisk (or something like it) be the origin of Isa 60's imagery?

While possible, especially insofar as the Black Obelisk represents many of the Assyrian motifs that will later figure prominently in Persian iconography, such a view is unlikely for several reasons. For one, the Black Obelisk, while certainly monumental, does not approach the scale of the Apadana, and there is nothing in its style or presentation that would indicate it was intended to have the same sort of function. In comparison, the Apadana's depiction is

Figure 13. Black Obelisk of Shamaneser III (ninth century)
(after Gressmann: Taf. LV Abb. 123; cf. Strawn: 430 fig. 4.40).

almost gargantuan and says as much (or more) about Persepolis as it does
about the king portrayed. Indeed, one cannot be sure which Persian king
it is that is represented in the original central panel! Here the overarching
nonhistorical nature of Achaemenid art must be remembered. This is altogether in line with Isa 60 (see further below) but in stark contrast to the Black
Obelisk. The latter is a monument set up by a particular king, Shalmaneser
III, to commemorate particular military victories. It is altogether *historical*.
The persons involved are identified not so much by dress and presentation
as by actual description; the same could be said of the tribute brought. Both
the presenters and their tribute are also rather limited in number and "sets"
compared to Persepolis (see Dandamayev and Lukonin: 260) and are broken
up by what would appear to be animal scenes from the wild, a motif altogether absent from Isa 60. Furthermore, the winged sun-disk is hardly central
to the relief program of the Black Obelisk. It is much too small and insuf-
ficiently portrayed to claim artistic centrality. It occurs only on one side of
the obelisk and there in two different panels; even then it must compete with
the eight-pointed star. This competition is further reflected in the obelisk's
inscription, which invokes a number of gods, including not only Shamash
but also Enlil, Ea, Sin, Adad, Marduk, Urta, Nergal, Nusku, Ninlil, and Ishtar.
Thus both the text and iconography of the Black Obelisk highlight more than
one god; the Apadana and Isa 60 focus on just one. Perhaps most significantly,
however, the tribute on the Black Obelisk is *forced*. Most of the tribute bearers
bend forward slightly "as if submitting to the burden of subjugation" (Root
1979:255).[24] They do not bear their burdens willingly or easily (i.e., in the
Atlas pose). Even more significant on this point, however, is Shalmaneser's
braggadocio regarding his exploits. The inscriptions describing these are violent and tyrannical (see *ANET*, 279–81; Thomas: 48; Miller and Hayes: 286).
This, while altogether typical of Neo-Assyrian practice and Divine Warrior
texts, is exactly what is missing in Isa 60 and the Apadana. The Black Obelisk,
in sum, lacks a correlation of a constellation of motifs (Keel and Uehlinger
1998:12–13, 394). Again, it is not only what is present but also what is missing
that proves critical to the discussion of interconnection.[25]

The Black Obelisk is but one possible antecedent, although it may well

---

24. See the previous note on Isa 60:14 and note again that the tribute is not mentioned
in connection with the שׁחות in this verse.

25. Cf. Ahn's comment: "Soweit sich für die religiöse Herrscherlegitimation konzepti-
onelle Diskrepanzen zwischen iranischen und altorientalischen Vorstellungen ausmachen
ließen, ergaben sich diese Unterschiede hauptsächlich nicht für die Legitimations*argumentation*, sondern für die *Ausdrucksformen* und *Bilder* dieser Legitimation, die dem jew-
eiligen weltanschaulichen Kontext entnommen sind" (306–7, emphasis original).

be the best, for the imagery found in Isa 60 and the Apadana. This and all other antecedents, textual or iconographical, are important; indeed, many are critical in the development of the later semantics of Persian art. However, as was the case with the textual antecedents, none of the iconographical precursors of which I am aware contains all of the motifs present in Isa 60 and the Apadana reliefs *with the same tenor.* As Root has stated:

> This monument [the Black Obelisk] notwithstanding, the ninth century tribute scenes seem as a rule designed to portray historical events rather than to provide, within one tableau, an emblematic, timeless vision of the abstract concept of the king receiving tribute from "all lands." (1979:255)

Such a tableau, present at Persepolis, is also found, however, in Isa 60.

4. Persian Text- and Art-Forms in Trito-Isaiah

Solar imagery and tribute procession are the most prominent examples of connection between Persian art- and text-forms and Isa 60, though others might have been mentioned.[26] But what is the nature of that connection? Might one not make the case that the two entities are, in fact, discrete? How might it be established that Isa 60 is truly *dependent* on the Apadana and not something else? At least two related issues must be addressed in order to begin to respond to these difficult questions: the issues of availability and chronology. Although these are closely related, it is instructive to treat them separately.

The question regarding availability, to put it baldly, is simply this: Would the Apadana reliefs have been available to Trito-Isaiah? Persepolis is, after all, a good distance from Jerusalem. Root has taken up a similar problem with reference to the relationship between the Apadana and the Parthenon frieze (1985:103–20). She concludes that it is altogether probable that the Greek artisans of the Parthenon were familiar with and consciously emulated the Apadana reliefs. Thus the north facade (perhaps completed as early as 500–490 B.C.E.) can be seen as a generative source for the imagery of the Parthenon (completed ca. 449 B.C.E.). Upon first blush, this period of roughly forty years may seem to be relatively short, but Root accounts for the rather speedy dissemination of the Apadana imagery to places far removed from Persepolis by

---

26. Cf., e.g., the sentiment of Isa 60:22 with the stock formula in the royal inscriptions, which state that it was Ahuramazda who made RN "king, one king of many, one lord of many" (e.g., DNa; DSe), or the garden imagery of Isa 60:13, 21 in light of the Persian *paradeisoi* (see Lipiński 1973:358–59; Brayley: 275–86; Dandamayev 1984:113–17; Stronach 1989:475–502; Steck 1991:101–5).

means of several important considerations. One of these is the fact that several prominent Athenians are known to have visited Persepolis during the period in question (Root 1985:116). These visitors could have served as carriers of the imagery back to parts west.[27] Moreover, and from the opposite direction, many of the artistic motifs present at Persepolis are clearly influenced by the west, if not by Greece itself (see Frankfort: 358–63; Collon 1995:178; Moortgat: 37; cf. also Root 1979; Calmeyer 1991:25–33; 1994:131–47). This is a direct result of both the exotic materials used and the multicultural nature of the artisans employed at Persepolis, a point already mentioned above (Root 1985:116–19; Collon 1995:177). These craftsmen, too, could have served as imagery- and style-carriers (Collon 1995:177; Frankfort: 366–67). In short, an accurate portrayal of the geopolitical situation must be one that includes dynamic interaction across the empire, including Persepolis (Root 1985:117; Collon 1987:90; Frankfort: 348–49; Cook: 107–10). This, undoubtedly, is what permitted cross-permeation of various art- and text-forms between Persia and other locales, including Greece but also perhaps Yehud.

However, a worker who actually saw Persepolis and its Apadana reliefs and then went home talking about it is only one possibility that exists for the dissemination of visual information. The minor arts are a more economical and practical—but just as successful—way to disperse themes found on larger monumental art (see Uehlinger 2000). It is quite interesting on this point to note that it is *exactly* in the Persian period that we find a revival of the cylinder seal (Collon 1995:181; 1987:90). Figure 14 is a nice example. It depicts a king on a lion hunt underneath Ahuramazda and is inscribed in Old Persian, Elamite, and Babylonian: "Darius, the great king," probably to be understood as Darius I (Collon 1995:183). Other Achaemenid seals that present Ahuramazda in the winged sun-disk have also been found (see Collon 1987: nos. 422, 424–25, 465, 574, 744–745, 747, 754, 865, 884, 895, 923). As important as the subject matter of these seals, however, is their distribution. Figure 14, for instance, was discovered in Thebes. Others have been found in such disparate locales as Turkestan (Oxus), Sinai, and Marathon, not to mention sites in the Levant—Kamid-el-Loz, Tell el Mazar, and Jericho—proving that they "have been found all over the Achaemenid empire and beyond" (Collon 1987:93). It would seem, then, at least possible that imagery like that found at Persepolis might have been known in Palestine by eyewitness, by tale, or by seal (see Stern 1982:196–228).

---

27. One should recall here the stories—or at least the literary motif—of Jews in high positions in foreign courts (Wills). Esther, e.g., takes place in Susa, which has a strong iconographical relationship with Persepolis.

Figure 14. Seal of Darius I (?), Thebes
(after Porada 1969:177 fig. 89; cf. Collon 1987: fig. 558).

But here again the issue of chronology raises its ugly head. A great deal would seem to hang on the dating of Trito-Isaiah, especially chapters 60–62, and the dating of the Apadana reliefs, if the former is to be truly and directly *dependent* on the latter. Root has made the case that it is the *planning* of an artistic piece, not its execution, that matters most in discussions of its chronology. If her estimation that work began on the Apadana about 515–513 (1985:108) is correct, then that provides the *terminus ad quem* of the planning. How much earlier the planning could be dated is, however, uncertain. If one were to argue that Isa 60 is directly dependent on the Apadana, then the former would need to be dated after the latter's planning. But the amount of argumentation involved to make such a case quickly becomes unwieldy. If one *could* establish a genetic relationship between the two, it would provide further data for discussing Trito-Isaiah's sociohistorical location (i.e., the planning of the Apadana would provide the *terminus a quo* for Isa 60); however, there are simply too many unresolved and insolvable issues that remain, including the precise dating of Isa 60–62 (cf. Westermann: 296 [537– 520 B.C.E.] with Albertz: 457 [515 B.C.E.]) and how Trito-Isaiah might have become familiar with this imagery in the first place (especially at its *planning* stage, if that is required by the chronology).[28]

---

28. Of course, it is not a matter of the Persian materials being known to Trito-Isaiah alone but also to his audience and cultural base. The latter need not have known the mate-

Figure 15. Behistun relief (drawing by Ulrike Zurkinden;
cf. Porada 1969:147 fig. 77; cf. Root 1979: pl. 6).

That being said, the possibility of visual dissemination through work-ers, visitors, tribute-bearers, and so forth, not to mention via the minor arts, is enough to indicate that exact dependence through chronological priori-ty-succession and/or by seeing the Apadana in person are not required steps in a process of dependence. Further, if the imagery at work in Isa 60 is in any way related to Persian iconography, say, through glyptic motifs, even then it may well be ultimately traced back to Persepolis because the "imperial Achae-menid style" that subsequently prevailed throughout the empire was created there (Dandamayev and Lukonin: 261).

Even so, the notion of direct dependence is not the best way to discuss the relationship between Isa 60 and the Apadana. "Connection" or "rela-tionship" may be both safer and more accurate. That is, both Isa 60 and the Apadana program may be understood as reflexes, one textual and one artistic, of Persian imperial propaganda. Instead of both of the former being directly related to each other, it is instead more likely that each is, in turn, dependent on the latter. As already demonstrated, the imperial ideology encapsulated in the reliefs of Persepolis is not limited solely to the Apadana, nor is it restricted to a narrow window of time. On the contrary, the themes found there are echoed throughout Persian art and literature. The well-known Behistun relief and inscription (fig. 15) are further examples (Blenkinsopp 1996:200). The same could be said of Achaemenid glyptic. If it is correct to track such motifs and themes—better, such imperial propaganda—into the text of Isa 60, then

rials, but some of them might have, and this would no doubt have cast further light on Trito-Isaiah's themes (see Tate: 10).

Trito-Isaiah becomes yet another example of the influences of Persian ideology and theology in the west (Root 1991:1–29), indeed in Persian-period Yehud itself (Uehlinger 1998:134–82).

5. CONCLUSIONS

It remains, then, briefly to address how this study impacts an assessment of the theology and ideology of Trito-Isaiah, especially as it is expressed in Isa 60. There has been a certain tendency in scholarship to characterize Trito-Isaiah as "abstract" or "de-historical" (Seitz 1996:226; Albertz: 456; Hanson 1979:46–77; Childs: 325–26, 333–34, 336–38). But these very same characteristics have often been noted in Achaemenid art, where one finds "static royal icons, frozen in time" (Collon 1995:179). That such are present, then, not only in Trito-Isaiah but also in Persian iconography would caution those who too quickly or too easily attribute Trito-Isaiah's sentiments to "apocalyptic fancy" or "eschatologizing." While such a perspective was argued most convincingly by Paul D. Hanson (1979; see Halpern 1998:625 n. 3, 641; Schramm: 108–82 for critique), it is now rather commonplace. Rainer Albertz, for instance, summarizes the Trito-Isaiah material as follows: "All this [data from Trito-Isaiah] points to [an] internal discussion within a small marginal group which does not enjoy any public respect and which has largely lost all connections with historical and political reality" (456; cf. Hanson 1979:62–63; 1995:218; Clements 1997:441–54, esp. 444–47, 452–53). *But the artistic material from the Apadana (and elsewhere) would indicate that the exact opposite conclusion is in order.* That is, Trito-Isaiah and Isa 60 may not be the literary product of a person(s) who has lost all connections to historical and political reality. On the contrary, if this person(s) was truly influenced by Persian imperial propaganda, then the sentiments found herein are exactly in tune with historical and political reality (see Halpern 1998, esp. 641–43). That is, I must be quick to add, *Persian* historical and political reality. In Isa 60, the timelessness, the stateliness, the endurance of Persian imperial propaganda is thus being co-opted and reapplied to Jerusalem. The *pax Persica* has become the *pax Jerusalem*. This, in turn, further explains what Albertz finds so hard to accept, namely, that the vision of the nations in Isa 60 "does not presuppose any violent upheaval among the world powers but [is] *a voluntary change* of consciousness" (457, emphasis added; see above). While Albertz takes this to be further evidence that Trito-Isaiah has left his historical wits behind him, this notion is, on the contrary, exactly what is found in the reliefs (and texts) from Persepolis, Naksh-i Rustam, and so forth. Albertz's and others' stumbling-blocks turn out to be, in short, *the exact things that demonstrate a close and strong relationship between Trito-Isaiah, the Apadana reliefs, and Persian imperial propaganda.*

To be sure, not all of this similarity is exact, nor is the adoption without modification. Not all of the nations in Isa 60 are peaceful volunteers—not, that is, if 60:12 is original, although that verse, too, is not without possible Persian precedent (Collon 1987:92; see nos. 574, 744–745, and 747)—it is the flip-side of the *pax Persica*! Furthermore, perhaps the designation of Yahweh as an *eternal* light that will *replace* the sun, while connected to solar/Ahuramazdan imagery, is nevertheless polemical against such (see Ackroyd 1990:1–16). Maybe the imperfect forms in Isa 60:2 indicate that the prophet realizes that the application of the Persian ideal onto a Jerusalemite reality remains but a future prospect and promise (Grabbe 1992:47; Albertz: 457; Blenkinsopp 1996:215; K. Koch 1982:152–53; P. A. Smith: 195). Even so, Trito-Isaiah's imposition of such a picture on Persian Yehud may indicate that this prophet, too, is no less optimistic or hopeful than his predecessor, Deutero-Isaiah. Whatever the case, the interface between Isa 60 and Persian iconography is evidence that attempts to utilize Trito-Isaiah (especially Isa 60) as a source for historical reconstructions of Persian Yehud or as a testimony to the development of eschatology, apocalypticism, and sectarianism in the Hebrew Bible may be misguided if they do not consider the relationship that exists between this text and Persian propaganda as encapsulated in Achaemenid art. How this relationship *should* affect critical questions such as these is a topic for another paper.

An Exile's Baggage:
Toward a Postcolonial Reading of Ezekiel

Jean-Pierre Ruiz

The word of the Lord came to me: Mortal, you are living in the midst of a rebellious house, who have eyes to see but do not see, who have ears to hear but do not hear; for they are a rebellious house. Therefore, mortal, prepare for yourself an exile's baggage, and go into exile by day in their sight; you shall go like an exile from your place to another place in their sight. Perhaps they will understand, though they are a rebellious house. You shall bring out your baggage by day in their sight, as baggage for exile; and you shall go out yourself at evening in their sight, as those do who go into exile. Dig through the wall in their sight, and carry the baggage through it. In their sight you shall lift the baggage on your shoulder, and carry it out in the dark; you shall cover your face, so that you may not see the land; for I have made you a sign for the house of Israel. I did just as I was commanded. I brought out my baggage by day, as baggage for exile, and in the evening I dug through the wall with my own hands; I brought it out in the dark, carrying it on my shoulder in their sight. (Ezek 12:1–7, NRSV)

I still recall that journey as if it had taken place but yesterday or last week, although I was only thirteen at the time.... The surprise call on a Friday to the effect that I would be leaving the following Monday, alone—as so many others did, though in the end a seat came open for my mother as well. The final weekend of visits to family, friends, places—the exchange of goodbyes, *sotto voce* in case somebody might wish to do us harm; the preparation of the one piece of baggage allowed, a sack that came to be known affectionately as *el chorizo* (the sausage) and that was stuffed with clothing for an unspecified period of time in the unknown *el norte*. (Segovia 1996:210)

Introduction: Echoes of Exile

To read Cuban-American New Testament scholar Fernando Segovia's still-vivid memories of flight from his native Cuba on 10 June 1961 side by side with the prophet Ezekiel's sign-act is to recognize the truth of Edward Said's observation: "To think of exile as beneficial, as a spur to humanism or to creativity, is to belittle its mutilations. It is produced by human beings for other human beings; it has torn millions of people from the nourishment of tradition, family, and geography" (Said 1983:50, cited in Smith-Christopher 2002:21). In the reminiscence of Cuban-American theologian Ada María Isasi-Díaz we hear the echoes of exilic lament across the centuries in the bittersweet poetry of Ps 137:

> It was the summer of 1961, in Santa Rosa, California, when I first read Psalm 137. I remember resonating with most of what the psalm says; I remember feeling it could appropriately voice the pain I was experiencing being away from my country against my will. After the Cuban Missile Crisis in 1962 I realized that my absence from Cuba was to be a long one. Shortly after there came the day when my visa status was changed from "tourist": I became a refugee.... I recall vividly the day I dared mention to a friend how much I identified with Psalm 137. Jokingly she answered me, "Are you going to hang up your guitar from some palm tree?" I knew that though she and many others around me intended no harm, in reality they were incapable of understanding the sorrow of my being away from *la tierra que me vió nacer* (the land that witnessed my birth). (Isasi-Díaz: 149)

More than forty years later, tens of millions of people continue to shoulder the burdens of an exile's baggage, as deportation, flight from armed conflict, and forced migration—raw and real—are neither ancient history nor old news for political, religious, and economic refugees and asylum seekers around the world. The Office of the United Nations High Commissioner for Refugees reports that at the beginning of 2002 some 19.7 million people—one out of every three hundred persons on earth—were persons of concern that fell under its mandate (http://www.unhcr.org/). These numbers do not include the millions who are classified as economic migrants, persons in economic need who leave their countries of origin in pursuit of a decent living elsewhere, among them the many Latin Americans who risk their lives to cross the militarized border between the United States and Mexico.[1] It is because the deep river of migrant and refugee tears continues to flow across the centuries from ancient Mesopotamia into our own time that this study of Ezekiel—himself deported from Jerusalem in 597 B.C.E.—makes no pretense

---

1. In the Tucson Border Patrol sector alone, one hundred "illegal entrants" died attempting to enter the United States between 1 October 2002 and 22 July 2003 (Ibarra). On pastoral and public policy responses to migration especially from Mexico to the United States, see the Mexican and U.S. Catholic Bishops 2003.

to detachment or neutrality (see Segovia 1995:68–69). As Lisa Malkki notes, "There has emerged a new awareness of the global social fact that, now perhaps more than ever before, people are chronically and routinely displaced" (52). The pressing reality of involuntary displacement and dislocation of so many in our own time may be said to frame a moral challenge for biblical scholarship generally and for the interpretation of exilic texts in particular. Daniel L. Smith-Christopher frames that imperative in the following terms:

> All biblical books are products of a community of transmission, and the community of the book of Ezekiel is clearly a community struggling with mobile identities and transnational culture and theology. *That* is why Ezekiel's crisis is our crisis. And that is why we listen to Ezekiel today. It was economics, control, and power that dragged Ezekiel to Babylon, and it is economics, control, and power that create our current situation. (Smith-Christopher 1999:110–11)

While I am quite sympathetic to Smith-Christopher's take on Ezekiel, I also find that Fernando Segovia's hermeneutics of engagement and otherness sounds a note of salutary caution, and I am inclined to believe that Smith-Christopher himself would not disagree.
As Segovia argues,

> Rather than positing any type of direct or immediate entrance into the text, the hermeneutics of otherness and engagement argues for the historical and cultural remoteness of the text. Such a hermeneutics begins, therefore, by recognizing that the biblical text comes from a very different historical situation and cultural matrix, a very different experience and culture; that all texts, including the biblical texts, are contextual products; and that no text—not even the biblical text—is atemporal, asocial, ahistorical, speaking uniformly across time and culture. (Segovia 1995: 68)

Likewise,

> [T]he reader is also to be regarded as socially and culturally conditioned, as other to both text and other readers.... Rather than seeking after impartiality or objectivity, presuming to universality, and claiming to read like anyone or everyone, the hermeneutics of otherness and engagement argues for a self-conscious exposition and analysis of the reader's strategy for reading, the theoretical foundations behind this strategy, and the social location underlying such a strategy. (Segovia 1995:69)

Thus, while Ezekiel's crisis is *not* our crisis, *our* crisis may well move us to read Ezekiel's crisis with urgently interested eyes. Let me suggest that postcolonial hermeneutics might provide us with one set of useful optics for this project. First I will offer a sketch of postcolonial theory as it has begun to gain ground in biblical interpretation, then I will offer a reading of Ezek 20 through the lens of postcolonial criticism's attention to the dynamics of deterritorialization, assimilation, and resistance.

What *Is* Postcolonial Hermeneutics and Why Does It Matter Anyway?

Postcolonial hermeneutics, a relative newcomer in the discipline of biblical studies, appeared on the scene in the last decade through the efforts of scholars from the so-called Third World and of scholars from the Third World diaspora with academic appointments in First World settings (Gandhi; Loomba). Arif Dirlik identifies the pedigree of postcolonialism in the following terms:

> [P]ostcolonialism has its intellectual origins in the poststructuralist revolt against the very real limits of Eurocentric modernity (in both its liberal and Marxist versions), and has answered a very real critical need: not only in calling into question the obliviousness to the local of generalized notions of modernity, but also in calling attention to problems of a novel nature that have emerged with recent transformation in global political and social relations. (Dirlik 1997:9)

Postcolonialism emerged when the subjects of empire—the British Empire in particular—began to *write back*, to borrow a phrase from the title of a key text of postcolonial theory (Ashcroft, Griffiths, and Tiffin). Dirlik goes on to locate the rise of "postcolonialism" on the academic horizon, suggesting that

> The term in its current usage acquired popularity in the late 1980's, and rapidly catapulted to the forefront of cultural studies, making an impact not only across academic disciplines, but through slogans such as "multiculturalism," in politics as well, especially the politics of academic institutions. The dynamic power moving the discourse of postcoloniality was the visible impact on cultural studies of intellectuals of Third World origin in First World institutions.... The emergence of postcolonialism to the forefront of consciousness has coincided over the last decade with the increasing visibility of the term "diaspora," which may well be the immediate social condition for a postcolonial consciousness. Diasporas have become a highly visible component of a global social landscape. (Dirlik: 8).

R. S. Sugirtharajah, who is among those who have taken the lead in transposing postcolonial theory from (nonbiblical) literary criticism into biblical studies, maintains that "the major achievement of postcolonialism is to inaugurate a new era of academic inquiry which brings to the fore the overlapping issues of empire, nation, ethnicity, migration and language," and he suggests, vis-à-vis biblical interpretation, that "postcolonialism is roughly defined as scrutinizing and exposing colonial domination and power as these are embodied in biblical texts and in interpretations, and as searching for alternative hermeneutics while thus overturning and dismantling colonial perspectives" (Sugirtharajah 1998a: 16; see also Sugirtharajah 2001; Donaldson; Boer). Fernando Segovia offers a similarly broad description of the range of postcolonial studies: "I take the by now common designation of 'Postcolonial Studies' to signify the study of the realm of the geopolitical—the relationship between center and margins, metropolis and periphery, on a global political scale: the imperial and the colonial. Such a relationship I further see as encompassing both social and cultural 'reality'—social formation and cultural production" (Segovia 2000:11–12).

In some sense, the concerns of postcolonial criticism do not appear unfamiliar to more conventionally conceived biblical studies. In fact, as Stephen D. Moore suggests,

> Much traditional biblical scholarship reads like postcolonial criticism *avant la lettre*—or else badly done. That hallowed gateway to biblical criticism, for example, the "Old" or "New" Testament introduction (whether the textbook or the course), has derived much of its efficacy and allure from its ability to summon "exotic" empires from the shadows of the biblical texts and parade them before the student: Egypt, Assyria, Babylon, Persia, Greece, Rome. So much biblical scholarship is already a reflection on imperialism, colonialism, and the resistance they inevitably elicit. (Moore: 188).

Sugirtharajah and others who have begun to employ postcolonial hermeneutics in biblical interpretation are not unaware of the controversies surrounding postcolonialism. The cynicism of Russell Jacoby is not atypical:

> "Oh it's something post-colonial," responded the gift giver to my friend's question about a birthday present, a piece of pottery with an unusual pattern. Was it a Mayan design? Or Persian? No, it was post-colonial—the latest catchall term to dazzle the academic mind.... If you think history or sociology or anthropology has an identity crisis, try post-colonial studies. Its enthusiasts themselves don't know what it is. Indeed, this is part of its charm. Post-colonial studies is obsessed with itself. Few agree on where it came from, what it includes, or where it is going (Jacoby: 30).

Marxist critic Terry Eagleton's voice is prominent in the chorus of postcolonialism's cultured despisers, as he observes "There must be surely be in existence somewhere a secret handbook for aspiring postcolonial theorists, whose second rule reads: 'begin your essay by calling into question the whole notion of postcolonialism.' (The first rule reads: 'Be as obscurantist as you can decently get away with without your stuff going absolutely unread')" (Eagleton 1998: 24).[2] Well aware of the hypnotic power of discourse for its own sake among academics, Sugirtharajah insists on the praxeological imperatives that impinge on the responsible postcolonial critic:

> A postcolonial critic's role is not simply limited to textual dealings or literary concerns. Postcolonial hermeneutics has to be a pragmatic engagement, an engagement in which praxis is not an extra option or a subsidiary enterprise taken on in the aftermath of judicious deconstruction and reconstruction of the texts. Rather, this praxeological involvement is there from the outset of the hermeneutical process, informing and contesting the whole procedure. If we neglect this, we may become ridiculous figures like the Lavatri Alltheorie portrayed in Rukun Advani's novel, *Beethoven among the Cows*. In the longest chapter of the book entitled "S/he, or A Postmodern Chapter on Gender and Identity", Lavatri Alltheorie is described as a "Post-modern theoretician, boa deconstructor, discourse analyst, post-structuralist critic, feminist historian of subalternity, colonialism and gender". A diasporic Indian academic, she offers courses to packed audiences of white students on "the semiology of Deconstruction and the Deconstruction of semiology". The danger is that we will be seen as deliberately using catchphrases and buzzwords as a form of posture and power play. (Sugirtharajah 1998b:113).

While the liberationist inclinations of postcolonial critics are clear, postcolonial critical practices are characterized by a very deliberate methodological eclecticism, an eclecticism that Sugirtharajah suggests is itself a strategic move:

> Postcolonialism's critical procedure is an amalgam of different methods ranging from the now unfashionable form-criticism to contemporary literary methods. It is interdisciplinary in nature and pluralistic in its outlook. It is more an avenue of inquiry than a homogeneous project. One of the significant aspects of postcolonialism is its theoretical and intellectual

---

2. Eagleton rightly critiques the sort of postcolonialism that is "a brand of culturalism, which inflates the significance of cultural factors in human affairs. This is a vice to which literary intellectuals are especially prone. It would, to be sure, be comforting for them if what was at stake between the north and south of the globe really was in the first place questions of value, signification and history, identity, cultural practice, rather than arms, trade agreements, military alliances, drug trafficking and the like. 'Postcolonialism' has been on the whole rather stronger on identity than on the International Monetary Fund, more fascinated by marginality than by margins" (Eagleton 1998: 26). See also Eagleton 1999, which is his review of Spivak 1999.

catholicism. It thrives on inclusiveness, and it is attracted to all kinds of tools
and disciplinary fields, as long as they probe injustices, produce new knowledge which problematizes well-entrenched positions and enhance [sic] the
lives of the marginalized (Sugirtharajah 2001:258).

In a similar vein, Moore explains that "postcolonialism is not *a* method of
interpretation (any more than is feminist criticism, say) so much as a critical sensibility attuned to a specific range of interrelated textual and historical
phenomena" (Moore: 183). The eclecticism of postcolonial biblical criticism is
neither random nor capricious. Postcolonial biblical critics such as Sugirtharajah neither conceal their own social locations nor mask their ideological
investment in and commitment to their constituencies.

Sugirtharajah lays out three intersecting tasks for postcolonial biblical
criticism:

> First, scrutiny of biblical documents for their colonial entanglements:
> the Bible as a collection of documents which came out of various colonial
> contexts—Egyptian, Persian, Assyrian, Hellenistic and Roman ... needs to
> be investigated again.... It will revalue the colonial ideology, stigmatization
> and negative portrayals embedded in the content, plot and characterization.
> It will scour the biblical pages for how colonial intentions and assumptions
> informed and influenced the production of the texts. It will attempt to resur-
> rect lost voices and causes which are distorted or silenced in the canonized
> text. It will address issues such as nationalism, ethnicity, deterritorialization
> and identity, which arise in the wake of colonialism.
>
> The second task of postcolonial criticism is to engage in reconstruc-
> tive reading of biblical texts. Postcolonial reading will reread biblical texts
> from the perspective of postcolonial concerns such as liberation struggles
> of the past and present.... it will interact with and reflect on postcolonial
> circumstances such as hybridity, fragmentation, deterritorialization, and
> hyphenated, double or multiple, identities. One postcolonial concern is the
> unexpected amalgamation of peoples, ideas, cultures, languages and reli-
> gions.
>
> The third task of postcolonial criticism is to interrogate both colonial
> and metropolitan interpretations. The aim here is to draw attention to the
> inescapable effects of colonization and colonial ideologies on interpretative
> works such as commentarial writings, and on the historical and administra-
> tive records which helped to (re)inscribe colonial ideologies and consolidate
> the colonial presence.... Postcolonial interpretation will also investigate
> interpretations which contested colonial interpretations and concerns. It
> will bring to the fore how the invaded, often caricatured as abused victims
> or grateful beneficiaries, transcended these images and wrested interpreta-
> tion from the invaders, starting a process of self-discovery, appropriation
> and subversion. (Sugirtharajah 2001:250–57).

To the growing body of postcolonial studies, biblical criticism informed
by postcolonial theory contributes a sense of depth by calling attention to
histories of empire and colonization that predate (and that have directly and
indirectly influenced) the development of European imperial and colonial
initiatives in Africa, Asia, and the Americas beginning in the early modern
era. While it makes little sense simply to set Queen Victoria's British Empire
side by side with Nebuchadrezzar's Neo-Babylonian Empire, postcolonial biblical critics argue that quite a bit can be learned by using the critical tools
crafted to investigate texts that emerged under the influence of the former
to reexamine texts that emerged under the influence of the latter. It is easy to
see how such categories as deterritorialization, diaspora, ethnicity, identity
(including hyphenated, double or multiple identities), hybridity, assimilation,
and resistance might be useful tools for sorting out some of the entangle-
ments of ancient texts with ancient empires. At the same time, the place of
the Bible close to the religious heart of the European imperial and missionary
enterprise makes biblical interpretation from a postcolonial vantage a valuable contribution to the intellectual history of the European colonization of
Africa, Asia, and the Americas.

To illustrate some of the moves of postcolonial biblical interpretation, I
offer two examples that suggest the wide range of approaches postcolonial
critics have explored. First I will discuss Francisco García-Treto's reading of
the Joseph story in Gen 39–41 from the standpoint of the subfield of diaspora
studies. Then I will turn to Daniel L. Smith-Christopher's provocative postcolonial treatment of Ezekiel from the standpoint of the subfield of refugee
studies. These two studies converge in their attention to the impact of exile
as a consequence of empire and colonialism. "The very nature of exile," says
Justo González, is "a life in which one is forced to revolve around a center that
is not one's own, and that in many ways one does not wish to own. Exile is a
dislocation of the center, with all the ambiguities of such dislocation. Thus the
exiled poet sings about not singing …'How could we sing the LORD's song in
a foreign land?'" (González: 92).

In "Hyphenating Joseph: A View of Genesis 39–41 from the Cuban
Diaspora" (García-Treto: 134–45), Francisco García-Treto offers a reading
of the Joseph story mediated through Cuban-American cultural critic Gustavo Pérez Firmat's analysis of a new exile's process of adaptation to a new
homeland, a three-stage process of substitution, destitution, and institution
(see also Behar). Substitution, the first stage, "consists of an effort to create
substitutes or copies of the home culture" (Pérez Firmat: 7; see also García-
Treto: 137). For the Cuban-American diaspora, this substitution took the
form of the creation of "little Havana" in Miami. With regard to the Joseph
story, in *Genesis Rabbah* 86:5 (on Gen 39:3) we find that "In the early days of

his captivity in Potiphar's house, Joseph goes about repeating (whispering) the Torah which he had learned in his father's house. This is his strenuous attempt to 're-member' his identity and culture, to keep 'God with him'" (Zornberg: 274; see García-Treto: 137). Destitution, Pérez Firmat's second stage of exilic adaptation, occurs when "the awareness of displacement crushes the fantasy of rootedness" (Pérez Firmat: 10; see García-Treto: 139). Here, García-Treto suggests, "Among the many factors that can bring about an awareness of being displaced, none is perhaps more frequent or disturbing in the experience of exiles than the experience of being 'put in one's place' by the prejudices and stereotypes of the dominant culture" (139). García-Treto suggests that in the Joseph story this stereotyping happens in several ways. For Potiphar's wife, Joseph is stereotyped as a sexual object, while for Pharaoh's baker, Joseph is "a Hebrew lad there with us" (Gen 40:12). García-Treto speculates, tongue in cheek, "Did the Egyptians have equivalents of the 'Latin lover' or of the 'hot-blooded *señorita*' stereotypes for Hebrews?" (140). The third stage, institution, is the construction of a hybrid, hyphenated self. Joseph becomes a Hebrew-*hyphen*-Egyptian, "so thoroughly at home, at least in the externals of Egyptian culture, that by the denouement of the story his constructed identity functions as a successful disguise to fool his own brothers" (140).

In his moves back and forth from the world behind and of the text to the world in front of the text, it is ultimately the praxeological dimension of postcolonial biblical hermeneutics that drives García-Treto's reading.[3] He concludes that the Joseph story "is the story of many diasporas, over many centuries and across many borders … a story of survival and success, of reunion and reconciliation, in a word, of salvation" (145). García-Treto's study of Gen 39–41 takes up what Sugirtharajah identifies as the second task of postcolonial biblical criticism, as a rereading of the Joseph story from the perspective of his own hyphenated identity as a member of the Cuban-American diaspora.

The clever title of Daniel L. Smith-Christopher's study, "Ezekiel on Fanon's Couch: A Postcolonialist Dialogue with David Halperin's *Seeking Ezekiel*," itself offers a clue to Smith-Christopher's approach. The Afro-Caribbean anticolonial activist, philosopher, and psychiatrist Frantz Fanon (1925–1961) is widely regarded by postcolonial theorists as "a romantic hero of decolonization" (Memmi: 39; cf. Loomba: 143; Macey; Gordon, Sharpley-Whiting, and White). Born in Martinique and trained as a psychiatrist in France after the Second

---

3. I employ the distinctions among the world behind the text, the world of the text, and the world before (or in front of) the text, following Schneiders: 97–179.

World War (in which he fought as a member of the Free French), Fanon's experiences both in France and in Algeria sensitized him to the crisis of colonialism. His first book, *Peau Noire, Masques Blancs* (*Black Skin, White Masks*) focused on the psychology of oppression (Fanon 1952; 1967; cf. Hussein 1985). In *L'An V de la Révolution Algérienne* (*A Dying Colonialism*) and *Les Damnés de la Terre* (*The Wretched of the Earth*) he advocated revolutionary resistance to French colonialism in Algeria (Fanon 1959; 1965; 1961; 1963; see also Macey).

Smith-Christopher writes: "Though Fanon is often remembered for his political philosophy, he was also a pioneer in the exploration of the psychological impact of colonization and of the sociopolitical context of psychological illness" (1999:141). Through this door, Smith-Christopher returns to revisit the question of Ezekiel's psychological condition. Critical of the Freudian approach adopted by David J. Halperin's *Seeking Ezekiel: Text and Psychology* (1993; cf. Broome), Smith-Christopher argues that "tendencies to read the psychological state of Ezekiel totally apart from the social and psychological experiences he suffered are symptoms of the same avoidance in other biblical scholarly analyses—an avoidance of the Exile as a real event where human beings deeply suffered. Any psychological assumptions about Ezekiel derived apart from serious attention to the Exile are thus tantamount to blaming the victim" (Smith-Christopher 1999:134–35). Therefore, "when Halperin ignores the social circumstances and realities of the Exile in order to read Ezekiel in order to read Ezekiel as struggling with sexuality, he is blaming the victim" (1999:144).

For Smith-Christopher, understanding the sociopolitical context of the exile and of Ezekiel's condition as a deportee to Babylon is key to understanding the prophet's peculiar behavior, especially the bizarre sign-acts: "What appears to have driven Ezekiel to act out the horrors of conquest—the scattering of refugees in fear, the butchering of prisoners captured, and the taking of exiles? The answer is what drives thousands of traumatized human beings to relive memories that can literally drive them to despair, alcoholism, silence, and suicide" (1999:134). Smith-Christopher finds a more coherent framework for considering Ezekiel's condition in the symptomatology and literature of post-traumatic stress disorder, insisting that this "forces us to ask serious questions about the adequacy of any psychological assessment of Ezekiel that does not appreciate the historical and social implications of the siege of Jerusalem, the deportations, and the executions by the Babylonian armies in the Exile" (1999:142). Thus, in Smith-Christopher's reading, Ezekiel carried painfully heavy baggage into exile, baggage that readers unpack in the text of the book as it witnesses to the impact of the exile.

Smith-Christopher's study stands as a contribution to postcolonial biblical criticism not so much in view of his deliberate nod in the direction of

Frantz Fanon but especially inasmuch as it demonstrates the entanglement of the book of Ezekiel with its sociopolitical context in the Neo-Babylonian imperial project, that is, with the forced dislocation of Ezekiel in 597 B.C.E. from Jerusalem to Tel-Abib by the river Chebar.[4] Smith-Christopher's study of Ezekiel, like García-Treto's study of Gen 29–31, is driven mainly by praxeological concerns. He reads Ezekiel "the refugee prophet" side by side with Homi K. Bhabha's assessment of the human costs of globalization: "The demography of the new internationalism is the history of postcolonial migration, the narratives of cultural and political diaspora, the major social displacements of peasant and aboriginal communities, the poetics of exile, the grim prose of political and economic refugees" (Bhabha 1994:5; see Smith-Christopher 1999: 110). It is his acute consciousness of this reality that ultimately led Smith-Christopher to articulate a biblical theology of exile in his book by that very title:

> In this work I am not exclusively focused on the exilic events of the ancient Judeans. I argue that ancient Israelite responses to exile and diaspora, as reflected in the biblical texts, can provide the building blocks for rethinking the role of the Hebrew Bible in informing the modern Christian theological enterprise.... I no longer have much interest in, or patience with, attempting to hide the theological agenda that partially motivates my interest in the subject of the Babylonian exile and the Hebrew textual and religious responses. (Smith-Christopher 2002:6–7)

BETWEEN ASSIMILATION AND RESISTANCE: A POSTCOLONIAL APPROACH TO EZEKIEL 20[5]

> What you are thinking will never happen: "We shall become like the nations, like the tribes of the countries, worshiping wood and stone." (Ezek 20:32)

Identity, hybridity, assimilation, and resistance are commonplaces in the

---

4. Both in this study and elsewhere, Smith-Christopher expresses strong skepticism toward "recent trends to discount the importance of the Exile and to minimize its impact" (1999:112 n. 9, 114–15), with reference to Grabbe 1998. See also Smith-Christopher 1989; 1997; 2002. In the editor's foreword to Smith-Christopher's *A Biblical Theology of Exile*, Walter Brueggemann writes, "There is now a powerful skeptical opinion among some scholars, especially in Britain, concerning the deep characterization of exile reported in the Old Testament text. That opinion suggests that exile is largely an ideological construct designed to advance the influence and legacy of one segment of emerging Judaism" (Smith-Christopher 2002:vii).

5. Here I revisit my earlier treatment of this text (Ruiz 1997; 1998).

idiom of postcolonial criticism. Frantz Fanon puts the issue before us more forcefully: "Colonisation is not satisfied merely with holding a people in its grip and emptying the native's brain of all form and content. By a kind of perverted logic, it turns to the past of oppressed people, and distorts, disfigures and destroys it" (1961:170). This is the perversely effective logic of the Neo-Babylonian imperial practice of forced deportation, of which the prophet Ezekiel was himself a victim. As Daniel Block notes:

> Mesopotamia had long been the benefactor of forced Israelite immigration. According to neo-Assyrian records hundreds of thousands of citizens from the northern kingdom had been dispersed throughout the empire.... Nebuchadrezzar continued this policy with the Judeans, bringing the cream of the population to Babylon and settlements nearby. These deportation policies were driven by several objectives: (1) to break down bonds of nationality and resistance; (2) to destroy political structures by removing civil and religious leaders; (3) to provide conscripts for the Babylonian army; (4) to bolster the economy of Babylon (Block: 5–6; see also Oded 1979).

Some scholars, at least since Martin Noth, have gone to considerable lengths to downplay the impact of the deportation on the Judeans exiled to Babylon. Noth contended that "the exiles were not 'prisoners' but represented a compulsorily transplanted subject population *who were able to move about freely in their daily life*, but were presumably compelled to render compulsory labor service" (Noth 1960:296). Bustenay Oded declares

> There is no clear and explicit evidence that the Mesopotamian exiles lived under conditions of suppression or were subjected to religious persecution at any time during the years 586–583 BCE.... One gets the impression that they had a certain internal autonomy and that they enjoyed the freedom to manage their community life (Ezek. 33.30–3).... The exiles had the benefit of personal freedom. (Oded 1977:483; cf. Smith-Christopher 2002:65–73)

With respect to religion as a marker of the persistence (or otherwise) of the identity of the deportees from Judah, Oded maintains that "many of them did not lose their national identity and their special religious nature, and they persisted in maintaining the link with their homeland, with Jerusalem and with the dynasty of David. The Assyrians as well as the Babylonians customarily permitted national-ethnic groups, exiles or not, to express their national and religious identity, obviously without national independence" (Oded 1995:209).

The sarcasm of Hans Barstad is downright disturbing:

When reading the commentators on the biblical texts relating to these events, one sometimes gets the Sunday school feeling that they regard the Babylonians as an evil people who came to destroy the true believers in Judah out of sheer wickedness, and that the bringing of Judeans into exile was a mean punishment or base revenge following the uprising of the Judean king. It is high time that we start thinking about the whole matter from a rather different perspective. The Neo-Babylonian empire represented a highly developed civilization, with an advanced political and economic structure.... Already at an early stage the economy of the Mesopotamian countries had turned into an aggressive and expansionist one, soon to be followed also by territorial expansion. The conquest of the neighbouring countries became necessary in order to secure control of vital trade routes, and taxes and tribute were needed for the consolidation of the empire. (Barstad: 63–65)

We cannot help but ask: was Neo-Babylonian imperialist adventurism just the necessary price of doing business, in which the fate of the Judean exiles constituted easily dismissed collateral damage? We need to recall that, although they belonged to the elite classes of the Judean population, Ezekiel and the other Judeans by the Chebar were in fact forced deportees, not voluntary expatriates. That being the case, Ezek 20:32 can be recognized—through a postcolonial optic—as an unmistakable expression of destitution, Pérez Firmat's second stage of exilic adaptation, in which "the awareness of displacement crushes the fantasy of rootedness." Pérez Firmat elaborates: at this point exiles feel "that the ground has been taken out from under them, that they no longer know their place, that they have in fact lost their place. Rather than nostalgic, they now feel estranged and disconnected" (10).

Translators and exegetes alike are of two very different minds when it comes to Ezek 20:32. Moshe Greenberg renders this verse "And what has entered your minds shall never, never be, your thinking, 'We will become like the nations, like the families of the earth, serving wood and stone'" (1983:362). He finds here an echo of 1 Sam 8:20, the adamant refusal of the elders of Israel to listen to Samuel's warning against their insistent request for a king to govern Israel: "we are determined to have a king over us, *so that we also may be like other nations* (והיינו גם־אנחנו ככל־הגוים)." Therefore Greenberg holds that Ezek 20:32 expresses "the wish of the people, not their despair," and that "It is this defiant wish that arouses God's indignation (here, vs. 33)," whereas to despair God "responds with encouraging exhortation (33:10ff.; 37:12ff.)" (371).

Walther Zimmerli takes the other side. He recognizes that ככל־הגוים "is as a rule interpreted as a cohortative" and that the phrase "has usually been understood as the expression of a definite idolatrous decision" (Zimmerli 1979:414; also Clements 1996:91). While aware of this, Zimmerli holds that "it is more correct to find in v. 32, in accordance with 33:10; 37:11, the expression of a deep despair.... If the judgment of being scattered among the nations ... [by YHWH] is already an accomplished fact (v. 23) ... is any hope left of any other future than dispersion among the nations with all its bitter religious consequences?"(1979:414). Thus, Zimmerli renders 20:32 as follows: "It will never happen, what has arisen (as a thought) in your spirit, that you say 'We shall become like the nations, like the families of the (heathen) lands and worship wood and stone'" (1979:402).

Leslie C. Allen's rendering of 20:32 is also in line with this: "The thought that is in your minds will never happen, the prospect of your being like other nations, like the communities of foreign countries, worshiping wood and stone" (3). As for "worshiping wood and stone," this practice is mentioned in Deut 4:28; 28:36, 64; 29:16; 2 Kgs 19:18; and Isa 37:19. Adrian Graffy argues that the phrase "is necessary to complete the sense and should not be deleted as a deuteronomic addition."[6] It would seem quite a stretch to take "We shall become like the nations, like the tribes of the countries, worshiping wood and stone" as a cry of defiance or as anything but an expression of the most abject despair. Its resonances echo in the sentiments of Lam 1:3: "Judah has gone into exile with suffering and hard servitude; she lives now among the nations and finds no resting place; her pursuers have all overtaken her in the midst of her distress."

Stepping back for a moment to consider Ezek 20:32 in its immediate literary context, I note, with Graffy, that while "Ezekiel 20 has sometimes been considered a unit," most commentators "find it necessary to divide the chapter" (65). Graffy suggests that the break should be made before 20:32 and that verse 32 marks the beginning of a disputation speech that continues until 20:44. The disputation begins by taking up a quotation attributed to Ezekiel's fellow exiles, a pattern also found in 12:27; 33:10; and 37:11. Graffy observes that "all the quotations in disputation speeches attributed to the exiles in Ezekiel express despair and hopelessness, whereas those of the people left in Jerusalem have a confident, arrogant tone" (66–67; see Ezek 11:3, 15; 12:22; 18:2; 33:24). He also insists that despite the echoes of 1 Sam 8:20, the tone we find in Ezek 20:32 "is similar to that found in Ezek 25,8, where Moab insults Judah by describing her as 'like all the nations,'" and that in Ezek 20:32 "The

---

6. Graffy: 66. Risa Levitt Kohn notes, "The idolatrous practice of worshiping 'wood and stone' appears predominantly in Deuteronomic passages that foretell Israel's future exile.... The people are thus portrayed as worshiping in this manner in foreign nations. The expression also describes the idolatrous practices witnessed by Israel in Egypt (Deut. 29.17)" (92). Also see Pons: 227–28. Eichrodt, who deletes "serving wood and stone" as an instance of Deuteronomic editing, suggests that Ezek 20:32 announces the plans of the elders of Judah to establish a cultic center to YHWH in Babylon (181).

people despondently accept this as a fact. They consider they have lost their special place among the nations" (Graffy: 66).

Following the quotation in 20:32 we find a programmatic refutation in verse 32 that is introduced with an oath: "As I live, says the Lord GOD, with strong hand and arm outstretched I will rule over you." The refutation then proceeds in three parts (20:34–38, 39–42, 43–44), each of which concludes with the recognition formula "you will know that I am YHWH" (וידעו כי־אני יהוה). The divine response to the despair of the deportees is a direct challenge to Nebuchadnezzar's sovereignty. Fittingly enough, in 20:34–38 the reestablishment and emphatic reaffirmation of sovereignty over the exiles by their deity takes place through a deterritorialization that is likened to the exodus from Egypt:

> I will bring you out from the peoples and gather you from the lands where you are scattered.... I will bring you into the wilderness of the peoples, and I will enter into judgment with you there face to face. Just as I judged your ancestors in the wilderness of the land of Egypt, so I will judge you, says the Lord GOD.... I will lead you into the obligation of the covenant ... and you will know that I am YHWH.

Contra Greenberg, who suggests that "the wilderness of the peoples" is the "Syro-Arabian desert, bounded by various peoples" (1983:372), the reference need not be geographically localized. "The desert is important here simply as the typological counterpart to the first 'desert of Egypt,'" the desert in which the identity of Israel in covenant with its god first took shape (Zimmerli 1979:416).

The promised deterritorialization into "the wilderness of the peoples" where divine sovereignty over the deportees is to be reaffirmed is followed in 20:39–42 by a reterritorialization, the reestablishment of the deportees in their deity's own land:

> On my holy mountain, the mountain height of Israel, says the Lord GOD, there all the house of Israel, all of them, shall serve me in the land; there I will accept them.... As a pleasing odor I will accept you, when I bring you out from the peoples, and gather you out of the countries where you have been scattered; and I will manifest my holiness among you in the sight of the nations. (Ezek 20:40–41 NRSV)

At this point the disputation speech addresses the despair of the deportees with an unmistakable expression of resistance against the Neo-Babylonian imperial ideology. David Stephen Vanderhooft cites a Neo-Babylonian inscription in which Nebuchadnezzar is presented as protector of humanity:

(As for) the widespread peoples whom Marduk, the lord, gave into my hand
… I continually strove for their welfare. (In) a just path and correct conduct
I directed them…. I stretched a roof over them in the wind, (and) a canopy
in the tempest. I brought all of them under the sway of Babylon. The yield
of the lands, the abundance of the mountain regions, the produce of the
countries, I received within it (Babylon). Into its eternal shadow I assembled
all the peoples for good.

Vanderhooft then explains:

This passage and its parallels emphasize the idea that the king is the protector of all humanity. Thus, the gods grant the king rulership over the
"widespread peoples," a phrase that refers to all populations under royal
control. The king is thus able to better their circumstances; he is, in short,
their divinely appointed protector and benefactor, not their conqueror. The
modern historian might argue that this is merely a pious fraud, designed
to blunt the crassness of the more important concern, also expressed here:
namely, the material exploitation of conquered populations for the benefit
of a ruling elite. The notion of the king as protector of humanity, however,
deserves attention as an important aspect of the imperial theory. (42)

Furthermore,

[A]ccording to the imperial ideology, the conquest … of non-Babylonian
populations is not to their detriment, since the Babylonian elite views "the
eternal shadow of Babylon" as a restorative one. Similarly, there is no reference in Nebuchadnezzar's inscriptions to the king placing his yoke (nīru)
upon conquered people, as there so often is in Assyrian royal inscriptions.
Rather, Nebuchadnezzar asserts that he gathers the people into Babylon's
shadow tābiš, "for good, peacefully." (43)

The disputation speech of Ezek 20:32–44 is especially striking in the face of
claims like these, claims that could easily have led the deportees to the level of
despair that the saying in 20:32 expresses. The Neo-Babylonian imperial ideology established clear and unmistakable distinctions between the metropolitan
center and the conquered subject peripheries, mapping their relationships in
ways that reflected the exploitative flow of labor and goods *from* Judah (and
elsewhere) *to* Babylon. The prophetic refutation of the despairing saying of
20:32 utterly rejects the Babylonian configuration of metropolis and peripheries out of hand, to present the Judean deportees with an alternate, resistant
worldview: "As a pleasing odor I will accept you, when I bring you out from
the peoples and gather you out of the countries where you have been scattered,
and I will manifest my holiness among you in the sight of the nations. You

shall know that I am the LORD, when I bring you into the land of Israel, the country that I swore to give to your ancestors" (Ezek 20:41–42). This promise anticipates the elaborate restoration vision of chapters 40–48, which includes the detailed mapping of the land "for inheritance among the twelve tribes of Israel (47:13; Stevenson). All this casts doubt on the label Greenberg assigns to Ezek 20:1–44, namely, "threat of a new Exodus," and suggests instead that it might be more fitting to see here the *promise* of a new exodus.

To fill out this postcolonial take on Ezek 20:32 just a bit more, I offer two further interrelated observations, both of which touch on the relationship between 20:32–44 and the first part of the chapter, 20:1–31. In that respect, I agree with Graffy's position that 20:32–44 has its own integrity as a disputation speech as well as with his explanation that the "lack of a full introduction to the disputation speech suggests that it was intended to be closely related to what precedes, perhaps to balance the negative tone of vv. 1–31 with brighter prospects" (65). On the basis of the relationship between the two parts of Ezek 20, a look at the beginning of the chapter may prove instructive, first with respect to the date and, second, regarding the audience: "In the seventh year, in the fifth month, on the tenth day of the month, certain elders of Israel came to consult the LORD and sat down before me."

Commentators note that the oracle is dated to 591 B.C.E., according to the pattern in Ezekiel whereby events are identified with Jehoiachin's exile as the *terminus a quo*. The "seventh year" is the seventh year since the deportation of Jehoiachin, two years after the first such date of Ezekiel's inaugural vision (1:2; Freedy and Redford; McKeating: 62–72). The first siege of Jerusalem in 597 B.C.E. is a constant reference point for the exiled priest-prophet, and the dated oracles are clear indication of how deep were the scars of this event (see 2 Kgs 24:10–20). Recall the autobiographical remarks of Fernando Segovia quoted at the beginning of this paper, the still-vivid memories of 10 September 1961, several decades after the fact, as he said, "I still recall that journey as if it had taken place but yesterday or last week, although I was only thirteen at the time" (Segovia 1996:210).

The occasion of the oracle in Ezek 20:1–32 is the arrival of "certain elders of Israel" in the presence of the prophet "to consult the LORD" (20:1). The inclusion in verses 3 and 31 ("As I live, says the Lord GOD, I will not be consulted by you") indicates that the elders are the audience for 20:1–31 and suggests (in the absence of any indication to the contrary) that they continue to be the audience for 20:32–44. This is the third time in the book that the elders approach Ezekiel (also see 8:1; 14:1), and it is also the third time that they face condemnation for the sin of idolatry (in 8:11–12 they are observed *in flagrante delicto*; Duguid: 117–18). While the accusation can be understood under the rubric of the self-destructive rhetoric of blaming the victim, it might also be suggested that the sin of devotion to deities other than the national received such intense condemnation because it already represented an assimilationist behavior that threatened the distinctiveness of the people's identity.[7] Thus, the remedies proposed in the refutation portion of the disputation speech (20:33–44) emphasize the recognition formula, וידעו כי־אני יהוה ("you will know that I am Yhwh," 20:38, 42). While the struggle over identity, between assimilation and resistance, was an issue before 597 b.c.e., the deportation of Ezekiel and the elders of Judah and the collapse of any viable notion of national autonomy and self-determination made it an even more urgent matter. The predeportation polemic against the worship of gods other than the national deity becomes escalated into a discourse of subaltern resistance for a population of involuntary deportees. While Oded may speak confidently about the survival of "the national religious identity" during the exile "because of the celebration of such traditional customs as Sabbath observance ... and circumcision and because of the activity of prophets like Jeremiah, Ezekiel, and the so-called Second Isaiah" (1977:484), there can be no doubt that the Babylonian military actions against Jerusalem and its population in 597 and 587 b.c.e. had a deliberately debilitating impact on individuals and on institutions: "Disaster comes upon disaster, rumor follows rumor; they shall keep seeking a vision from the prophet; instruction shall perish from the priest, and counsel from the elders. The king shall mourn, the prince shall be wrapped in despair, and the hands of the people of the land will tremble" (Ezek 7:26–27a).[8] This was the heavy baggage of exile, which the prophet symbolically packs and takes up in Ezek 12. How many are the refugees and asylum seekers, undocumented economic migrants and other itinerants in our own century who just might recognize in Ezekiel's baggage something of their own?

Conclusion

Edward Said writes:

> Exile is one of the saddest fates. In premodern times banishment was a particularly dreadful punishment since it not only meant years of aimless wandering away from family and familiar places, but also meant being a sort of permanent outcast, someone who never felt at home, and was always at odds with the environment, inconsolable about the past, bitter about the present and the future.... During the twentieth century, exile has been

---

7. On the question of identity and the mechanisms of ethnicity in the context of exile, see Smith-Christopher 1989:58–63. See also Barth.

8. On the impact of exile on Ezekiel as a priest-become-prophet, see Mein: 199–213.

transformed ... into a cruel punishment of whole communities and peoples, often the inadvertent result of impersonal forces such as war, famine and disease. (1996: 47)

By taking another look at Ezek 20 from a postcolonial perspective, this essay has suggested that in some sense that the river of deportees' tears that daily grows wider and deeper in our own day flows from as far upstream as the waters of Babylon in the sixth century B.C.E. Taking Ezek 20:32 as an expression of what Pérez Firmat identified as destitution proves helpful in taking sides on the question of whether that verse describes defiance or despair. Reading the disputation speech in 20:33–44 as an expression of resistance, the call for a new exodus and a new settlement of the land of Israel acquires new significance as a minority discourse that rejects the mapping of metropolis and margins imposed on the Judeans by the Babylonian imperial ideology. Not everyone who was compelled to live under Babylon's eternal shadow found the shade comforting. For many it spelled the gloom of shattered hope. Is it any surprise that they sat and wept?

Finally, the praxeological turn, the question of real-world payoff of reading. Recall Surgirtharajah's admonition to the would-be postcolonial biblical critic: "Postcolonial hermeneutics has to be a pragmatic engagement, an engagement in which praxis is not an extra option or a subsidiary enterprise taken on in the aftermath of judicious deconstruction and reconstruction of the texts" (1988b:113). In some sense, it is the present predicament of refugees, asylum seekers, and migrants that sent me back to Ezek 20 in the first place. If that is where I stay, then the work remains unfinished (Schüssler Fiorenza). If, on the other hand, this rereading of Ezek 20 returns us to the world in front of the text with eyes and ears wide open to those in our own time who shoulder an exile's baggage, and if the deportee prophet Ezekiel urges us to seek and to enact deeds (and not just words) of resistance and hope, then perhaps this sort of reading makes a difference.

Diaspora and Homeland in the Early Achaemenid Period: Community, Geography and Demography in Zechariah 1–8

John Kessler

1.0. Introduction

One of the most intriguing features of Judean history in the Persian period is the emergence of several widely dispersed communities in various parts of Mesopotamia, the Levant, and Egypt consisting of inhabitants of the former northern and southern kingdoms. Persian-period scholarship has devoted significant attention to various issues such as the population, borders, and governance of Yehud, the region's internal sociopolitical structure, as well as the impact of Achaemenid imperial policy upon polity in Yehud. More recently, fresh attention is being devoted to the issue of how the community in Yehud and the other Israelite/Judean communities beyond its borders defined and understood themselves, as well as how they viewed other Yahwists who stood at some distance, either ideologically or geographically, from themselves. The present study will seek to contribute to this discussion by analyzing Zech 1–8 with a view to determining this text's particular understanding of the composition, nature, geographic location, and future of the community of Yahweh. Such an analysis will enable us to glimpse one distinct perspective on the question of how the *pastiche* of Judean communities described above understood one another in the context of the Achaemenid period.

1.1. Zechariah 1–8 as a Source for the Persian Period

The question of the literary history of Zech 1–8 is a complex one and cannot be discussed in detail here. Nevertheless, the present study assumes it to be a relevant source for the period at hand and makes four assumptions. The first is that Zech 1–8 is a discrete and distinct literary entity, separate from (albeit related to) both Zech 9–14 and Haggai and should be read as such.[1] Second, redactional complexities notwithstanding, Zech 1–8 can be viewed as consisting of two major blocs of material: (1) a sermonic framework (henceforth SF) consisting of 1:1–6; 7:1–8:23 and (2) a visionary-oracular complex (VOC) consisting of 1:7–6:15. It is generally agreed that, while both sections reflect complex literary development and contain both earlier and later material, the SF represents the work's last major compositional stage (Beuken 1967; Redditt: 40–43; Amsler: 43–46; Petersen: 124). The date of this final form is ascribed by some to the time around 515 B.C.E. (Redditt: 42; Meyers and Meyers 1987:xlv), by others to the late sixth or early fifth century (Amsler, Lacoque, and Vuilleumier: 63; Petitjean: 440; Rudolph 1970), or to the mid- to late fifth century (Ackroyd 1968; Beuken 1967; Coggins: 31).[2] While I personally favor a dating in the late sixth or early fifth centuries, this only marginally affects my conclusions. The creation of such texts as Haggai and Zech 1–8 in the early Achaemenid period should not be deemed improbable. Despite its reduced size (see below), Yehud was nevertheless the locus of significant literary activity (Carter 1999:286–88; Ben Zvi 1996; 1998; Kessler 2001). Third, while significant portions of the material contained in Zech 1–8 likely date from various moments early in the Achaemenid period, this material has been subject to ongoing reflection. As Chary (43) appropriately comments, the older material "is not an immutable monolithic piece. It is rather the property of the community which meditates upon it and completes it as new religious needs arise." Thus Zech 1–8 may be read as a textual unity comprising ongoing theological reflection at various moments. Fourth, Zech

1. On the relationship between Zech 1–8 and 9–14 in current scholarship, see Floyd 2002:303–8; Boda 2003. Zech 1–8 is frequently read together with Haggai (so Meyers and Meyers 1987) or with Haggai, Zech 9–14, and Malachi (thus Sérandour; Bauer). My reading of Zech 1–8 does not deny that Haggai and Zech 1–8 share certain thematic and ideological preoccupations and a common historical matrix. Nor do I deny the possibility that at some point Haggai and Zech 1–8 were incorporated into a common literary and theological collection. What I do affirm, however, is that in form and content Haggai and Zech 1–8 are sufficiently distinct to be evaluated independently from one another (Kessler 2002: esp. 56–57; Coggins: 44–45; Boda 2003:49–54, with bibliography). Furthermore, the arguments adduced in favor of a late-sixth-century composite redaction of Haggai-Zech 1–8 (thus Meyers and Meyers 1987; Lux) or a mid-fifth-century work including Malachi (Sérandour: 75–84, esp. 76) appear inconclusive in that they could all equally be used to demonstrate that Zech 1–8 and/or Zech 1–8; 9–14 and Malachi were all united to the book of Haggai *already in existence*.

2. Lipiński (1970) views 8:20–23 as a far later addition, stemming from the late Persian or Hellenistic period, due to its use of the pilgrimage motif. This, however, is far from certain; see Petitjean: 419–38).

1–8 reflects a Yehudite, rather than a diasporic, perspective (Petitjean: 442–43).[3] Zion is the central point from which the world is viewed or to which the world comes.

1. 2. YEHUD AND THE DIASPORA IN THE EARLY PERSIAN PERIOD

Amidst the torrent of scholarly interest in the Persian period over the past twenty years one can speak of a certain emerging critical consensus that views Yehud as a Persian province whose territory and population were vastly diminished when compared with the situation at the end of the monarchic period. In contrast to the position proposed by Albrecht Alt and followed by several scholars such as Galling (1964), Petersen (26–27), and McEvenue, wherein Yehud/Judah was annexed to Samaria and governed from there until the time of Nehemiah, or to the approach taken by Sacchi, Bianchi, and Niehr, which views Yehud as a quasi-independent kingdom within the Persian Empire ruled (at least in the early period) by a Davidic scion, a significant number of scholars view Yehud as a subunit within the fifth satrapy, initially ruled over by a governor of Davidic stock (Avigad; Williamson 1998; Lemaire 1994; Carter 1999:50–52; Na'aman). The province itself consisted of a rather small swath of territory lying around Jerusalem. Two major positions have emerged here. The first is that of Ephraim Stern (1982), who favors a somewhat larger province, including such sites as Lod and Ono in the northwest, Hazor in the north, and Beth-zur in the south. This contrasts with the narrower boundaries proposed by scholars such as Carter (1999:97) and Lemaire (1994:21). Lemaire views the province as consisting of the area within a radius of some twenty-five miles around Jerusalem (1994:20–21). Despite some extremely high estimates of the population of the province (Weinberg 1996:37), the application of modern demographic analysis, which involves such matters as spatial analysis, carrying capacity, water supply, and the establishment of a population co-efficient, has yielded far lower estimates.[4] Two major positions appear in the recent literature.[5] The first is that of Carter (1999:201–2), who suggests that the maximal population

---

3. Cf. Redditt (42), who argues on the basis of 2:10–17 (2:6–13) that the visions and accompanying oracles were formulated in Yehud and sent back to Babylon. Thus the exiles were the "original audience to whom the visions were directed." Similarly Petitjean (127–28) sees the purpose of 2:10–17 as being "to support the return-from-exile movement."

4. For a history of modern demographic analysis, including the work of Y. Shiloh, R. Gophna, M. Broshi, I. Finkelstein, and J. Wilkinson, see the surveys in Carter 1999:195–99; Lipschits 2003:324–26.

5. Cf. The earlier suggestion of Albright (87) of about twenty thousand in Yehud.

of the province during the Persian period to have been approximately twenty thousand. Oded Lipschits is critical of Carter's methodology[6] and suggests a maximal population of about thirty thousand for the Persian period as a whole (2003:363–64). While an increase of 50 percent from Carter's suggestion (or a decrease of 30 percent from Lipschits's) is certainly significant in relative terms, in absolute terms both estimates reflect a sparsely populated province, especially when compared with the situation on the eve of the Babylonian conquests, at which time the population of Judah was about 110,000 (Lipschits 2003:363–64). Especially striking here are Carter's and Lipschits's perceptions of the situation in Jerusalem. Carter (1999) assumes Jerusalem to have had a population of less than one thousand in the period between 538 and 450.[7] Lipschits (2006) and also independently Lemaire (2003:291–92) view Jerusalem to have been largely desolate until its refortification in the mid-fifth century. Both view the capital of Yehud as having been situated at Mizpah until that point. Blenkinsopp (1998:34) views Mizpah as the political and religious capital of Babylonian Judah until the *coup d'état* of Ishmael, after which the religious center moved to Bethel. David Ussishkin similarly views Jerusalem as having been territorially quite large but severely underpopulated during the Persian period. Lipschits (2006) further argues that the presence of an elite in the mid-fifth century initiated the redevelopment of Yehud but that real growth did not occur until the emergence of an even more significant elite in the Hellenistic period.[8]

Concurrent with this developing consensus regarding a reduced Yehud there has been a growing body of evidence regarding the presence of descendants of the inhabitants of the northern and southern kingdoms in a variety of locations beyond the borders of Yehud. This population is frequently designated by the term "Jewish"; however, such a term is problematic in that it is somewhat ambiguous, potentially anachronistic,[9] somewhat ill-fitting for the inhabitants of Samaria, and in danger of homogenizing quite disparate groups. Elsewhere (2006) I have suggested the designation "Yahwistic." However, this

---

6. Specifically Carter's periodization of the evidence into Persian I and Persian II (Carter 1999:199; Lipschits 2003:359–60). Readers of the two works may become confused here. Lipschits refers to Carter's two periods as Persian A and B, while Carter himself actually dubs them Persian I and Persian II.

7. Carter posits a settled area of 25–30 dunams of settled area in the early period (1999:148). Using his population coefficient of 25 persons per dunam—a figure Carter views as maximal—the result would be 625–750.

8. On the fortification of Jerusalem in this period, see Bodi: 37–55.

9. See Knauf (2002), who seeks to avoid anachronism by speaking of a "pre-biblical Judaism" at Elephantine.

is also not without problems of its own, since the terms *yehudi/yehudim* were widely used at the time as self-designations in Yehud and at Elephantine (Neh 1:2; Esth 2:6; Porten and Yardeni: A.4.7; Cowley: 30).[10] For the present study I will use the term "Israelite/Judean" to describe these communities. Whatever term is used, however, evidence of the presence of such a population, in such forms as biblical texts, extrabiblical literary materials, Yahwistic names in inscriptions and numismatics, is available for the following regions: Samaria, Egypt, Babylonia-Elam, and several of the regions surrounding Yehud, including Edom, Galilee, Ashdod, Idumaea, Moab, and Ammon (see Japhet 1983 for an earlier survey and Kessler 2006 for a survey of the more recent evidence, both with bibliography). Given the highly fragmentary state of our knowledge of these communities, it is virtually impossible to suggest any specific estimate of their demographic proportions vis-à-vis Yehud.

1.3. STUDYING THE JUDEAN COMMUNITIES IN THE ACHAEMENID EMPIRE

We thus are faced with a highly disparate mosaic of diverse yet related communities tracing their origins to the earlier kingdoms of Israel and Judah. One may summarize this complex tapestry as follows: (1) *golah* returnees in Yehud; (2) *golah* remainees in Babylonia;[11] (3) Yehudite remainees; (4) Israelite/Judean residents in Egypt; (5) Israelite/Judean inhabitants in the province of Samaria; and (6) other Israelite/Judeans in the various regions of the Levant. As noted above, one of the most fascinating questions to emerge in the analysis of these diverse communities is how they viewed one another. Certain studies have begun to address this question. Significant attention has been paid to the relationship between the returnees and the nondeported Judean remainees (Kessler 2001; Ben Zvi 1995:109–10; Williamson 1998:159) and between the returnees and the population in Samaria to the north (Ben Zvi 1995; Diebner; Knoppers). Others have investigated relations between the returnees and the Babylonian remainees (Bedford), between the Egyptian Diaspora and the communities in Jerusalem and Babylon (Bar-Kochva; Garbini: 133–50; Phillips; de Pury and Römer) or between the population in Yehud and the surrounding provinces (Rappaport). Still others have reflected upon Jewish identity formation (Hamilton; Cohen; Berquist 2006; Dombrowski).

---

10. For a summary of the use of the term, see Schmid.

11. The existence of other Israelite/Judean communities in the east is often speculated upon; see Smith-Christopher 2002:71, who suggests that Judeans may have been conscripted for military service by Nabonidus and scattered in Arabia. See also Oded (481), who suggests that exiles from the former northern kingdom were found among the Babylonian-Elamite Judean population.

Other studies have sought to understand the community in Yehud in terms of broader sociological dynamics. Most significant here are Causse's pioneering study (1937), Weinberg's citizen-temple community (1992), and Smith-Christopher's study of the impact of the exile on the Golah (1989; 2002).[12]

In a recent study (2006) I proposed viewing the Yehudite returnee community as a charter group. Based on the sociological model elaborated by John A. Porter in his study of colonial elite groups, I define a charter group as a *geographically transplanted elite*. As described by Porter, such an elite moves into a depopulated or underpopulated territory and establishes itself as the hegemonic sociopolitical force within the region, controlling its social, political, and economic institutions and leaving its impress for generations to come. Such hegemony is frequently achieved and maintained via political and economic support from outside the region itself. Viewing the returnees as functioning as a charter group is not meant in any way to predict outcomes or to form a grid through which to read the data. Rather, it offers a heuristic vantage point from which to observe the social, religious, and political dynamics at work in Persian Yehud and to view the similarities and dissimilarities that may exist between that situation and other analogous contexts. One especially significant issue is how such groups deal with questions of identity, membership, exclusion, and inclusion. It is to such questions that we now turn.

2.0. THE VIEW FROM ZECHARIAH 1–8

The present study, however, seeks to address the question of Israelite/Judean identity from the ideological perspective of one contemporary literary source, Zech 1–8. As such, I am not engaging in any kind of "concordist" enterprise, that is, asking this text to confirm or deny any of the historical, demographic, or sociological reconstructions mentioned above. My purpose is rather to examine the text in order to ascertain its own ideological perception and evaluation of the community in Jerusalem/Yehud and its relationship to the Israelite/Judean communities external to it. Once this ideological perspective is ascertained, I will seek to reflect on how the perceptions in Zech 1–8 relate to two specific and critical questions in the Achaemenid period: Jewish identity; and the future of Jerusalem and Yehud. In conclusion, I will offer some reflections on what such a perspective might reveal about the community that

---

12. See also Fried; Tollefson and Williamson. On the need for extreme caution in the use of sociological analogies, see Carter 1996.

produced it, when read against the backdrop of the realities of life in early Persian Yehud.

As noted above, Zech 1–8 views the world from the vantage point of Jerusalem (Petitjean: 442–43). The primary addressee, then, is the community in Yehud that is in the process of restoring the temple and reconstituting communal life. This provides a fixed point of reference and center of focus for the text as a whole (Petersen: 119; Meyers and Meyers 1987:lvi). However, it is also immediately apparent that the world of the text radiates outward from this one fixed point both chronologically and spatially. Chronologically, the text's purview extends to both past and future communities related to the one in Jerusalem. Spatially, the text's interest emanates outward from Jerusalem, to the cities of Judah, to Israel, Babylon, and beyond.[13] The present study will look at the data from the perspective of the narrative continuum created within the world of the text, as it moves from past to present to future. Within this framework, the text's geographical/spatial movement, from Israel, Judea, and Jerusalem, to the distant regions of the earth and back again, will become apparent. Methodologically, each segment of the narrative continuum will be analyzed first from the perspective of the SF, then from that of the VOC.

2.1. The Community of the Past

2.1.1. The Sermonic Framework: 1:1–6; 7:1–8:23

Zechariah 1–8 opens with a word from Yahweh in the eighth month of Darius's second year, thus October 520.[14] The reader is immediately struck by absence of any specified audience for the oracle (cf. the clearly expressed addressees in Hag 1:1; 2:1, 10, 20). Rather, attention is immediately focused upon a community of the past—consisting of "the ancestors" (’btkm)—who lived prior to the community presently addressed. No further designation of the identity of this earlier group is given in the opening section. The text simply describes the fact that they refused to hear (sm‘) or pay heed (hiphil of qsb) to Yahweh's warnings to them through the "former prophets" (1:4). This resulted in Yahweh's intense anger (1:2; where the verb qsp is strengthened via a cognate accusative) and judgment, (described as his word "overtaking the fathers" [hiphil nsg, 1:6]). Zechariah 7:1–8:23 likewise mirrors this perception of the past, albeit in greater detail. While the term "ancestors" does not

---

13. Meyers and Meyers (1992) and Floyd (1997) discuss the cosmic aspects of our text, but this theme cannot be pursued here.

14. On the scribal computation system in Haggai and Zech 1–8, see Kessler 1992; 2002:41–51, with bibliography.

reappear in this section, the same group is clearly referred to in the oracles in 7:1–7 and 8–14 (on the structure of these sections, see Floyd 2000:418–27). They refuse to hear (infinitive absolute of *smʿ*, 7:11; cf. 1:4) or pay attention (hiphil of *qsb*; cf. 1:4). This section adds the further terms "to refuse," "to set a defiant shoulder," and "to block the ears and make the heart as stone" (7:11–12; Meyers and Meyers 1987:403–4). As a result, Yahweh became exceedingly angry with them (here *qsp gdwl*; cf. 1:2), scattered them (*sʿr*; only here for scattering in Zechariah) among the nations they had not known (7:14, a Deuteronomism; cf. Deut 13:2; 28:36, 64; Jer 22:28; cf. 8:13 and 8:7).[15] As a result, Jerusalem, the cities of Judah, the Negev, and the Shephelah were depopulated (7:7), the land was desolated (*ʾrs nsmh*), and the beautiful land made a desolation (*ʾrs hmdh smh*, 7:14).

2.1.2. VISIONARY-ORACULAR COMPLEX: 1:7–6:15

A similar perspective is found in the VOC. While there is no explicit mention of the "ancestors" here, the concept is clearly present and implicit in the description of the nations' (2:2 [1:19]) and Yahweh's (2:10 [2:6]) scattering of the community. The second vision (2:1–4 [1:18–23]) refers to the scattering (*zrh*) of Judah, Israel, and Jerusalem by the "horns" (*qrnwt*). Several points are worthy of attention here. First the verb *zrh* ("to scatter") is a crucial one used to describe the exile and is found in a variety of traditions (Lev 26:33; 1 Kgs 14:15; Jer 31:10; 49:32; Ezek 5:2, 10, 12; 6:8; 12:14, 15; 20:23; 22:15; 36:19; Ps 106:27). Second, the precise localities to which these dispersed ones have been scattered are not explicitly stated in the vision. The mention of the four horns in 2:1 (1:18) may refer to Assyria and Babylon as the agents of this dispersion (Boda 2005) or may have a more general referent.[16] However that may be, the location of the dispersed persons is not specified. Third, the text links all the dispersed Israelite/Judean communities to this scattering. No account is taken of any who have engaged in voluntary emigration[17] or mili-

---

15. 8:7, 13–15 will be discussed in greater detail below.

16. Boda 2005 suggests the image of two animals with two horns each. He notes Vanderhooft's evidence for the Assyria-Babylon amalgam in various contexts (207). Alternately, Chary (64–65) among many others suggests that the four horns do not designate Babylon in particular but rather "the collective responsibility of all the Gentile nations for the evil done to the elect people." The number four is thus an expression of universality, similar to the four winds of 2:10 (6) and 6:5; see also the same image in Jer 49:36; Ezek 37:9; Dan 7:2; 8:8; 11:4.

17. It could be argued that any such emigration was redactionally subsumed under the concept of scattering. This appears to be the assumption of Petitjean (100–101). On

tary colonization (such as the community at Elephantine).[18] Fourth and most significantly, in 2:2 (1:19) the dispersed ones include "Israel." The mention of Israel in such a context is surprising, given the more frequent exilic designation of the objects of the nations' dispersal and Yahweh's renewed favor as "Judah and Jerusalem" (Zech 1:12; 2:16 [12]; 8:15; 2 Kgs 23:1, 2, 5, 24; 24:20; Isa 40:9; 44:26; Jer 1:15; 11:3; 18:1; Joel 4:1 [3:1]; 4:6 [3:6]; Zech 12:2, 5, 6, 7; Mal 2:11, 3:4). Furthermore, in 2:4 (1:21) only Judah is mentioned. However, despite the absence of the name "Israel" in the LXX, with Barthélemy (936–37), Meyers and Meyers (1987:138), Petersen (161), and Chary (64) but *pace* Redditt, I retain the entire phrase.[19] "Israel" here likely refers to those Israelites exiled by the Assyrians (Petersen: 163; Barthélemy: 977) and also possibly to those northerners who may have come south after 722 and were exiled by the Babylonians (Meyers and Meyers 1987:138). Later in the same vision (2:4 [1:21]) the exile is said to have been enacted upon "Judah" (*yhwdh*) and "the land of Judah" (*'rs yhwdh*). The reason for the absence of the name Israel here (cf. 2:2 [1:19])[20] may be due either to a desire to focus on the south (Petersen: 164) or because the activity of the "smiths" (*hrsym*)[21] is seen as consisting in the eviction of all foreign powers from the territory of Yehud (Chary: 66) or due to the specific interest in the "the restoration of self-governance in Yehud" via Persia's routing of Babylonian hegemony (Meyers and Meyers 1987:140, 145–46). In this vision it is the Gentile nations who have done the scattering.

The oracular additions to the third vision provide further detail. The exiles have been dispersed to a wide variety of locations, as symbolized by the four winds (2:10 [6]),[22] specifically to the north (*spwn*, 2:10 [6]), to Babylon (*bt bbl* 2:11 [5]). Here it is noteworthy that Yahweh is the author of the dispersion and that, unlike 2:2 and 4 (1:19, 21), where *zrh* is used, here *prs*

questions of immigration and the movement of persons, see Limet; Garelli; and on roads, see Graf 1993. Mobility is an absolutely critical issue for the understanding of our period; see below.

18. On the origins of this colony, see Knauf; Porten 1984:378–83; 2003.

19. Amsler (67) follows Duhm, Mitchell, Sellin, Jepsen, Elliger, Delcor, and Rudolph in retaining Israel but seeing it as a secondary insertion intended to further generalize the referent of the vision. Barthélemy (937), however, notes that this is a literary, not a textual, judgment.

20. LXX does add "and Israel" at 2:4 (1:21); however, this is clearly an interpolation from 2:2 (1:19; see Barthélemy: 932).

21. The meaning and identity of the image here cannot be discussed in the present study; cf. the extensive literature in the commentaries.

22. Also 6:5 and the same image in Jer 49:36; Ezek 37:9; Dan 7:2; 8:8; 11:4 (Petitjean:100–101).

is employed.[23] The text would thus appear to recognize a past, widespread dispersion and a more focused one (Babylon). A careful distinction must be made here. On one hand, Assyria and Babylon are widely recognized as the agents of dispersion in the Deuteronomistic tradition, as well as in Chronicles and various prophetic texts.[24] This should not, however, be used to collapse all the expatriate communities into the one in Babylon.[25]

In sum, then, both the SF and the VOC view the addressees of Zech 1–8 as the descendants of an earlier community that had hardened its hearts and refused Yahweh's word and that was scattered abroad, leaving the land a desolation. Thus the community of the past is perceived as having once existed in Jerusalem, Israel, and Judah but as having been dispersed to various localities. While certain differences in vocabulary and emphasis exist between 1:1–6 and 7:1–8:23, on the one hand, and 1:7–6:15, on the other, the basic perspective of the two blocs is the same.

2.2. The Community of the Present

In contrast with the community of the past, which was portrayed as having been dispersed, the community of the present exists in two geographical/spatial foci: (1) Jerusalem (and possibly elsewhere in Yehud);[26] and (2) various regions beyond Yehud where Israel and Judah's descendants are now found. This perspective is present in both the SF and the VOC.

---

23. On the use of *prs* here, see Petitjean: 98–100.

24. Boda 2005 cites the following: 2 Kgs 20//Isa 39; 2 Kgs 24–25; 2 Chr 32:31; 33:11; 36; Ezra 5:12; Jer 21:11–12; 29–30; Ezek 17–32; Isa 13:1–14; 21:1–10; Hab 1:5–11.

25. Lust argues that the notion of a widespread regathering in Ezekiel is a late Persian or Hellenistic creation. He seeks to distinguish the notions of *galut* and diaspora, arguing that the notion of *galut* is limited to Babylon, in contrast to the wider diaspora. He does not deal with Zech 1–8, which seems to locate the *golah* (8:10, 14) in the context of the wider dispersion.

26. Clearly a community is implied as present at Jerusalem. If Bethel is read as the subject of 7:2 (on which, see below), population is recognized in that city as well. In 7:7 a former time is described when Jerusalem, the cities of Judah, the Negev, and the Shephelah were inhabited (*ysbt*). As will be argued below, however, this implies that Zech 1–8 views these regions as still totally deserted.

2.2.1. THE COMMUNITY IN YEHUD

2.2.1.1. The Sermonic Framework: 1:1–6 and 7:1–8:23

As noted above, Zech 1:1–6 opens with a word from Yahweh to the community in Jerusalem.[27] The oracle implies a direct link and inherent continuity between the community of the past and the addressees. Thus the oracle in 1:2, set off by a *Wortereignisformel* preceding it (1:1) and a *Gottesspruchformel* formula following it (1:3), confronts the community of the present with the extreme anger of Yahweh vis-à-vis "your ancestors." The present community is then called to manifest behavior that stands in contrast to that of the ancestors, who were overtaken by the judgment[28] proclaimed by Yahweh through his prophets. Zechariah 1:6 ends on an optimistic note. Members of the present generation[29] have returned/repented (on the double significance of *swb* here, see Petersen: 110–11). A similar perspective is found in 8:1–17,[30] where the themes of the nonrepentance of the ancestors, the result of their actions, and the renewal of the present generation are taken up. The foundational unity between the community of the past and that of the present is expressed in the strongest of terms in 8:14–15. Here Yahweh states: "Just as I purposed to do evil to *you* [*lkm*] when *your ancestors* [*'btkm*] provoked me … so I have thought to do good to Jerusalem and to the house of Judah." The implication is that the judgment on the ancestors can be seen as having been experienced by the present generation (*you*), in that the two groups constitute an extended unity. The use of the vocatives "house of Judah and house of Israel" (8:13) or the terms "Jerusalem and the house of Judah" (8:15) similarly reveal the book's

---

27. This localization is not explicitly stated but may be implied from the parallel in 7:1–14.

28. This is the sense of *nsg* here. In the Jeremiah prose tradition it refers both to literal pursuit and capture (39:5; 42:16) as well as to a more generalized description of destruction (42:16) and captivity (Lam 1:3). Rudolph 1970:70 stresses the importance of Deut 28:2, 15, 45 here.

29. 1:6b could be an allusion to the return to Zion by the present generation, thus Petersen (100–101) or Meyers and Meyers (1987:96), who relate it to the effects of the preaching of Haggai. Amsler (57) following Rothstein, Beuken, and Petitjean, views it as a narrative conclusion describing the effect of the preaching of Zechariah in 1:1–6a upon his hearers. In favor of this latter position is the fact that Hag 1:1–15 follows a very similar pattern: 1:1–3 contains a complex and somewhat idiosyncratic merging of date formula, addressees, and oracles; and 1:12–15 contains a summary of the effects of the preaching of Haggai (Kessler 2002:112–12; Floyd 2000:266–72). The exact group that constitutes the subject of *swb* in Zech 1:6b remains, however, rather ambiguous.

30. Floyd 2002:427–36 affirms the essential unity of this long section.

understanding of its addressees as members of a broader unity, such that the present generation can be said to have been the recipients of Yahweh's actions in the past. This is identical to the perspective in Hag 2:5, where the text[31] speaks to the Persian-period community of "the covenant I made with *you* when *you came out of Egypt*." Similarly, 8:13 also extends this unity in both a past and a future sense. There Yahweh declares to the (present) Yehudite community, "just as *you* were a curse among the nations so I will save [*ysʻ*] *you*." Thus the first "you" is tied to the present community in Yehud (contextually the "you" in 8:13 is the same "you" addressed in 8:9 and described as being "those who in these days hear these words from the mouths of the prophets present on the day of the foundation of the house of Yahweh Sebaoth." The second "you" clearly refers to the diaspora members whom Yahweh will bring back to Yehud as a future date. Thus the Yehudite community is the visible manifestation of the broader entity that extends chronologically into both the past and future and that radiates geographically outward form Jerusalem.

The present community in Yehud is further glimpsed in 7:1–7. Zechariah 7:2 has been the subject of extensive inquiry due to its extreme ambiguity. Neither the question of the subject and objects of the verb *slh* nor their identities, functions, or places of origin can be discussed in detail here.[32] It is widely affirmed that a question is sent to the Jerusalemite temple,[33] with its functioning priests and prophets, by those living at a distance from it. What is significant for our purposes, however, is that a new designation for the community in Yehud is introduced here. The prophet uses the question as a springboard for a response to "all the people of the land" (*ʼl-kl-ʻam hʼars*). As in Hag 2:4, the term describes the general population of Yehud (Nicholson 1965:66; Rudolph 1970:144; Boda 2003:398–99; Amsler, Lacoque, and Vuilleumier:115).[34] It is significant to note that the present community in the land is called to a renewed commitment to Yahweh. This hortatory tone, largely ethical in nature, is a hallmark of Zech 1:1–6; 7:1–8:23 (see Boda 2003:60–61). The generation of the ancestors has passed. Now the present generation is called to return (*swb*) to Yahweh (1:3), not to be like (*ʼl thyw*

31. On the textual issue here, see Kessler 2002:160.

32. See, provisionally, the analysis in Meyers and Meyers 1987:379–84; Baldwin: 141–42; Petersen: 281–82; Barthélemy: 967–98.

33. Thus, Meyers and Meyers 1987:384–85; Amsler: 114; Lemaire 1970; but cf. Blenkinsopp 1998, who argues that the question is sent to Bethel but responded to from a Jerusalemite perspective.

34. Amsler (15) suggests that the term is explicitly inclusive of the remainees, on which see below. Gunneweg views the reference here as to the upper-class land owners, but this limitation is not warranted by the context.

k-) the ancestors (1:4), and to pursue diligently (*'hb* here, as in Prov 4:6) "truth and peace" (8:19).

Finally, in 8:6, 11 the present generation is described as a remnant (*s'ryt*). As in Hag 1:12 and 2:4, the term here clearly refers to the numerically small proportions of the Yehudite community (vis-à-vis the diaspora) as well as, albeit subtly, to their renewed relationship to Yahweh (cf. Hag 1:1–15; Zech 1:6b).[35]

2.2.1.2. *The Visionary-Oracular Complex: 1:7–6:15*

The VOC similarly views a community present in Yehud. However unlike the SF this section does not describe the community in relationship to earlier generations, few epithets are attached to it, and it receives no commands or exhortations as a group. An appellative for the community as a whole does occur, however, in 2:14 (10), where the term "daughter of Zion" (*bt sywn*) is employed.[36] Here the personified Jerusalem designates the community gathered in proximity to Jerusalem, which is called to rejoice due to the greatness of the future blessing of Yahweh. If the oracle here specifically addresses Jerusalem (as opposed to Yehud as a whole), [37] the contrast between present *petitesse* and future *grandeur* is indeed an immense one, given the fact that Jerusalem may have been a mere village at the time.[38] Amsler (76) suggests that the term "Jerusalem" includes both returnees and remainees; however, such a suggestion remains conjectural.

---

35. On the use of *s'ryt* here, see Meyers and Meyers 1987:417, who affirm the theological significance of the term in Zechariah but deny any such significance in Haggai. However, the fact that the term is used in Haggai only *following* the people's obedience in 1:12 is surely significant. Amsler (122) sees the term only as an image of smallness. A similar perspective is found in Conrad (144–45). On Hag 1:12–15 as a covenant renewal, see Beuken 1967:45–46; Kessler 2002:550 n. 327.

36. On the sense of the feminine term here, see Petersen: 179–80.

37. Petitjean (129–30) notes that while the term *bt sywn* frequently refers to the city of Jerusalem here as in Mic 4:10, 13; Zeph 3:14; Zech 9:9, Jerusalem has a metonymic value, and designates the broader community gathered around it. Amsler (1988:76) and Meyers and Meyers (1987:417) appear to limit it to the population of Jerusalem. On the one hand, the unity of Jerusalem and the cities of Judah, seen elsewhere in the book (1:12, 17; 2:4, 16), the reference to the desolation of the "beautiful land" in 7:7, 14, and the fact that the basic division in Zech 1–8 is between two groups (homeland and diaspora) rather than three (Jerusalemites, Yehudites, and diaspora members) would favor Petitjean's view. On the other hand, however, the Jerusalemite temple, as the dwelling of Yahweh, receives special attention in Zech 1–8 (1:14, 16 [2x], 17; 3:2; 8:3).

38. Carter 1999; Lipschits 2003.

The VOC mentions various specific members of the community in
Yehud, as well as their roles and activities: Joshua the high priest (3:1);
Zemach/the Branch (3:8; 6:12) and servant of Yahweh;[39] Zerubbabel (4:6,
7, 9, 10) the temple builder.[40] Zerubbabel and Joshua may be clearly identified as returnees (see Hag 1:1). Zechariah 6:10, 14 mentions Heldai, Tobijah,
and Jedaiah,[41] all of whom are associated with the community of returnees
(*gwlh*, 6:10), who have come to the house of Josiah. Commentators see either
all of these individuals as returnees from the diaspora who have come with
an offering for the temple (Amsler, Lacoque, and Vuilleumier: 105; Rudolph
1970:129; Redditt: 77) or, alternatively, only Heldai as a recent returnee, while
the others are earlier returnees now resident in Yehud (Meyers and Meyers
1987). Petersen (274) suggests that Josiah's father Zephaniah may have been
a remainee. However one understands the time of their arrival, the presence
of these individuals forms a bridge between the community in Yehud and
the broader Israelite/Judean community beyond it.[42] Just as 1:1–6 and 7:8–14
presuppose a unity between the ancestors and the present generation, and
8:13–15 envisages a unity between the returnees and the diaspora, here this
text views the nonreturned exiles in the diaspora as an extension of the community in Yehud. [43] If these individuals have indeed come to Yehud to take
up residence, bearing gifts from the diaspora (thus Chary: 109), this event
prefigures the yet-future and greater ingathering of the exiles spoken of elsewhere in Zech 1–8.

---

39. The identity of this individual has been much discussed. Rose and Meyers and
Meyers (1987:372–73) see it as a symbolic-messianic figure. Amsler (108–9), following a
long interpretive tradition, sees it as a reference to Zerubbabel. Lemaire (1996:51) notes
the presence of Zemach-Zerubbabel as a double name in the inscriptional evidence.

40. Note that, unlike Haggai, Zechariah mentions neither Zerubbabel's political status
not his Davidic genealogy.

41. On the various possibilities for understanding *hn* in 6:14, see Meyers and Meyers
1987:340–43. The hypothesis of a double name seems quite probable, given the frequency
of such names at the period; see Demsky; Lemaire 1996:51.

42. As noted, mobility is an absolutely critical issue for the understanding of home-
land-diaspora relations in our period. The degree to which the community in Babylon
may have been involved in the life of the community in Yehud is contingent on the degree
of facility of interchange between the two; see Limet; Garelli.

43. Meyers and Meyers (1987:339) aptly comment, "The ambivalence of the term
'exiles' helps to demonstrate the unity of a community acknowledging Yahweh as God,
apart from the form or identity of the political state in which those who acknowledge
Yahweh may live." See also Rudolph 1976:129, who sees this as a demonstration of the
participation of the nonreturnees in the project in Yehud.

2.2.2. The Community outside Yehud

2.2.2.1. The Sermonic Frame: 1:1–7; 7:1–8:23

Zechariah 1:6 makes only an oblique reference to Judeans outside Yehud. Thus, as noted above, Yahweh's judgment upon the ancestors (1:4–6) is a way of speaking of destruction and, by extension, exile. Zechariah 8:1–7, however, makes it clear that dispersion is an ever-present reality. In 8:7 a further designation for the Judean community ("my people" ['*my*]) is added to those already mentioned. Here, then, the members of the people of Yahweh are seen as living in the east and the west (*m'rs mzrh wm'rs mbw' hsms*; cf. Ps 50:1). This may be a simple merism, thus designating the exiles wherever they may be (thus Meyers and Meyers 1987:418, who note the parallel with Isa 43:5–7; Rudolph 1970:148), or the mention of the west may be an explicit inclusion of the Egyptian diaspora (Ackroyd 1968:213; cf. Phillips). In 8:13 the community outside Yehud is seen as belonging to the "house of Israel and house of Judah" whom Yahweh will deliver in the future. Finally, in the concluding oracle, 8:20–23, the diaspora community is described via the locution *'ys yhwdy*. The term *yhwdy* carries ethnic (Jer 34:9, 40:11–12; 41:3; Neh 5:8), territorial (Jer 43:9; 44:1; 52:28), and linguistic (2 Kgs 18:28; Neh 13:24) overtones. In a more general sense it is used, as here, to denote members of the southern kingdom or their descendants living in exile (Esth 2:5; Lemaire 1970: 43–44).[44]

2.2.2.2. The Visionary-Oracular Complex: 1:7–6:15

The VOC similarly takes into account the existence of the diaspora beyond Yehud. Zechariah 2:2 (1:19) understands the past scatterings to be an ongoing reality. As already noted, the oracle in 2:10–17 (6–13),[45] while acknowledging a broader diaspora, focuses on the community in Babylon (*bt bbl*).[46] In this

---

44. See Schmid. Meyers and Meyers understand the term *Yehudite* here as meaning "citizen of Yehud who has accepted the new reality of postexilic Israel: its new administrative structure, its restored temple, and Yahweh's sovereign presence" (1987:441). This however, seems, unwarranted, as the term is more naturally to be taken as a simple gentilic-religious designation here.

45. On the delimitation of this oracle, see Amsler: 73; Petitjean: 91–94; Floyd 2002:365–70.

46. On the sense and use of this expression, see Petersen: 175–76, who renders it "fair Babylon." Meyers and Meyers (1987:164) render it simply "dwellers of Babylon." As Petersen (175) notes, in the Jeremianic tradition the exiles in Babylon appear to function

context the exiles are called "Zion" (2:11 [7]).[47] Significantly, whereas in the second vision the focus of interest was the territory of Yehud, here the use of the term *Zion* lays stress on the identity of the exiles as those who, despite their dwelling in places far removed from Yehud, still stand in relationship to Jerusalem as the religious center of the territory and the place where Yahweh's future dwelling will be realized.[48]

In the analysis of the community in Yehud, mention was made of the individuals named in 6:10 and 14. These individuals have come from the *golah* and in some sense represent the nonreturnee community.[49] A further designation of the diaspora community occurs in 6:15a, at the end of a section that Floyd (2002:409) labels a report of a prophetic symbolic action. In this context it is promised that "those who are afar off" (*rhwqym*) will come

---

as the concrete manifestation of the more general exile (see Jer 6:22; 16:15; 23:8; 31:8). The implication of this would be that the specific call to flight addressed to the exiles in Babylon would be paradigmatic and applicable by extension to the exiles as a whole.

47. I take Zion here to be a vocative (see Petersen: 172–73). Meyers and Meyers (1987:164) treat Zion here as an accusative of direction. This is possible but unlikely due to the clear parallelism between Zion and "the one who dwells in Babylon." In a similar vein Petitjean (105–7) prefers a vocative due to the likelihood that a vocative would follow the interjection *hwy* and the similarities between our text and Isa 40:9; 52:1–2; Zeph 3:16; Zech 9: 13; Pss 146:10; 147:12. He further notes the parallel between 2:11 (7) and the calls to the "daughter of Zion" in Isa 52:1–2; Zeph 3: 14, 16, and Zech 9:9, 13.

48. See Petitjean: 105–7 for a detailed discussion of the terms *Jerusalem* and *Zion* in Isa 40–55 and Zech 1–8. Petitjean discerns two principal referents for these terms: (1) Jerusalem/Zion as the capital and religious center of the new community (Isa 51:3; 52:7–8; Zech 1:14, 17; 8:2–3); and (2) a designation of the people as a whole (Isa 40:9; 41:27; 46:13; Zech 2:11). In summary, he states, "The use of Zion to designate the deportees in Babylon serves to place the dramatic situation created by the exile in stark relief. Israel has been snatched away from its land and from the religious centre which Yahweh has assigned to his people—Jerusalem and the hill of Zion. Put another way, Zion is no more in Zion." Amsler (74) similarly suggests that Zion is used to stress the relationship of the exiles to the promises made to Zion in Isa 40:9 and 51:16. Ackroyd (180) similarly comments, "It is significant that the sense of belonging to the community even while in exile is expressed so strongly that the exiles can be described as 'Zion who dwells in Babylon.'" See also Meyers and Meyers 1987:339.

49. Meyers and Meyers (1987:368–68) view each of the individuals in the list as constituting "a carefully chosen set" in which "each individual represents a group of Yahwists that has a special relationship with the territory of Yehud and to the Temple of Yahweh being rebuilt there.... [T]heir inclusion by Zechariah in his account of such an event apparently reveals the prophet's awareness of the geographical diversity that characterized the Yahwist community in his day." This suggestion is an interesting one that cannot be evaluated here.

and build the temple of Yahweh. The term is one frequently used for the diaspora population (Isa 33:13; 43:6; 49:12; 60:4, 9; Jer 30:10; 51:50; Dan 9:7).

3.0. Demographics and the Future of Jerusalem and Yehud

The narrative continuum of Zech 1–8 can be summarized as follows. The SF and VOC both portray a similar image of the community of Yahweh. Yahweh's people formerly dwelt in Judah, Israel, and Jerusalem. The city of Jerusalem was of special importance, as it was there that Yahweh also dwelt, in his temple. Due, however, to their refusal to heed the word of Yahweh, his people were scattered to diverse nations, and the land and its cities became desolate. A new era, however, had dawned. A community now existed in Jerusalem and Yehud that was in the process of rebuilding and reconsecrating the temple. Nevertheless, a significant portion of the people of Yahweh remained outside the land, particularly in Babylon. From the perspective of Zech 1–8, however, this bifurcation into two groups, one in the land and the other outside of it, is, in the final sense, anomalous and provisional. The text therefore looks ahead and depicts the relationship between Yahweh and his people as having a future phase. A survey of the data in both major sections of Zech 1–8 will demonstrate that Yahweh's ultimate purposes are understood as involving an undoing of the earlier scattering, and a restoration to the land.

3.1. The Sermonic Frame: Zechariah 1:1–6; 7:1–8:23

Zechariah 1:1–6 has little to say about either the existence of the diaspora or its return. That theme, however, does appear in 7:1–8:23. Zechariah 7:7 bemoans the depopulation and economic devastation of all of the southern kingdom: Jerusalem, the cities of Judah, the Negev, and the Shephelah; 7:14 similarly reflects on the land's devastation. The theme of its restoration is taken up in 8:1–17 and 18–23.[50] Zechariah 8:3 announces Yahweh's imminent return to Zion.[51] In addition to the religious and ethical components of

---

50. On the division of these sections, see Floyd 2002:427–36.

51. See Petitjean (1969:369–71), who notes the parallelism here with 1:14–16b and 2:14–15 (10–11). The perfects *sbty* in 1:16 and 8:3 would thus be read as examples of the *perfectum confidentiae* stressing the certainty of Yahweh's return (see Amsler, Lacoque, and Vuilleumier:66) and the imminence of the event expressed by the *futurum instans* in 2:14–15. Alternatively, Meyers and Meyers (1987:122) see the perfect in 1:16 as indicating that the oracle viewed Yahweh's return as having already taken place, whereas the *futurum instans* in 2:14 (10) is a real future, indicating that the oracle stems from a time before the rededication ceremony (1987:168). At 8:3 they argue that the implication is that the dwell-

Jerusalem's future described in 8:3, a demographic dimension is introduced in 8:4–6. Zion's future is unveiled in three stages. First, an image is drawn of an inhabited Jerusalem (note the use of *ysb* in 8:4, parallel to Yahweh's own dwelling in 8:4). The description of the city's inhabitants is significant. The reference to old men and women leaning upon their staffs and to children of both genders playing describes a situation of blessing, peace, and security.[52] Zechariah 8:7–8 indicates the source, at least in part, of this future population. Through a *futurum instans* indicating imminence (cf. Hag 2:6, 21) it is stated that Yahweh will deliver his people (*hnny mwsyʿ*)[53] from the east and west (likely inclusive of the Egyptian diaspora) and bring them (hiphil of *bwʾ*) to dwell (*ysb*) in Jerusalem. Zechariah 8:13 takes up the same theme and describes this event as a coming deliverance.[54] This future repopulation is seen as a manifestation of Yahweh's decision to do good (*ytb*) to Jerusalem and to Judah (8:15). In the concluding oracles of this section (8:20–22, 23) reference is made once again to the exilic community at large as well as to the Gentiles. To stress the extreme value placed upon the exilic community by the Gentile nations around them, ten non-Jews[55] are said to take hold of the garment of an individual of Israelite/Judean origin (*ʾys yhwdy*) who is en route to Jerusalem.[56]

---

ing of Yahweh has already begun. On the ambiguity of *swb*, see Petersen: 156. However the chronology of Yahweh's return is understood, all three passages go on to demonstrate the *effects* of this return.

52. For a description of the meaning of the various elements in the description, see Ackroyd: 212).

53. This combination of *hinneh* and the verb *ysʿ* is frequently used in connection with Yahweh's coming repatriation of the exiles (Isa 25:9; 35:4; 62:11; Jer 30:10; 46:27; Zeph 3:19).

54. Hiphil of *ysʿ*; however, a simple imperfect is used here, different from the participial construction in 8:7 noted above.

55. *Pace* Lipiński 1970:44–46, who views the referent of *ʿmym rbym* and *gwym ʿswmym* in 8:22 as being diaspora Jews. The argument is unconvincing in the light of the frequent use of such terms for Gentiles (cf. Isa 2:1–4; Mic 4:1–4).

56. It is difficult to determine exactly what brings these *yehudim* to Jerusalem. Petersen (315–18) sees the notion of pilgrimage as implicit in 8:20–22 but notes that in 8:23 the language is more vague. If one reads 8:23 in the light of 8:8, then a definitive return to dwell permanently is in view. However the verb *ysb* is absent from 8:23, and the language here is far closer to that of pilgrimage (Amsler, Lacoque, and Vuilleumier: 125). If this is indeed a reference to diaspora members returning to Jerusalem only for pilgrimage, 8:23 stands in significant tension with the dominant vision of Zech 1–8, which foresees a total return. If such were the case, Lipiński's suggestion (1970:42–46) of a later addition would be the most likely explanation.

3.2. THE VISIONARY-ORACULAR COMPLEX: 1:7–6:15

A very similar perspective is found in the VOC. In the first vision and oracle (1:7–17) the angel of Yahweh expresses discontent with the status quo. The fact that the earth is at rest is viewed as a reflection of Yahweh's lack of compassion (*rhm*) toward Judah and Jerusalem (1:12). The resolution to this dilemma is the return of Yahweh to Jerusalem in compassion (*rhm*, 1:16, 17b) and election (*bhr*, 1:17). The result of this return will be twofold: (1) Yahweh's house will be rebuilt; and (2) a measuring line (*qw*), frequently used in connection with judgment (2 Kgs 21:13; Isa 34:11; Lam 2:8) but also salvation (Ezek 47:3), shall be stretched forth over Jerusalem. Zechariah 1:17 advances this description by asserting that Yahweh's cities (*'ry*) will overflow (a rare use of *pws*; cf. Prov. 5:16) with prosperity (*twb*). This corresponds to their former prosperity (cf. 7:7 *slwh*) and populous state mentioned in 7:7. The theme of repopulation is similarly taken up in the second vision (2:1–4 [1:18–21]), albeit implicitly. There judgment is pronounced on the horns (i.e., nations) that scattered "Judah, Israel and Jerusalem" (2:2 [1:19]). The implication of the terrifying (i.e., destruction; see Boda 2005) of these nations in explained in the third vision (2:5–9 [1–5]) and accompanying oracles (2:6–13 [10–17]). In 2:5–6 ([1–2]) a figure appears with a measuring line (*hbl mdh*, which here symbolizes hope, as in Jer 31:39; Ezek 40)[57] and goes forth to measure (*mdd*) Jerusalem. The significance of this is explained in 2:8–9 (4–5). Jerusalem will be so full with a multitude (*rb*) of people (*'dm*) and cattle (*bhmh*)[58] that[59] it will be like an unwalled village (*przh*; cf. Ezek 38:1; Esth 9:19), its population having far surpassed the boundaries of the city walls.[60] However, the lack of fortifications naturally raises problems of defense. Thus the security of the city will be guaranteed by Yahweh himself 2:9 (5), who will protect it like a wall of fire.[61] The origins of this multitude are not specified in the vision, but the following oracle implies that, at least in part, it will be made

---

57. Cf. the same image but using the term *qw* in 1:16.

58. Cf. the similar description of a multitude of people and cattle in Nineveh in Jonah 4:11, using identical terms.

59. The *min* in *mrb* is causal, indicating that Jerusalem's unwalled state stands in direct causal relationship to the multitudes present within her (the Hebrew is specific: *btwkh*).

60. Clearly in Darius's reign Jerusalem's walls were in ruins. Meyers and Meyers (1987:154–55) see the description here as rooted in the realities of the early Persian period. Perhaps the implication here is that, from the perspective of Zech 1–8, the reconstruction of the walls is unnecessary (cf. Ackroyd 1968:179).

61. See Amsler, Lacoque, and Vuilleumier: 71–72, who note that the imagery here recalls the pillar of fire of Exod 13:21–23. Note also the contrast with the walls and gates that are destroyed by fire in Jer 49:27; Amos 1:7, 10, 14; Neh 1:3; 2:13, 17.

up of exiles who heed the call to flee Babylon in 2:10–13 (6–9).[62] This call
is presented in the most urgent of terms. The exiles are called to flee (*nws*;
2:10 [6]) and to escape (*mlt*; 2:11 [7]). These terms, individually and more
especially taken together, suggest an urgent flight and seeking of refuge in the
context of an impending disaster (see Gen 19:20; Isa 20:6; Jer 46:6; 48:6, 19;
51:6; Amos 9:11). The disaster in context here is Yahweh's impending judgment on Babylon for its mistreatment of his people (2:12–13 [8–9]). A further
indication of the source of Jerusalem's population is given in the subsequent
oracle (2:14–17 [10–13]). Many nations (a frequent prophetic designation of
the Gentile world, especially in the sixth century [Jer 25:14; 27:1; Ezek 26:3;
31:6; 38:23] and in eschatological descriptions [Mic 4:2–3]) will join themselves to Yahweh (*lwh*; cf. Isa 14:1; 53:3, 6; 50:5; Esth 9:27; Dan 11:34) and
become his people (*l'm*). Such language is frequently used in the sixth century
for the renewal of the relationship between Yahweh and his people (Jer 24:7;
31:1, 33; Ezek 11:20; 36:28; 37:23; esp. Zech 8:8) but is also used for the inclusion of foreigners (Ruth 1:16; Isa 14:1; 19:27; 53:3, 6; Jer 50:5; Esth 9:27). The
exact form that this "becoming the people of Yahweh" would take is not specified.[63] Judgment on Babylon (here called *'rs spwn*, 6:6, 8) is likely in view in
the vision in 6:1–8 (e.g., Amsler:104–5).[64] The quieting (*hnyhw*) of Yahweh's
Spirit in the north country is seen by a long exegetical tradition as permit-

---

62. On the issue of the origin of this oracle and its function in its present literary
context, see Petitjean:127, who sees it as support for the movement to return. Amsler (76)
views it both as an appeal to the diaspora members to return, which could have been transmitted by word of mouth to those in Babylon, and as an encouragement to those who had
already made the move back to the homeland. Meyers and Meyers (1987:172–73) make a
similar point. Rejecting the notion that Zechariah's prophetic activity had begun in exile
(see Ackroyd 1968:148–49), they maintain that we hear "in the imperatives of this oracle
pulling its distant audience to Zion the voice of one who has already made the return and
who is involved in the temple restoration project." It is destined to "be heard by fellow
returned Yehudites needing assurance that they have chosen wisely or by exiles still pon-
dering the choice." The suggestion that the oracle is destined to reassure the returnees is
certainly correct. That the oracle should have been transmitted to the Babylonian communities remains speculative, as it presupposes significant movement between the homeland
and Babylonian diaspora in our period—by no means a certainty. As noted above, personal mobility is a complex issue that is of critical importance for our period.

63. For a discussion of this, see Rudolph 1976:91, who notes that what is being
described here goes far beyond the simple notion of a pilgrimage to Jerusalem on the
part of the nations; see also Amsler:76. Meyers and Meyers (1987:175) maintain that this
expression indicates that the nations will "share in the special arrangement which had
heretofore characterized Israel as a 'people.'"

64. But cf. the alternative approaches of the vision in Meyers and Meyers 1987;
Floyd 2002.

ting the return of the exiles.[65] The report of the prophetic symbolic action in 6:10–15 concludes with the promise that "those that are far off" (*rhwqmym*) will come and build the temple. As noted above, these are diaspora members who return to Jerusalem.

In sum, then, we have seen that for both the SF and the VOC the present situation is viewed as temporary and somewhat anomalous. The narrative continuum of the text looks forward to a time when the exiles will ultimately return to dwell in Yehud, and Gentiles will come and join with them. Jerusalem will be filled to overflowing and the population and prosperity of Judah restored.

4.0. ZECHARIAH 1–8 AND PERSIAN-PERIOD REFLECTION

Zechariah 1–8, then, presents a comprehensive and self-consistent image of the community of Yahweh. The broadest designation for this community is the simple epithet "my people" (2:11 [7]; 8:7–8). This community includes past generations (1:1–6; 7:11–14) as well as those alive in the present (6:15). Furthermore, the text envisages the ongoing life of the community in the future (8:1–8). While consisting in its foundational sense of the "house of Israel and the house of Judah" (8:13), this community is open to the inclusion of Gentiles (2:15 [11]; 8:20–23). Moreover, Zech 1–8 displays a strong geographic focus. It uses the metonymic expression "Judah, Israel, and Jerusalem" (2:2 [19]; see also 1:12, 14, 16, 17, 2:4, 16; 3:2; 8:13) for the people of Yahweh, thus profoundly connecting them to their places of origin. Through the activities of the nations (2:2 [1:19]) as well as Yahweh (2:11 [6]) they have been scattered into a variety of locations (2:10 [6]; 8:7), especially Babylon (2:10–12 [6–8]). Such a situation, although persisting until the time of the book's production, was merely provisional and would ultimately give way to a new reality. The dispersed communities in every location would be regathered by Yahweh and restored to the land (2:8 [4]; 6:15; 8:1–8), which would overflow with abundance and prosperity (1:17). Most important, Yahweh himself would dwell in Jerusalem amidst his people (1:16; 2:9 [5], 14 [10];

---

65. Amsler (104–5) disputes the inference that the return of the exiles is in view but cites Sellin, Elliger, Rudolph, Delcor, and Rothstein as supporting it. Chary (108) affirms, "The poverty and demographic insignificance of the tiny community will be overcome when the diaspora returns, having been touched by the movement of the Spirit. [They will come] not only from Babylon, the largest community, but from many locations.... Such was the assurance and comfort that the then-present moment required." Similarly, Petersen (272) comments that the vision "is designed to elicit another exit, that of the return of those in the north country to their homeland."

8:3, 8). Such an understanding of the Israelite/Judean community is highly significant when set in the context of two burning issues in the Achaemenid period: (1) requirements for membership in the people of Yahweh; and (2) the future of Yehud and especially of Jerusalem.

4.1. Exile and Identity

Zechariah 1–8 paints a general image of exile and return that is quite similar to that of Ezra, Nehemiah, the Deuteronomistic History, Jeremiah, Ezekiel, and Chronicles. However, it is immediately apparent that Zech 1–8 does not use the experience of exile in Babylon as a means by which membership in the community of Yahweh is defined and demarcated. This stands in tension with several near-contemporary texts. Jeremiah 24:8 clearly distinguishes the deportees from both the remainees and the Egyptian diaspora and asserts that Yahweh's favor lies with the former group, to the exclusion of the latter two (on the complexities of this passage, see Carroll 1986:480–88). The Egyptian diaspora is singled out for special disapprobation in Jer 42:15–43:13. Similarly, Ezek 11:15 identifies the *golah* as the exclusive embodiment of the true Israel (Allen 1994:163–64). Ezra-Nehemiah furthers this concept by making membership in the assembly contingent on three requirements: genealogical roots in the former southern kingdom; exile to the east; and obedience to the "law of Moses" (Kessler 2006; Gunneweg 1983). In Ezra-Nehemiah the experience of Babylonian exile is specifically used as an exclusionary strategy vis-à-vis the Samarian population (Ben Zvi 1995) and the Yehudite remainees.[66] The stability of such a definition of communal boundaries was reinforced through the prohibition of intermarriage with members of the nonapproved groups, on pain of excommunication for noncompliance (Ezra 7:26; 10:8, Neh 13).

Zechariah 1–8, however moves in a very different direction. As noted above, it would appear that all the descendants of the inhabitants of both the northern and southern kingdoms are eligible for inclusion in the community. While a certain interest is expressed toward the Babylonian community in 2:6–7 (10–11) and 6:10,[67] this interest is never expressed in exclusionary terms. The relevance of this may be seen with reference to three groups. The first of these is the Egyptian diaspora. Zechariah 8:7 speaks of Yahweh bring-

---

66. Note, however that various strategies may have been deployed to facilitate the inclusion of the Remainees (Kessler 2006; Japhet 1983:114; 2003; Dyck, 2000; Bedford:150).

67. Petersen (280) opines that "it is difficult to avoid the inference that Zechariah has particular sympathies with those who have been in exile." It is commonly assumed that Zechariah himself was a returnee.

ing back those in the east and west, which leaves the door wide open for the inclusion of the Egyptian community. The absence of any exclusionary designation here is especially relevant in light of the commonly recognized similarities between Zech 7:1–8:23 and the prose tradition of Jeremiah (Boda 2003:59), a tradition that was certainly aware of the rejection of the Egyptians in Jer 37–43[68] and 24:8. Judith R. Phillips has argued that Zechariah's visions are intended to reinforce the rejection of the diaspora and a focus on Jerusalemite expressions of Yahwism. The clear openness to all diasporic communities in both sections of Zech 1–8, however, speaks against the rigid lines she draws. The second of these groups is the nondeported population, whether resident in Yehud or in other neighboring provinces.[69] Indeed, the perspective of Zech 1–8 seems somewhat unconcerned by existing Achaemenid provincial divisions[70] in that two of the four regions mentioned in 7:7 (Shephelah, Negev) lay outside the boundaries of Yehud (Lemaire 1994). The implication may be that for the compiler of Zech 1–8 the "real" Yehud (whatever the Persian administrative system may have provisionally ordained) included all the territory of the former Judah.[71] Care needs to be exercised here so as not to extract too much from Zech 1–8. Thus despite Amsler, who affirms our text to be *inclusive* of both the returnees and the remainees (Amsler, Lacoque, and Vuilleumier: 115), it is perhaps better to affirm that Zech 1–8 makes no explicit reference to the exclusion of such a population. The use of *'am h'rs* in 7:5 cannot be used as an explicit reference to the inclusion of the remainees, since the term's referent is most likely the general population, not the community from which the returnees distinguish themselves, as in Ezra-Nehemiah. As noted above, both the mention of Israel in 2:2 (1:19) and the parallelism between the "house of Israel and the house of Judah" in 8:13 (Japhet 1983:111) would indicate that Zechariah favors the inclusion of this group.[72] Third, Zech 1–8 is open to Gentile inclusion. Gentiles join themselves to Yahweh and become part of his people in 2:15 (11)

---

68. Note the treatment of this section in Lohfink.

69. On the tension between Zech 1–8 and Ezra-Nehemiah on this issue, see Petersen: 182. On the mixed marriages, see Eskenazi.

70. Issues of borders and their significance have received attention in the recent literature. Fantalkin and Tal (2006), discuss the actual situation of the Shephelah in our period and argue for a fluidity of borders in transitional periods. On the issue of the relevance of the concept of borders in the study of the ancient world, see Wright. On the broader question of the construction of identity, see Berquist 2006. On the relationship between borders and the movement of persons, see Limet: 167–68.

71. Such a perspective may be reflected in the town lists in Ezra 2 and Neh 7; 11.

72. Japhet (1983:111) appropriately comments, "As for the people of the north ... although the 'house of Israel' is not the immediate audience of the prophet, ... they are

and join returning exiles on their journey to Jerusalem in 8:23.[73] It needs
hardly to be mentioned that such openness to Gentiles stands in tension to
the separation from them in Ezra-Nehemiah, which appears to preclude even
the possibility of conversion as a response to the question of mixed marriages
(see Cohen: 306).

Concurrent with this nonexclusivist interpretation of the exile is a somewhat more general and less polemical presentation of the fate of the land
subsequent to the Babylonian devastations. Whereas various other traditions enter into far greater detail regarding the extent of the depopulation of
the land and its significance, the presentation in Zech 1–8 is quite reserved.
No ideological or theological reason for the deportations is provided other
than the anger of Yahweh (1:4–6; 7:13–14).[74] What is more, in Zech 1–8 the
descriptions of the state of the land after the Babylonian devastations are
quite restrained when compared with other sources, and no insistence is
made upon absolute emptiness.[75] Zechariah 7:14 is the only passage in the
corpus where a description of the state of the land following the Babylonian
invasions is given, and only two highly general terms are used. First, 7:14a
describes the land as having been desolated (*smm*) and laid desolate (*smh*).
The verbal form occurs frequently in Lev 26 (26:22, 31, 32, 33, 34, 35, 43),
Isa 40–55 (48:8; 49:19; 54:3; it occurs once in Isa 56–66 at 61:4), Jeremiah
(10:5; 12:11; 18:16; 19:8; 33:10), Ezekiel (6:4; 35:15; 36:4, 34, 36), Lamentations (1:4; 3:11; 5:18), and once each in the Deuteronomistic History and
Chronicles (1 Kgs 9:8; 2 Chr 36:21) but nowhere in this sense in Ezra-Nehemiah.[76] The adjectival form occurs in Isa 1–39 (5:9; 13:9; 24:12), once in the
Deuteronomistic History, twice in Chronicles (2 Kgs 22:19; 2 Chr 29:8; 30:7),
and very frequently in Jeremiah (2:15; 4:7; 18:16; 19:8; 25:9, 18; 42:18; 44:22)
but not in Ezra-Nehemiah. The themes of destruction, exile, and abandonment figure prominently in the use of this root. The two terms are found

---

nevertheless within the scope of his prophecies and of his conception of the people of
Israel. On the similar perspectives in Chronicles, see Braun.

73. It is noteworthy that the motif of the servitude of the nations, present in texts such
as Isa 60 (see Morgenstern), is absent from Zech 1–8.

74. See Gangloff, who surveys the various sources and underlines their distinctive
usages of the "empty land" motif. His article, however, paints an unduly negative view of
the *golah* (cf. Smith-Christopher 1989; 2002) that underlines only the strategies of exclusion utilized by the *golah* and does not take into account some of the strategies of inclusion
present in our sources; see above.

75. See, e.g., the extensive use of the roots *hrb*, *smd*, *yst*, *ysm*, *'bd*, *klh*, *krt* in other
sources and their absence in this sense in Zech 1–8.

76. It appears in Ezra 9:3–4 but in the polel participial form and refers to the devastated emotional state of Ezra himself.

together only in Jer 18:16; 19:8; 49:17 and Zech 7:14. The use of such terms is closely paralleled in the Deuteronomistic-Jeremianic tradition (Petitjean: 358–59). Zechariah 7:14b adds a further general description: "with no one passing through or returning" (cf. Petitjean, who notes the parallels in Isa 33:8; Jer 9:11; 51:43; Ezek 14:15; 29:11; 33:28; 35:7).[77] Both terms constitute general descriptions of a devastated land where cities are in ruins and normal socioeconomic life has been shattered. However, no explicit implications are drawn from the devastation of the land or the experience of exile relative to membership in the community.

Furthermore, while the language in Zech 1–8 stresses the radical disruption of the Assyrian and Babylonian conquests, it does not view that situation as having come to an end as yet. The complaint of the angel of Yahweh in 1:12, set in the second year of Darius (1:7), still laments the depopulated state of Jerusalem and the cities of Judah. Thus from the perspective of Zech 1–8 the depopulated state caused by the disobedience of the ancestors persists *despite* the arrival of such figures as Joshua, Zerubbabel, and Zechariah himself in Jerusalem.[78] Thus the perspective of Zech 1–8 is that of a sparsely populated land looking forward to a better future. In sum, then, Zech 1–8 does not make exile to Babylon a *sine qua non* of inclusion and holds a view of the community of Yahweh that is open to all those who have genealogical links with the northern and southern kingdoms as well as, through acknowledgement of Yahweh, Gentiles who join themselves to him.

4.2 THE RETURN OF THE EXILES AND THE END OF THE DIASPORA

Zechariah 1–8 views the existence of the diaspora as provisional and somewhat anomalous. Several commentators have noticed this theme. Amsler (74) suggests that the oracle in 2:10–11 "reminds the exiles of the abnormal situation in which they find themselves, living in a foreign land." Petitjean

---

77. The allusion need not be one of total emptying but may reflect the absence or impossibility of normal human travel and economic activities (Meyers and Meyers 1987:405).

78. Petitjean (442) captures the perspective of Zech 1–8 as viewing the present moment as a decisive juncture. He states, "From this perspective the present moment marks a decisive change form the preceding decades. The recent past has been dominated by the anger of Yahweh against the ancestors … and the consequences of that judgment still darken the existence of the community called to restoration." He views the temple refoundation ceremony as the definitive harbinger of better days ahead and the completion of the temple as ushering it in (443). Coggins (30) comments that "neither [Haggai nor Zechariah] seems to be in any way aware that a turning point in the community's life—the ending of the exile—has been reached" (cf. Galling 1952)

(109) similarly suggests that via the language of 2:11 "the prophet places the tragic condition of Israel in exile in stark relief." Two elements in Zech 1–8 may account for such a *malaise* with the status quo. The first would appear to stem from religious tradition. Like Haggai, Zech 1–8 draws significantly upon broader Deuteronomistic theology. In that theological stream, particularly as reflected in Deuteronomy, the Deuteronomistic History, and Jeremiah, there is a close association between people and land. Disobedience to the covenant results in loss of land (Deut 4:25–28; 28:64; 1 Kgs 14:15; 2 Kgs 17:18; 24:1–4; Jer 7:34; 9:16), and renewal of covenant brings blessing in the land (Deut 28:1–14) or return to the land (Deut 30:3; Jer 29:14; 32:36–44). The hope of regathering the exiles is found widely in a variety of prophetic traditions (Isa 11:12; 43:5; 54:7; 56:8; Ezek 11:17; 20:34; 37:21; Mic 2:12; Zeph 3:20; Zech 10:8, 10). The situation created by the events of the sixth-fifth centuries has sometimes been described as a transition from a territorial to a nonterritorial Yahwism or, alternatively, to a multicentric Yahwism (Petersen: 119–20). While Zech 1–8 clearly accepts the reality of such a situation, it clearly views it as an interim measure. In line with the broader Deuteronomistic and prophetic outlook, Zech 1–8 sees Yahweh's ultimate purposes as being fulfilled only with the return of his people to the land.

In addition to the weight of tradition, a second source of frustration was the actual situation in Yehud, mentioned several times in the text. Zechariah 1–8 is painfully aware of the existential reality of a depopulated Yehud (1:12; 7:7, 14) and an extensive diaspora (2:2 [1:19]; 2:10–13 [6–9]; 7:14; 8:7). With the announcement of Yahweh's return to Jerusalem (1:16; 2:9 [5]; 15–16 [11–12]; 8:3), such an ongoing state of affairs would be incongruous in the extreme.

It will be immediately noticed that such a perspective stands in significant tension with other contemporary and near-contemporary sources. Haggai makes no explicit reference to the exile or return of the exiled population.[79] While Ezra-Nehemiah recognizes the reality of the diaspora and the potential for return (Neh 1:8–9) it also recognizes the possibility of remaining in exile and supporting the returnees (Ezra 1:3–5; see Williamson 1985:14–15). Esther makes no mention of Jerusalem and affirms the presence and protection of Yahweh for those in exile.[80] While it is sometimes assumed that Zech 1–8 acknowledges the ongoing existence and legitimacy of the diaspora,

79. See Galling 1952:76. On the hermeneutics of the book of Haggai and the possible reason for such an omission, see Kessler 2002:271–75.

80. Esther is usually assigned to the late-Persian or Hellenistic period; however, see Friedberg 2000 for an argument in favor of an earlier dating. As a sideline it is interesting to note that, from the perspective of Zech 1–8, the question of alternative cult sites would

whose members periodically come in pilgrimage to Jerusalem, no unambiguous allusion to such a community can be found.[81]

Finally, it should be noted that, from a Zecharian perspective, the return of the diaspora members is in some sense contingent upon the faithfulness of the remnant community already in Yehud. The notion of the community's return to Yahweh is one that underpins 1:1–6 and 7:1–8:23. At times such an ethical and religious renewal is described by the general terms *swb* (1:4) or *smr* (6:15), while at other times more detail is given (5:3–5; 7:9–10). What is most noteworthy is that in 6:15b the return of the exiles to rebuild the temple is made conditional upon the diligent obedience (note the infinitive absolute of *smr*) of the community in Yehud. Some commentators would attach this condition to either 15a (the recognition that the prophet has been sent by Yahweh) or the entirety of 6:10–15.[82] However, both suggestions are unlikely. It is most probable that it is the return of the exiles to participate in the rebuilding of the temple that is conditioned upon the obedience of the community. In this sense the perspective here is like the "tent peg" imagery of Ezra 9:8, where the refounded community at Jerusalem is viewed as a "foothold" that has been gained through Yahweh's grace but that may ultimately be lost if the community is unfaithful. The prophetic call to obedience is far from optional: the community's own future, in some sense, hinges on it. The formulation in 6:15 is stock Deuteronomistic phraseology (Meyers and Meyers 1987:366). The return of the exiles and the resumption of normal existence in the land, a situation for which the tiny community longed, are thereby made conditional upon their own fidelity. Thus, in good Deuteronomistic form, Zech 6:15 asserts that, just as the unfaithfulness of the fathers resulted in the loss of the land, so the obedience of the present small remnant in the land will play a role in the fulfillment of Yahweh's ultimate purposes. Petitjean (444) concludes, "In conformity to the ideology of the covenant, [Israel's] privileges demand in return a complete faithfulness to the demands connected with divine favour. This explains the importance and the extent of the exhortations which Zechariah sets forth … to call community to a valid response to the grace of the covenant."

---

be a temporary one at best. Given the ultimate return of Yahweh's people to Zion (not to mention his presence there), what need would there be of such installations?

81. As noted above, 8:23 could depict a diasporic pilgrimage to Zion, but even this is not explicitly stated. If, however, such were the case, it would likely stand in tension with the rest of Zech 1–8 and reflect ongoing theological reflection on the reality of life outside the land.

82. Meyers and Meyers (1987:366) make the establishment of a new temple in Yehud, under the aegis of a Davidic dynasty, conditional on the people's obedience.

4.3. The Vision of Zechariah 1–8 and the Israelite/Judean Communities of the Early Persian period

We turn, in conclusion, to the question with which we began: According to Zech 1–8, how did the community in Yehud understand itself and its relationship to the other Israelite/Judean communities beyond it? I would suggest that Zech 1–8 allows us to draw the following conclusions. (1) the people of Yahweh, consisting primarily of the inhabitants of the northern and southern kingdoms, constitute an expansive, multigenerational, and geographically widespread body. (2) The center of this expansive entity is Jerusalem, wherein Yahweh dwells. It thus forms the fixed point of reference for the people of God. (3) The tiny community in Jerusalem (and, by extension, Yehud) constitutes the firstfruits of a new epoch in the history of Yahweh and his people. This small remnant is called to manifest worship and ethical integrity as a means of demonstrating their solidarity with Yahweh in the ushering in of the age to come. (4) In light of Yahweh's return to Jerusalem and his coming intervention in world history (see below), his people in exile are called to an immediate and hasty return to Jerusalem/Yehud. If Zech 1–8 has a political agenda with reference to other communities, it is surely at this point: the time of dispersion is over; it is time to return home. (5) Whatever divisions may have existed between the north and south or between various sectors of the population, these fissures belonged to the past. Yahweh's renewed presence in Jerusalem served to vouchsafe the return and reunification of all who had been scattered and the removal of the divisions between them. One diaspora community was no "better" than another. (6) Although the new era of Yahweh's dwelling with his people had dawned, the present situation constituted the initial phase of a dramatic intervention of Yahweh, soon to be realized. This element, stated boldly via the shaking of the cosmos and nations in Hag 2:6–9, 20–23, although less explicit in Zech 1–8, is still clearly present. Zechariah 1–8 looks forward to a future decisive act of Yahweh. The "smiths" will appear to put the "horns" to rout (2:4 [1:21]). Yahweh will surround Jerusalem as a wall of fire (2:9 [5]). Babylon would soon be judged as Yahweh "shook his hand" (2:13 [9]) over it.[83] The destruction of Babylon would be fully accomplished (6:1–8). In the light of such an intervention, the exiles were called to flee (2:10–11 [6–7]). But such flight was to be no mere human effort, since Yahweh himself promised to save them and bring them safely to Jerusalem and cause them to dwell there. In that great day (3:10, *bywm hhw'*,

---

83. On the various terms involved in the imagery of shaking, and their origin and significance, see Kessler 2002:175–79.

a clearly eschatological term; see Hag 2:23) the community would dwell in perfect peace.

We have seen, then, that Zech 1–8 presents a vision of a regathered community around the reconstructed temple in Jerusalem. What kind of a vision is this? How does it relate to the actual life situation of the community in Yehud in the earlier years of Persian rule? What can it tell us about their hopes, dreams, fears, and aspirations in the context the realities of life in an economically struggling, sparsely populated, territorially reduced province of the Persian Empire? First, this view of life is markedly concerned with ritual and ethical concerns (evidenced in the construction, ordering, and cleansing of the temple and its personnel [3:1–10; 4:1–14; 6:9–15] and the call to ethical behavior [1:1–6; 5:1–11; 7:1–8:19]) but *profoundly unconcerned* with the more mundane matters such as authorization and funding for travel and its attendant dangers (2:10–13 [6–9]; cf. Ezra 1:1–6; 7:21–24; 8:15–36; Isa 43:1–21; 49:19–26), economic viability and land-tenure struggles in the land (1:17; 7:7, 14; 8:4–5; cf. Hag 1:3–11; Neh 5:1–5), political boundaries (see 7:7; cf. Ezra 6:6–12), and the like. Such concerns are evident in other sources. In Zech 1–8, however, the exiles are called to return and viewed as coming to reside in Jerusalem and Yehud without any apparent attention to such practicalities as imperial authorization for travel, the dangers of the journey, financial considerations, land allocation and economic opportunities in Yehud, or even the presence of provincial borders. All this suggests a highly *idealized and schematic* image, formulated by a tiny community dreaming of its future and reflecting on its past. The harsh realities of life in the land, together with the undesirability of Yehud as a place of immigration (Blenkinsopp 2000:133–34), would engender ongoing reflection on the timing, nature, and even feasibility of such a return. Both the emergence of the pilgrimage as an interim measure and the eschatologizing of the motif of the return would appear to be the fruit of such reflection. Second, Zech 1–8 presents a highly *inclusivistic, nonpolemical, nonexclusionary* perspective. There is no evidence of priestly disputes or competition, no conflict between political and religious authorities, and no heterodox and ethnically suspect worshipers of Yahweh from whom to keep separate (cf. Ezra 2:62–63; 3; 10; Neh 9). Rather, the twin criteria of the correct worship of Yahweh and commensurate ethical behavior form the defining features of the community. Even Gentiles may be included among the people of Yahweh (2:15 [11]). If the text unwittingly reveals any fears or threats felt by the community, it would perhaps be that of the overpowering smallness and insignificance of their undertaking and the risk that it might all come to naught. As in Hag 2:1–4, the danger of "despising the day of small things" (4:10) may have been (alongside ethical failure; cf. 5:1–4; 8:16–17) the community's greatest peril. Third, the vision reflected here is *nostalgic* and *restorationist*, without being tied to the precise forms of the past. Floyd (1997:142–43) has pointed out this aspect of the text with reference to the text's reconfiguration of earlier monarchic hopes. This is very much akin to the adaptation of earlier traditions and institutions to changes circumstances evident in Haggai (Kessler 2002:273–74). Zechariah 1–8 expresses the fervent hope that Judah, Israel, and Jerusalem will once more be found in their former abodes and that the ongoing life of Yahweh and his people, disrupted by the disobedience of the ancestors, will resume. Fourth and finally, the vision here reveals the profound anticipation of a *coming, decisive intervention of Yahweh*. Babylon would be judged, the exiles would return, and even non-Israelites would join in the worship of Yahweh and become his people. All of this would come in short order. A new day was about to dawn.

These four characteristics would seem to me to reflect the vision of a community whose future stood before it and who painted upon that *tabula rasa* enthusiastically with broad and bold strokes, anticipating the future acts of God that would turn the impossible into reality. Such a perspective appears to fit better in the late sixth/early fifth century than a later period.

In conclusion, then, Zech 1–8 envisages the people of Yahweh as a collective entity comprised of all the historic people of Yahweh, the "house of Israel and the house of Judah" as well as those from among the nations. These are gathered around Yahweh, who reigns from Jerusalem, in lives of ethical integrity and in worship. Only a moment's reflection is required to reveal the highly enduring impact that this image has had.

THE STRANGE WOMAN IN PERSIAN YEHUD:
A READING OF PROVERBS 7

Herbert R. Marbury

Clearly Prov 1–9 has attracted a great deal of scholarly interest. In comparison to the balance of the book, the first nine chapters have been the subject of a disproportionate number of inquiries. Who can blame the exegete? What other texts are populated by such provocative literary figures as Woman Wisdom and her strange, foreign, and dangerous twin? One wonders: Who is the implied speaker, this instructor, whose pedagogy frames for pupils a world where sex, women, and men figure so prominently and hold such grave consequences? What might Woman Wisdom and Woman Folly, cosmic figures who wield the power of life and death, represent? Such a text beckons one to engage it with careful, varied, and creative inquiry. Traditional readings have viewed Woman Wisdom and Woman Folly as oppositional figures, twin poles between which young men would navigate a moral landscape.

More recent treatments, however, have raised new and interesting questions. Reading the unit through a trickster motif, Claudia Camp deconstructs the absolute opposition between the strange, foreign woman and Woman Wisdom. Her reading offers "a positive valuation of women's power as anti-structural, regenerative because of its liminality" (1995:155). Carole Fontaine has argued that both Woman Wisdom and Woman Stranger embodied the public and private social roles of women in ancient Israel. For her, these twin figures emerged out of the "actual lived experience" of women in Israelite society (1995). Gale Yee has argued that the discourse in the unit is a father's instruction to a son. She has shown structurally how the words of Woman Stranger are arranged as a counterbalance to Woman Wisdom (1989:62). Carol Newsom has shown that Prov 1–9 is androcentric discourse that constructs the Strange Woman as a threat to male power, thereby creating a basis for father-son bonding (1989). Focusing on the economic concerns of the Second Temple community, Harold Washington reads the Strange Woman

as the object of exogamous marriage. He shows how such a marriage would
have disastrous economic consequences for the *golah* community (1995).

On the whole, most scholars agree that the material contained in the
collection of Proverbs as a whole stems from the monarchic era (Crenshaw
1985:614; 1990; von Rad; Whybray 1990), while more recent discussions
argue that the class of sages, who composed Israelite sapiential literature, was
circumscribed by neither social class nor gender (Fontaine 1995:47). While
this material may have emerged from diverse chronological and demographic
origins, it most likely took its final form in the Persian province of Yehud
(Berquist 1995a:161–65). To an already well-developed discourse, this essay
adds an exploration of the social and political dimensions of the text in an
attempt to show that Prov 7 functioned to serve the political and economic
interests of the early Second Temple priesthood by communicating an admonition against the practice of exogamy among the members of the Second
Temple community. Central to my reading is the recovery of an *unmarried*
אשה זרה in Prov 7. She is the subject of the exogamy dreaded by Second
Temple elites. I attempt to recover her voice by employing a strategy of close
reading with deconstructive insights to decenter the interpretation of the
text as solely an "eschewing the adulteress woman" instruction. Second, by
way of an ideological critique, I argue that the text plays on the meanings of
the language of the Song of Songs by employing metaphorical reversals in a
new system of significations, using the symbolic specter of death to signify
upon the sexuality and the "foreignness" of the אשה זרה. Ultimately, Prov 7
resolves in the world of the text the ideological conflict between the Second
Temple elites and the foreign women of the populace in the social matrix of
Yehud.

A Married Prostitute and an Unmarried Adulteress?

The work of both translators and interpreters of this unit have functioned syn-
ergistically to establish the primacy of an "eschewing the adulteress woman"
interpretation. Raymond C. Van Leeuwen, in his treatment of the unit, writes,
"The main character in chapter 7 is the adulterous woman who represents
Folly" (84). R. B. Y. Scott gives a translation under the rubric, "The Temptress"
and translates אשה זרה as "stranger-woman"/"adulteress" (63) Moreover, the
NRSV translates 7:5 as "loose woman"/"adulteress," while the NIV translation is
similar, "adulteress"/ "wayward wife." However, these translations and interpretations are slippery. I shall argue that they indeed "slip" away.

Why is the phrase אשה זרה translated and subsequently interpreted as
adulteress? Upon what evidences could one sustain such a translation and
interpretation? Most of the treatments of the אשה זרה in Prov 7 assume that

she is married. Many of these arguments are based on: (1) a conflation of the אשה זרה of Prov 6 (who is explicitly identified as an adulteress) with the one of Prov 7 (Yee 1989; Camp 1995); (2) an acceptance of Gustav Boström's argument that the אשה זרה is a prostitute, a זנה, and the conflation of זנה with "adulteress" (McKane: 334); and (3) a reading of verse 19 כי אין איש בביתו as "for my husband is not at home" (Camp 1995; McKane: 170; Yee 1989; also NRSV).

The text's presentation of the instructions in Prov 1–9 leads one to read them as a unity. Certainly the value in this approach is that it takes up the text as given and reflects an appreciation of the broader ideologies, complex and conflicting character constructions, and voices within the unit. However, engaging such a broad swath of textual landscape also risks not attending to the individual voices and characters of smaller units, voices that by their very construction exist because they resist a composite construction. The varied and disparate attributes assigned to the אשה זרה in Prov 1–9 offer one such example. Several readings have conflated the various descriptions of the אשה זרה, synthesizing them into a single character, both married and adulterous. The text does not speak univocally for such a reading and assigns irreconcilable attributes to the אשה זרה in Prov 6 and 7, making it difficult to read her as a single character. For example, Washington recognizes this problem and reads both the women in Prov 6 and 7 as married but claims that the woman in Prov 7 is not an adulteress (1995:167). Only if one denies the occurrence of sexual intercourse between the woman and her paramour as described in verses 15–18 can she be married and not an adulteress. The characterizations in Prov 6 as אשת איש "wife of a man" (6:26) and אשת רעהו "neighbor's wife" (6:29) appear to be the only references that indicate a married אשה זרה. The other instances of an אשה זרה in Prov 1–9 do not. Similarly, only the אשה זרה of Prov 6 in verses 26, 29, and 32 (the last reference is to the man) is identified as an adulteress, since she is "the wife of a man" or "neighbor's wife." The biblical writers of Prov 1–9 characterize none of the other strange/foreign women this way.

In his *Proverbiastudien*, which has been followed by more recent scholars (Scott: 65; McKane: 338–39), Boström approaches the difficulty another way. He has argued, based upon the cultic language of 7:14 and the reference to the lunar phase in 7:20, that the woman was a cultic prostitute devoted to the deity Ishtar. Boström's only evidence for this argument are these two textual references. Even if one accepts the argument that she is a prostitute, a זנה, this does not mean that she is an "adulteress." Phyllis Bird clarifies the use of זנה, arguing that the term for adulteress often coincides with זנה but that the two are by no means synonymous.

> In Israel's moral code, a woman's sexuality was understood to belong to her
> husband alone, for whom it must be reserved in anticipation of marriage

as well as in the marriage bond. Violation of a husband's sexual rights, the most serious of sexual offenses is signified by the term נעה, "adultery"; all other instances of sexual intercourse apart from marriage are designated by the term זנה. These include premarital sex by a daughter, understood as an offense against her father or family ... whose honor requires her chastity (Deut 22:13–21; Lev 21:9; cf. Gen 34:31); or sex by a levirate-obligated widow (Gen 38:6–11, 24–26), understood as an offense against her father-in-law or her deceased husband's family (Bird: 222).

If Bird is correct, the narrator's use of the term זנה in Prov 7:10 to describe the אשה זרה precludes her from being an adulteress, since זנה implicitly refers to one who is unmarried.

Is He My Husband or Just Some Man and His House?

Even more problematic is the phrase כי אין איש בביתו in 7:19, which typically is translated by Scott (64), Washington (1995:167), the NRSV, and the NIV as some variation of "my husband is not at home." Translated this way, the phrase implies the sense of an illicit relationship. Yee writes, "The love of the אשה זרה is transitory. It lasts until morning, until the return of her cuckolded husband" (1989:63; cf. 2003:149–51). At first blush, this phrase lends itself to the assumption of marriage between the absent האיש (man) and the אשה זרה. However, other instances of האיש in the Hebrew Bible are translated simply "the man" or "the one," except Gen 20:7 where the phrase אשת־האיש is translated "man's wife." There, האיש, in conjunction with אשת clearly indicates a marital relationship. Since this is the only use of האיש in Proverbs, there are no comparisons. The term איש alone and without the definite article is never used in Proverbs to indicate a married man. So, an argument for such a particular translation in this instance with respect to the remainder of its occurrences in the Hebrew Bible is at least not closed, leaving the meaning(s) deferred. When the phrase כי אין איש בביתו is read "for the man is not in his house," there is nothing in the unit that indicates a present relationship between the man and the woman. She simply refers to him as "the man" and "his house." Bird argues, "There is also no specific term for 'husband' [in Hebrew] though the relational term ('master') was frequently used in the corresponding genitival construction instead of the general word for man" (Bird: 37). But this term for master is also missing from the present verse.

Neither is the second component of the phrase in verse 19, בביתו, often rendered "home," closed to a plurality of meaning. In 7:19 the translation "home," read in conjunction with "my husband," communicates the idea that the house is the dwelling place of both the man and the woman. However,

בביתו may also be rendered "his house," which would retain the sense of the possessive pronoun, would remove any sense of cohabitation, and possibly would imply separate residences. In the overwhelming majority of occurrences in the Hebrew Bible, בביתו is translated as "his house." The NRSV translates בביתו as "home" in 1 Sam 25:1 and 1 Kgs 5:14 and "household" in Job 21:21. However, in each of these three occurrences the translation retains the sense of the masculine possessive pronoun.

The Proverbs narrator/instructor's use of the possessive in reference to the house is telling. In both verses 8 and 11 the instructor identifies the woman's residence as "her house" but claims that "her feet" are never there. The אשה זרה, however, speaks of another place, his house בביתו. She never refers to the residence in a way that would clarify the question, stabilizing the meaning. Here the use of both feminine and masculine possessives appears to indicate an understanding of separate residences. By referring to different places, the language of the teacher and the speech of the אשה זרה appear to agree concerning the existence of separate residences. Thus, a reading of בביתו as "(at) home" is no longer stable. Other meanings arise encoded within the language and rhetorical constructions of the text, challenging the assumption of cohabitation.

If my recovery of the unmarried אשה זרה is tenable, then the traditional interpretation of an admonition against an adulterous woman is likely not the only voice encoded within the rhetorical structures of Prov 7. Instead, we also hear the voice of another woman, unmarried and foreign, from within the text. The instructor does not describe her using marital language. Even if we accept Boström's argument that the אשה זרה is a prostitute, then his reading also precludes her from being an adulteress, since the term זנה is reserved for unmarried women. Neither are the translations of איש as "husband" and the term בית as "home" closed. They may also be rendered "the man" and "his house" respectively. So out of univocal stability, multivocal chords and (dis)chords emerge. The meaning(s) of the language slip and erode, rise and fall, each voice giving way to another, all of them vying for a hearing within the text.

From Adulteress to Strange Woman: An Ideological Critique

In the study of the Hebrew Bible, ideological critiques have generally focused on describing the direction, flow, and use of power among the social classes of ancient Israel. Pioneering ideological treatments such as those of Norman Gottwald adopted Marxist categories and focused on Eagleton's "measurable absences." To date, the fullest explication of this Marxist trajectory of ideological critique has been articulated by Gale Yee (1995; cf. 2003). My own

ideological reading borrows insights from both Gottwald and Yee and follows
the line of inquiry developed in critical social theory among members of the
Frankfurt School.

At its best, an ideological critique connects text and context by unmasking power arrangements in the social world and demonstrating how those
relationships are worked out in the rhetorical structures of a given text. Generally, such readings proceed in two modes: one thickly descriptive and one
pejorative (Geuss: 12). At the purely descriptive level, an ideological critique
refrains from value judgments about the social world it examines. It may identify modes of production (Tucker: 143), perceived or real interests (Geuss:
45), or a class that controls means of production, and thus it may show how
this group benefits from such an arrangement. It ultimately attempts to render
as fully as necessary the multiple and complex structures and social arrangements of the ancient world (Geertz: 10). At the pejorative level, an ideological
critique takes insights from the descriptive mode and moves from description to judgment. It may focus on a text's ability to obscure the activity of
various forms of power, the masking of real interests, and identifying forms
of consciousness that the critic considers to be false. The pejorative mode
intends ultimately to reveal a text's discursive deception: the gross inconsis-
tency between what the text says and the intentionalities of such language in
the social world.

What type of social world might have been concerned with the activities
of an unmarried אשה זרה? A brief sketch of the internal dynamics of the province and its external relationship to the imperial bureaucratic apparatus show
how the strange and foreign woman fit into the variegated society of Yehud
and why her status threatened the maintenance of the Second Temple cult.

At one level Yehud remained under a foreign tributary mode of production (Gottwald: 44; Yee 1995:150) in the Achaemenid imperial system.
Tributes exacted from the masses were funneled on to Persepolis. So economically, not much had changed for the average inhabitant of Neo-Babylonian
Judah, now a Persian Yehudite. Persian governors simply replaced Neo-Babylonian ones, although with an enhanced bureaucracy that was more efficient
at taxation. Persian administration, however, differed from the Neo-Babylonians in an important way: Cyrus, Cambyses, and Darius understood the
value of making capital investments in local cults in order to secure their loyalty and enhance their ability to collect tributes from their devotees.

Unlike the economy of Yehud that remained fueled by imperial expansion
through the reign of Darius, the *political* fortunes of Yehud were in transition. The influx of new populations under the aegis of Cyrus and later Darius
engendered a struggle between competing interests, loyalties, and groups in
the province. Two groups relevant for the present discussion are the *golah*,

"the children of the exile" or "returned deportees," and those whom they designated עם־הארץ "the people of the land" (Smith-Christopher 1989:179–97; Carroll 1992).

In the absence of the political and social elite removed in the 597 deportation and the cultic elite removed in the 587 deportation, the *golah* created a reflexively integrated society with its own reconstituted political, economic, and cultic systems. Prior to the return, Yehud had recovered from the deportation of a mere 10 percent or less of the population just five decades prior (Weinberg 1992:37). Thus, the land was not the fallow "homeland" waiting to be repopulated as prophesied in the vision of Deutero-Isaiah, nor were the indigenous people awaiting or welcoming the "glorious return" of a new population with whom they would be forced to compete for resources and for cultural and political ascendancy.

On the other hand, Cyrus shrewdly encouraged the loyalty of the deportees. Niels Peter Lemche argues, "By allowing elite groups of the Jewish society to return to their homeland, which few or none of them had ever seen, the king [of Persia] created a bond of personal loyalty between his regime and this new Jewish group, whom he could count on to help him govern his far-flung empire" (180). Even if one follows Davies's argument that these new immigrants, the "returning exiles," were probably not the descendants of those removed in the deportations (1992:112), it still follows that, not only did the Persians want the immigrants to attain and maintain power in this western province of the empire, but the "returnees" themselves saw this as an opportunity to gain a measure of power and affluence that they may not have enjoyed in Babylon (Lemche: 180). To this end, the Achaemenids appointed individuals loyal to the empire from the elite of the Second Temple community to serve as local officials in the province (Neh 5:14; Weinberg 1992:136).

Receipt of such Persian largesse was not without obligation. It was incumbent upon the "returnee-elite" to cultivate and maintain order and control over the province, and equally as important to ensure that tributes were exacted from the populace and sent to Persia. Therefore, logically sympathetic to Cyrus, whom the literature claims was their liberator from Babylon, and to Darius, who financially supported the cult, these elites became agents of Persia and facilitated its imperial hold on Yehud.

Under the Persian satrap, the political interests of the empire worked in tandem with those who returned. The empire sought to expand and maintain order, leaving the "returnee-elite" no choice but to control a "homeland" in order to stay in power. So, the "returned deportees," inspired by the portrayal of the glorious homecoming in Deutero-Isaiah, in the face their own precarious social reality, and at the behest of their Persian benefactors, initiated the rebuilding of the cult with the construction of the Second Temple at its center.

This cultic center, the Second Temple, whose construction was supported by the Persian authorities, held at least two significations: one external and imperial; and one internal and cultic. Within the imperial system, the temple functioned as a part of the regulating tools that the Persians used to collect tributes. Within the province, the temple mediated the political, economic, and (ideological) religious power for the region. In doing so, the Second Temple cult constructed the significations that became the "grand narrative" under which the people would interpret their existence in the province of Yehud. In this metanarrative, the *golah*, the "returned deportees," were the sole, legitimate heirs to the land of the province. In a manner that recalled Israelites in the stories of Joshua, the members of the Second Temple community reenacted the conquering of an "empty" land promised to them (Ahlström: 283; Carroll 1992). Those outside of the *golah* community became typified as the enemies of this new Israel. These new enemies were, of course, analogous to Israel's traditional enemies (Deut 7:1–6; Ezra 9:1–2). Within this "grand narrative," the "returnee-elite," cultic officials and aristocracy, and those they co-opted sought to preserve their power by constructing a community with a clearly delineated and orderly hierarchical social structure and fiercely maintained boundaries of inclusion and exclusion. The cult itself was jealously guarded to prevent the incursion of outside membership. Smith-Christopher is instructive here:

> [T]here is little doubt that Ezra's constant use of exclusive terms regarding these "sons of the Golah," the frequent exhortations against intermarriage with the impure of the land, thus possibly corrupting the "pure seed," the priestly reforms of Lev. 25 and Neh. 5, all add up to a self-conscious community that is occupied with self-preservation, both as a pure community in a religious sense and also preservation in a material sense. (1989:197)

This cultic construction of "ethnic purity" functioned as a way of controlling access to power in the province. Such power was probably mediated along the kinship structures of official registries such as those found in Ezra 2:8 and Neh 7.

These boundaries were not only circumscribed by a fictive ethnicity but functioned to maintain and enforce strictly delineated gender roles. The postexilic period brought about a society of increased stratification based on gender, eroding the former, more egalitarian social structures (Fontaine 1995:35–36). With the ascendancy of the Second Temple cult came the reinscription of values and mores, ensuring that women were beholden to their בית־אבות, the primary unit of social organization, according to Weinberg

(1992:49–61). Women's access to public authority was severely limited in comparison to earlier eras. Further, this increased stratification and role definition extended especially into the realm of sexuality, consigning a woman's sexuality to her father's, then subsequently her husband's, control. Concerning Hebrew wives, Bird argues, "She defers to him [her husband] in speech and action, obeys his wish as his command, and puts his welfare first. She employs her sexual gifts for his pleasure alone" (1997:38). Women outside the Yehudite temple community may not have shared these Yehudite cultic mores. In neither Ezra nor Nehemiah does one read of foreigners being forced to adhere to "Israelite" law. Without a husband or ties to a בית־אבות, a "foreign" woman might be freer than a woman of the *golah* to employ her sexuality for her own pleasure or survival in whatever fashion she chose. Clearly, this freedom was marginal. Even foreign women were subject to some degree to Persian civil authorities, who often worked in tandem with the local cultic authorities. "Foreign" women would have also been subject to the authorities of their own communities. So the "foreign" woman was then a liminal figure in Second Temple Yehud; she probably wielded more power and enjoyed more freedom among the *golah* than her *golah* counterpart, but she was still subject to the governing authorities and to her own community. Consequently, in a society that sought to maintain order and genealogically circumscribed in-group/out-group designations, these liminal women and the Yehudite men who married them or who blurred genealogical structures by sexual association with them were dangerous to the Second Temple elite. By their associations with foreign women, these men widened the circle of those who had access to power and influence over the affairs in the province (Berquist 1995a:118).

Specific to this discussion of Prov 7 are the political events of the first half of the reign of Artaxerxes I, who inherited an empire in severe economic decline. At that time, the colony of Yehud had experienced two decades of Xerxes' policy of economic depletion. At the beginning of his reign, Xerxes destroyed temples throughout the empire to quell local ethnic nationalisms (Berquist 1995a:89–90). Although no such fate befell the cult in Yehud, it still had not been funded by the empire since Darius's administration. Consequently, because of imperial financial neglect, priestly activity abated and the priesthood turned to seeking internal sources of funding (91–92).

In the seventh year of Artaxerxes I's reign, 458 B.C.E., Ezra arrived in Yehud along with funding that indicated a reversal in imperial economic policy toward the Yehudite cult and reflected the empire's concern over the Hellenic influence encroaching upon its western frontiers (regarding the dating of Ezra, see Miller and Hayes: 468; Grabbe 1992:88–92; Berquist 1995a:110). The wealth that accompanied Ezra, along with his own civil and religious authority, were to be directed toward the completion of the new

cultic and imperial administrative center, the Second Temple. The elites in
the colony, particularly the priesthood, sought very quickly to restrict the distribution of this wealth to those who were members of the *golah* community.
Ezra 4:1–5 reflects this proscription from participating in the building of the
temple (Miller and Hayes: 457–60; Ahlström: 848 n. 2; Berquist 1995a:43 n.
16; Smith-Christopher 1989:109).

While the province struggled to meet its own internal challenges, geopolitical events external to Yehud affected the province as well. During this
era, the rise of the Delian League and its support of the Egyptian revolt was a
major concern of the Persian Empire. Egypt had always been a restless colony
and had revolted many times before. This time, however, its alliance with
Greek forces challenged Persia's control of the entire Mediterranean corridor.
Persia needed to fortify its territories and to define the populations in close
geographical proximity to Greece and the Mediterranean. Its response to this
threat was twofold: (1) it set up garrisons and fortresses along its western frontiers (Hoglund 1992:165–206); (2) it sent Ezra and Nehemiah to legislate the
means by which the Yehudite population would be defined under the control
of Persia (244–45). They accomplished this task by their admonitions against
mixed marriages and the separation of foreign nations from the *golah* community (Ezra 9–10; Neh 13). In this way, they assisted the wider imperial program
of clarifying loyalties and populations along the empire's western frontiers.

Ultimately, in concert with imperial political interests, postexilic Yehud
maintained strict control over ethnicity, gender, and sexuality. Succinctly
put, those men who were listed, who were landed, and who were wealthy had
access to power. Women on the whole were subordinate in the בית־אבות,
and a woman's sexuality was to be controlled by her husband. A "foreign"
woman, on the other hand, one of the עם־הארץ, whose sexuality, culture,
and access to wealth were not totally dominated by the Second Temple cult,
would be perceived as a serious threat to the nascent aristocracy struggling to
create ethnic cohesion and to maintain its legitimacy in the eyes of the empire
and the populace (Bailey; van der Toorn). While still marginally subjugated,
she could marry or associate with whomever she chose; more important, her
loyalties were not to the Persian Empire, nor was she invested in the maintenance of the Second Temple cult. Even more important, as a wife of a *golah*
man her power and influence in the domestic realm could rival that of cultic
authorities in the public realm. If she were not a devotee of the religion of
the Jerusalem temple, then she might encourage the household to support
a local shrine, thereby diminishing the funding vital to cultic maintenance.
Nehemiah appears to encounter a similar situation in which foreign wives
had so influenced *golah* offspring that they no longer even spoke the language
of the community (Neh 13:23–24). If such instances were widespread, the cult

might experience the catastrophic loss of a generation of devotees. Such a loss would mean disastrous consequences for the community and for the cult's relationship with imperial authorities.

In the final analysis, Yehud was replete with significations under which the *golah* community would construct their existence over against other religious and ethnic groups. The phenomenon that gave rise to the construction of these significations was a complex configuration of geopolitical events both internal and external to the province. I have described them only briefly here. They included a temple constructed by imperial foreign tributary economy that fueled imperial expansion, the influx of new populations and the increased competition for resources, social stratification, the imperial-financed temple and the correlate predominance of the Second Temple priesthood as the religious and quasi-civil authority of the province, and the imperial responses to the Greek-Egyptian threat.

A text purportedly taking its final form in a world characterized by complex webs of social relations—imperial and cultic, male and female, landed gentry and peasant, *golah* and עם־הארץ—would reflect the high stakes of such struggles. Berquist is instructive here:

> Proverbs presented a world-view of control, especially self-control. Yehud, as did all societies, required social control mechanisms of some sort. That is, in order to remain stable, it must find ways to encourage its population to hold to the basic behavioral norms of that society. Force was too expensive as a long-term widespread option, but the propagation of *an ideology of control* proved much more effective. (1995a:173, emphasis added)

Proverbs 7 encodes the language of fear and control even as it purports to be instructive to young Yehudite men. The text resolves a conflict between the Second Temple elite and the אשה זרה, ultimately silencing and signifying upon her, warning that any relationship with a woman of such social status ends in utter calamity.

In its presentation of the אשה זרה, Prov 7 reflects Barthes's understanding of a "second order semiological system" within a *golah* "grand narrative." Barthes argues that a "myth" takes up an "associative total" and appropriates it as a "second-order semiological system" (see Lyotard; Barthes: 109–42). Barthes defines his use of myth:

> In myth, we find again the tri-dimensional pattern which I have just described: the signifier, the signified and the sign. But the myth is a peculiar system, in that it is constructed from a semiological chain which existed before it: it *is a second-order semiological system*. That which is a sign

(namely the associative total of a concept and an image) in the first system, becomes a mere signifier in the second. (114)

The first system of significations is simply the speech of the אשה זרה, *prima facie.* Ostensibly romantic, her language signifies the amorous intent of a woman to engage a prospective lover. Such is the meaning of the same language in the Song of Songs. The second system, more complex than the first, comprises the self-understandings, ideologies, power arrangements, and social relations constitutive of the *golah* metanarrative. It particularly reflects the worldview of the cult and its concern with self-preservation and the maintenance of the community. Once the first system, the love language of the אשה זרה, is taken up into the second, the *golah* metanarrative, it is emptied of its original meaning and left bereft of its former history. The narrator effectively exchanges "love" as the former signified and replaces it with "death." As such, the speech of the אשה זרה no longer functions as a part of a sign that speaks to a romantic searching and a passionate consummation; rather, the book of Proverbs assigns new values to her language and in doing so controls within the text behavior that the Second Temple cult would have had little power to regulate within the social world.

It is at least curious that a proverb that brandishes death as consequence for a relationship with an אשה זרה never quite gives a real picture of how such a "death" might occur. Beyond metaphorical allusions, death is absent. Proverbs 7:22–27 threatens the pupil with his own demise, but the nature of the calamity is never revealed. Even more intriguing in 7:16–18, 22 is the narrator's use of the language and images of the Songs of Songs, placing them in an entirely different system of significations, so that the language of Eros in the Song becomes the language of Thanatos in the instruction (see Trible). The rhetoric associated with life, love, and fulfillment in the Song is reconstructed rhetorically using the image of death (7:27) to warn young men of inevitable catastrophe. In the process of reordering the meaning of the rhetoric, the language encodes values concerning the sexuality of women, foreign women in particular, those not under the authority of a *golah* husband or father.

Similar to the sociopolitical liminality of the marginally subjugated strange/foreign woman in Yehud, a comparable spatial and temporal liminality is reproduced in the discourse of the text. Throughout Prov 7 the אשה זרה exists in a liminal space, neither at his house nor at her house but outdoors. In Prov 7:15 the woman comes out to meet her lover. She recounts her search for him and her encounter with him. In Songs 3:1–4 we find a similar search. Here also the woman comes out to meet her lover. The activity of both women's searches for their lovers occurs in the streets (Prov 7:12; Song 3:2). In other words, they occur out of the purview of male household authority and, by extension, cultic authority. We encounter her not during the day or night but at twilight (7:9), when she is virtually invisible. This spatial and temporal liminality may be reflective of the sociopolitical liminality of women who were not part of a בית־אבות and subjugated by the Second Temple authorities. It symbolically places the אשה זרה under the auspices of neither the man's house (nor his בית־אבות) nor her own house. She occupies a space in society over which the Second Temple cult had little ability to control.

While her location with the world of the text may be liminal, her speech is, however, unambiguous, transparent in its romantic intent. Yet with each statement of her intent toward her lover, the instructor turns her words back upon her, reordering their intentionality. Although the teacher in Prov 7:5–12 instructs the pupil that the אשה זרה desires to prey upon any foolish or naïve young man, she, like the woman in the Song, is definite concerning the identity of the lover she seeks. Using language very similar to her counterpart in the Song, she recalls the search for her companion.

So now I have come out to meet you to seek you longingly; now I have found you. Proverbs 7:15	I will seek him whom my soul loves … Song of Songs 3:15b

The search in the Song is resolved in 3:4 when the lover is brought into her mother's house. In Proverbs, however, we hear only the report of the teacher, recasting the words of the אשה זרה concerning her search, informing the pupil that this search will inevitably end in catastrophe for her prey. In Prov 7:17 the spices spread upon the couch are the same ones used in Song 1:13; 3:6; 4:14; 5:1, 5, 13. In the Song they are the trappings with which the woman prepares for love, while in Proverbs the teacher's rhetoric recasts them as enticements intended to lure the unsuspecting man to her bed. In 7:18 the אשה זרה speaks an invitation to her lover making her intentions toward him clear, "let us drink our fill of love," that is similar to the invitation of the woman in Song 5:1, "let us be drunk with love." The words of the אשה זרה are for the narrator, however, merely the devices of "her seductive speech" (7:20), the same phrase as that used to describe the sages' teaching (Camp 1995:137). Without the set of significations provided by the instructor, the words of the אשה זרה convey the same intent as the female lover in the Song of Songs. However, at every turn the narrator matches the strange woman with rhetorical reversals.

While there are many similarities in the behaviors of the אשה זרה of Prov 7 and the woman in the Song, Song 8 illustrates a significant distinction. In Song 8:1–2 the woman can only muse longingly, wishing that her lover were as a "brother" to her so that she could meet him in the streets without fear of reprisal for a public display of affection. In Prov 7:12 the אשה זרה enters into the streets "boldly"; in 7:15 she says that she has come out to meet her lover; in 7:13 she "grabs him and kisses him." This difference may reflect the marginal freedom of the אשה זרה over against the restricted existence of the woman in the Song. In Song 5:7 the woman is beaten and raped by the sentinels for entering the streets at night (Weems 1997:412). In Prov 7, where the אשה זרה as a foreigner steps out of the strictures of the constructed gender roles of her society, the woman in the Song remains self-consciously aware of gender-defined boundaries. Perhaps this episode illustrates a distinction between treatment of women of the *golah* community who were subject to a בית־אבות and women like the אשה זרה, who enjoyed some measure of freedom.

The narrator allows the אשה זרה to speak for herself in Prov 7:14–20. In 7:14 she speaks to her lover saying that she has made her sacrifices and has come out to meet him. Intentional about courting him, she recalls her search and celebrates finding him. She has made all the necessary preparations for their rendezvous: "I have decked the couch with coverings, colored spreads of Egyptian linen; I have perfumed my bed with myrrh, aloes, and cinnamon" (7:16–17). Having prepared lavishly for her lover, she offers her invitation, "Come, let us drink our fill of love until morning; let us delight ourselves with love" (7:18). Finally, she gives her lover the assurance, "for that man is not in his house" (7:19). The reader is left to speculate who "that man" might be: a thinly veiled reference to a בית־אבות, to a previous lover, or maybe an allusion to a relative who would prevent her from seeing her paramour—she gives no clues. Extricated from the signs invoked by the instructor's introductory and concluding rhetoric, her language is not signified with death or calamity. Instead, she speaks simply of meeting her cultic obligations and of courting her lover.

Next the instructor uses introductory and concluding verses to recast her words, signifying upon her by using the metaphor of death. Ostensibly, this is the instructor's tale. Out of twenty-seven verses, the woman's voice is allotted only seven. Even then the teacher supplies thirteen verses of introduction, carefully constructing the system of signs under which the implied audience, the pupil, would interpret the upcoming speech of the אשה זרה. The pupil is instructed in 7:1–2 to "keep my words" and "keep my commandments." In 7:3 the admonitions become more emphatic. The pupil is instructed to "bind" these words/teachings upon his fingers and to "write" them upon the "tablet" of his "heart." As if these warnings were not severe enough, the instructor directs the son to marry "wisdom" (חכמה) in 7:4. Only then is the purpose of this fivefold admonition revealed in 7:5. All of this "to guard/keep you from the אשה זרה." The insistent nature of the narrator's counsel to the young lover makes explicit the seriousness with which this woman is perceived. She is dangerous to the pupil and to his community.

Finally, as if the remonstrances were not enough, the narrator shifts from admonitions against associating with the אשה זרה to a sharply contemptuous characterization of the young lover, identifying him in 7:7 as one "lacking intelligence" and as one "from among the simple ones." The narrator does not make clear the reason for such a characterization until after the conclusion of woman's speech. There, the consequence is metaphorically death.

Raising eightfold the specter of death, the instructor resorts again to reversals of the language of the Song of Songs. The lover in the Song is told twice to be as a "young stag" (2:17; 8:14) high on a mountain. Similarly, in 7:22b the lover in Proverbs also is characterized as a stag, but unlike the Song this lover is "like a stag toward a trap." Not the symbol of a strong and virile lover. Rather, the stag is recast as a foolish, helpless animal being seduced to its death (Weems 1995:23–25).

In 7:24 there is yet another admonition to listen/obey. Finally, as if the admonitions and the warnings have not made their case, the instructor makes a last and this time explicit connection signifying upon the sexuality of the אשה זרה with death in the fourfold metaphor:

For many she has laid low [חללים הפילה],
    and many are those she has killed [הרגיה].
Her house is the way to Sheol [שאול],
    going down to the chambers of death [חדרי-מות]. (Prov 7:26–27)

Only a resistant pupil would need such repeated and forceful admonition. Interestingly, the lover's words, like nature of the lover's death, are absent from the unit. The reader does not hear of the lover's intention toward this woman. We are not informed as to his reasons for rebelling against the dictates of the Second Temple cult. But the teacher describes him as one "lacking intelligence" and as one "from among the simple ones" for loving an אשה זרה. The insistent, almost pleading tone of these last instructions may indicate an attempt to regulate the behavior of the men of the temple community who marry foreign women. Only a group whose behavior the governing authorities considered threatening would warrant such vigorous remonstrance and contemptuous characterization. In fact, in the Nehemiah Memoir (Neh 13:25) one reads of Nehemiah himself contending with, beating, and cursing those Jews who had married foreign wives.

In verses 26–27, with the specter of death now completely and emphatically associated with the sexuality of the אשה זרה, the rhetorical structures of the text have symbolically resolved the real social and ideological conflicts between the אשה זרה of the *golah* and the governing elite of the Second Temple cult. In the text, her sexuality, which she expresses with a marginal freedom and from her liminal status and which operates out of the purview of the Second Temple cult, is, in effect, controlled. While her speech is not absent from the text, nonetheless she is effectively silenced. The narrator trumps her with each phrase, turning her words upon her with shrewd reversals, transforming the words of Eros into Thanatos.

By the end of the proverb the speech of the אשה זרה has been completely recast. It has been emptied of its former meaning. Once filled with the language that signified love between the two paramours in the Song, it is "resignified," inscribed with new meaning. So the spices the woman used in the Song to prepare for her lover (7:17) become the lures for the trap of the אשה זרה. The words that are elsewhere the perspicacious rhetoric of the sages are now only "the smooth persuasion of her lips." The stag (Song 2:9, 17; 8:14; Prov 7:22b) symbolizing a robust lover is now a foolish beast lured to its demise. Each of these symbols has taken on new meaning.

Each new signification takes its place within the "grand narrative." In the larger grand narrative, they are now only signifiers. This *golah* narrative constructed new significations for the Second Temple community. Providing the foundation for constructing meaning around all other symbols, the narrative gave explicit instructions as to how the community was to negotiate their precarious position under the dominion of the Persian Empire and how to maintain group cohesiveness in a land where they were forced to compete with the indigenous people for cultural and political ascendancy. Therein, love with an outsider, an אשה זרה, was risky business.

It appears, finally, that the postexilic era was one of many challenges and tensions for the province of Yehud and its new population. The struggles of the cult to wrest political, religious, and social power found venues not only in the land but in the production of its literature as well.

QOHELETH IN LOVE AND TROUBLE*

Jennifer L. Koosed

Who Is Qoheleth? Because the book is a knot of contradictions, this question has proved troubling but also irresistible to readers. It has been a central question in the history of scholarship. How does one explain the contradictions in the text? Various groupings of authors, redactors, and glossators have been paraded up and down in the commentaries, yet all of these theories of authorship are based upon a commentator's assumptions about the consistency of identity. The integrity that interpreters search for in the text is a mirror of the integrity they assume about themselves. However, beginning with the linguistic theories of Saussure, translated into psychoanalysis by Lacan, and furthered in philosophy and literary criticism by Barthes and Derrida, the stability of language and identity has been undermined. Postmodern theories have revised our notions both of the self and of the text. Both can be incoherent, fragmented, lacking a stable center, contingent. This describes the text of Qoheleth, and insofar as the text creates a speaker, the identity of the speaker as well.

But neither texts nor identities are disembodied. Both are material objects. Language is an organ of the body, and this physicality manifests itself in writing. The body is embedded in the text through the naming of body parts (eye, hand, heart), and this same body is encoded in form, structure, and syntax so that the text becomes a body with organs, systems, and even a life of its own.

Who is Qoheleth? This is Qoheleth. We pick up Qoheleth's body every time we pick up the text, we read the body, turn its pages, touch its body with our own.

---

* An expanded version of this essay appears in my *(Per)mutations of Qohelet: Reading the Body in the Book* (Library of Hebrew Bible/Old Testament Studies 429; New York T&T Clark, 2006). Reprinted by permission of The Continuum International Publishing Group.

1.

I am a body marked by sexual difference and inculcated in a gender ideology that names me "woman." And I begin this paper with a concern. I am troubled by the way that this text portrays women and how this portrayal has been read throughout the history of interpretation.

> And I found more bitter than death the woman.
>> She is a snare,
>> And her heart is nets;
>> Her hands are fetters.
>> Good before God is
>> The one who escapes from her,
>> But the sinner is captured in her.
> See, this I found, said the Qoheleth:
>> Add one to one to find the reckoning,
> Which my soul still sought but I did not find.
>> One man in one thousand I found,
>> And a woman in all of these I did not find.
> See, this alone I found:
>> God made humanity right,
>> But they sought many contrivances. (7:26–29)

I begin my interrogation of the usual suspects. After all, I am not only a woman but a biblical scholar—another aspect of my identity sometimes in concert and sometimes in conflict with my sexual identity. I arrange my interrogating instruments before me: source criticism, form criticism, rhetorical criticism. But my impatience grows. I chose this passage because it bothers me. But none of these analyses has allowed me to get close to this bothersome phrase: "more bitter than death the woman" (7:26). It does not contradict other parts of the passage. It does not differ in structure or genre from the surrounding text. No space opens up for me to challenge this phrase. Even a shift to rhetorical criticism fails to yield the desired results, for I get snared in the rhetoric. I must break out of the inclusios and the chiasms, for they construct a prison of words that call me more bitter than death and claim that I am not wise. I am alternatively wicked and foolish and mad.

I begin again, this time with Judith Fetterly's theories on reader-response criticism and the resisting reading. Rather than implied readers, her interpretive community is a politically engaged, feminist community, and I find myself within it. Fetterly argues that the books in the American canon are "relentlessly androcentric and misogynist, as is the educational establishment in which the canon is taught" (Bible and Culture Collective: 37). We are all taught to identify male. For women, this means internalizing and identifying with androcentrism and misogyny and thus reading against their interests. Fetterly urges people to become resisting readers: "the first act of the feminist critic must be to become a resisting rather than assenting reader and, by this refusal to assent, to begin the process of exorcising the male mind that has been implanted in us" (Fetterly: xxii).

For Fetterly, the misogyny and androcentrism are inside the text itself. We can enter into the world of the text and be inculcated in its ideology, or we can refuse. Qoheleth 7:26–28 is a misogynist passage in the Hebrew Bible. There have been other negative portrayals of women in the Hebrew Bible, especially of women in the wisdom traditions. However, this is the only statement that categorically condemns all women. Tikva Frymer-Kensky (205) calls this "the first openly misogynistic statement in the Bible," and I would have to concur. These verses describe women in general; they do not limit the type of women who are called "more bitter than death." Arguments that this passage is not misogynist smack of apologetic. And, empowered by Fetterly to read against the grain, I resist this text.

2.

Turning now to the scholarly literature, I notice something strange. This verse troubles me, and this discomfort has compelled me to write about it. Yet few commentators devote the space to these verses that I believe they warrant.

In *A Feminist Companion to Wisdom Literature,* this verse is discussed briefly in a survey essay on the portrayal of women in wisdom literature (Brenner: 59–61), but there is not one feminist interpretive essay on Qoheleth alone. Why this gap? This verse seems to be ripe for interrogation from a feminist standpoint. Is it because it is too easy? In *The Women's Bible Commentary,* the only major commentary that squarely faces the misogyny in the text without excuse or qualification, Carole R. Fontaine writes that "the misogyny expressed (7:26) is no surprise" (1992:154). She does not elaborate further.

Other commentaries fall into three main camps. The first group, represented here by Whybray, denies that there is misogyny in the text:

> It has also been alleged, on very flimsy evidence, that Qoheleth was that very rare phenomenon among the Jews of the Old Testament period, a bachelor, and even a misogynist. This notion is based mainly on a single very obscure passage, 7.23–29, which is certainly capable of being interpreted as expressing contempt or hatred of women in general, but is also capable of other interpretations. (1989:22)

This is the only place in his commentary where he speaks of this passage. He does not state why these verses are "obscure," nor does he offer any other interpretation.

The second interpretive strategy in the commentaries is to upload on the relative pronoun *ăšer* in verse 26. The entire passage is not a condemnation of all women, then, but only the condemnation of a particular type of woman. Roland Murphy represents this position: "The description fits a certain type of woman against whom the sages railed; it is not a description of the female sex *per se*" (1992:76). He goes on to note that this "certain type of woman" is the adulterous woman. It is only adulterous women who are as bitter as death. To emphasize his point about the particular woman whom Qoheleth hates, Murphy chooses to translate *'iššâ* as "harlot" in his form-critical analysis of chapter 7 (1974:82), but he does retain the translation "woman" for his commentary (1992:74).

Choon-Leong Seow also pursues this line of argumentation, but he believes that it is Woman Folly who is "more bitter than death." Seow also argues that the following line in 7:28 was inserted by a later copyist, perhaps as "an ancient sexist joke" (1997:28).

The final interpretive strategy is one that does not necessarily deny that Qoheleth's statement is misogynistic or at least androcentric, but it does place the discussion of this androcentrism within its own androcentric frame. James Crenshaw opens his discussion on this passage with the following statement: "This section discusses two profound mysteries: wisdom and woman" (1987:144). Even though he does confront the contempt and hatred for women expressed in these verses, he has already excluded women from the conversation by foregrounding it in a statement on their mysterious nature. This is a biblical commentary's version of Freud's infamous statement, "What do women want?" Before he even addresses the misogyny of the text, Crenshaw makes a stereotypical statement about women himself. He places them all in a category outside of the knowable.

In these three ways, the commentators of Qoheleth extend and perpetuate the ideology of the text. The resisting reader, specifically the resisting feminist reader, not only questions the text but also questions these readings of the text. No attempt to salvage this passage is convincing.

When I look at the book of Proverbs, a comparable text within the wisdom tradition, it quickly becomes apparent how Qoheleth has intensified the condemnation by taking a criticism directed at the *'iššâ zārâ*—translated alternatively "strange woman," "harlot," "loose woman" and connected to the "foreign woman"—and making it a blanket statement about all women (see Brenner: 51–56 for a full description of female characters in Proverbs). The *'iššâ zārâ* is characterized as one who leads men astray away from wisdom

(Prov 7:5, 8, 10–23, 25–27)), who captures men (6:25; 23:27; 22:14), and whose bitterness leads to death (5:4-5). Her negative characterization is due to her actions, and she is opposed by Woman Wisdom and the faithful wife. In contrast to this, the woman in Qoheleth is not negatively characterized because of her actions. Rather, her person is already corrupt.

The personification of wisdom as a woman (Ḥokmâ or Sophia) in Proverbs is avoided altogether in Qoheleth. In fact, instead of wisdom being a woman, no wisdom whatsoever is found in any woman: "And a woman in all of these I did not find" (7:28c). The lack of a female personified wisdom is particularly evident in the Hebrew text. There are no neutral pronouns for inanimate objects in Hebrew; in other words, there is no Hebrew equivalent to the English word "it." Whenever the passage refers to wisdom, the feminine third person pronoun (hî') is used (Qoh 7:23). But unlike Proverbs (Prov 8, for example), Qoheleth never takes the next step of representing wisdom as a woman. Within the bounds of the statements against women in 7:26 and 7:28, the author is unable to equate wisdom with woman. It would transgress the ideological boundaries of the text.

Despite the fact that Proverbs characterized certain women as foolish and dangerous to men, there are many other women in the text who are good and helpful. There is the mother whose counsel the son is commended to listen and to obey (Prov 23:22; 31:1). There is the "woman of valor," who is the wife who supports and aids her family (31:10–27). She is a blessing to all (31:28–31). While it is true that these roles are still within the parameters of an androcentric society and that there is still a binary opposition between the good and the bad woman, the variety of images continually challenge each other, and the positive portrayals offer alternatives for women that are absent in Qoheleth.

This negative characterization of all women is not mitigated by the positive spin Qoheleth places on the pleasures one can derive with (or from?) one's wife (Qoh 9:9). (Qoh 9:9 and 7:26–29 are seen as contradictions by most commentators. Delitzsch [363–64] was the first to frame the problem of women in Qoheleth as the problem of resolving the contradiction between the negative 7:26–29 and the positive 9:9.) The woman is not valuable and worthy in and of herself, but only the pleasure she can give to her husband in this limited and harsh world. The full verse reads thus: "Enjoy [literally 'see'] life with the wife whom you love, all the days of your vain life that are given you under the sun, because that is your portion in life and in your toil at which you toil under the sun" (9:9). To read this verse as a direct contradiction of 7:26–29 is to make misogyny and love antithetical, a proposition refuted by any critical look at the history of the relationships between men and women. An androcentric and misogynistic worldview simply does not make love of one's wife (or mother, sister, daughter) impossible. If this were true, either misogyny or marriage would have failed a long time ago.

Qoheleth 9:9 is hardly a ringing endorsement of womankind or even a praise of the good wife. A second look at Prov 31 will confirm this. The wife in Prov 31 is good and praiseworthy because of her own actions, not just because she can provide pleasure. This wife provides clothes and food, takes care of the financial concerns of her family, is charitable and compassionate to others in need, is wise and kind and industrious. Contrast the endorsement at the end of this passage in Proverbs—"Many women have done excellently, but you surpass them all" (Prov 31:29)—to the end of the passage in Qoheleth: "And a woman in all of these I did not find" (Qoh 7:28c).

Certainly men do not fare much better in 7:28. Only one man in a thousand is wise, but at least there is this one man. Also, the voice of the text (the narrator or the implied author) is male, the entire book assumes a male audience, and men are characterized in a variety of ways and in a variety of contexts. Therefore, the statement in verse 28 does not become a general condemnation of all men (or even 999 men). A feminist interpreter must conclude that this text is unredeemable.

3.

Do I really mean that the text is unredeemable? Is the passage as simple and stable as I have portrayed it? The feminist stance that I have taken mirrors the one-dimensional woman of the text. Such a feminist reading suppresses other readings in order to argue a single point. This reading also invests the text with an androcentric and misogynist core, then reads from there. Fetterly's interpretation of the canon of literature does the same. As it is written in *The Postmodern Bible*:

> To argue that the canon of American fiction is at its core androcentric and misogynist presumes there is a determinant core already there in these texts. To read against the grain of these texts is to operate on the assumption that there is a grain against which to read. (Bible and Culture Collective: 38)

The same can be said of the Bible and my reader-response and feminist interpretation of Qoheleth. But no text has a stable core of meaning. The mask that I have used to be a feminist critic begins to show fissures and cracks as I recognize the instability of any "core meaning." The text cracks as well. I notice the text mutating.

The first step in any interpretation is to read the text in Hebrew, attend to the marginal notes, and stabilize the text. In the margins are variations, problems, inconsistencies. These marginal notes threaten to pull the text apart, they challenge its integrity, and the interpreter must tame them before she can go any further. Before I had even begun this paper, I was the text critic searching for the original, striping off layers of scribal error, clarifications, and theological glosses. Specifically, text-critical analysis requires the emendation of Qoh 7:22–27 in order to preserve the coherent gender identity of the speaker. But what I thought I had stabilized in the beginning now begins to shimmer and shake, shift and change. The letters are moving again, back to how they appear without emendation in the Masoretic Text. The stability that I have been seeking is an illusion. And when I read the MT without text criticism, coherent gender identity is absent.

Language is not an absolute system inextricably bound to an external reality. Instead, language is a system of differences. It is only possible to know the meaning of a word through other words. The connection between the signifier (the word or sound) and the signified (the concept or object) is a matter of convention, and this relationship is inherently unstable. The words themselves are unstable: letters can break off, change to another, or come together. With each mutation of a letter, meaning can change subtly or radically. Only the difference of a letter (a sound) separates "tree," "thee," "the," and "tee," and each of these words (sounds) are intelligible only because of what they are not (Bible and Culture Collective: 124). Words also change meaning depending upon their contexts; they change as they wander in and out of texts.

Texts are composed of these letters and these words. The instability of the language undergirds the instability of the ideology of that text. Systems—language and text—are always "systems of exclusions" (Bible and Culture Collective: 120). They mask these exclusions and attempt to appear whole and coherent. But no matter how tight or how masked its ideology may seem, the system always contains slippages, contradictions, and gaps where a reader can enter and unravel the text/ideology. Texts always deconstruct themselves.

The feminist analysis above relies on a misogyny found in the text itself and a reading of the text that resists that misogyny. However, such a reading suppresses the instability of the text and the inherent undecidability of language. A unified reading suppresses the moments in the text where the feminine unexpectedly erupts, thus undermining the androcentric ideology.

If one regards the unemended MT, the gender of the one spoken and the gender of the one speaking wavers. The first case is in verse 22. It reads, with vowels: "For also your heart knows that many times you [masculine singular] also cursed others." But, without pointing and without emendation, it reads: "For also your heart knows that many times you [feminine singular] also cursed others." The masculine and feminine second-person pronouns differ by only one letter: *'at* (feminine "you") and *'attâ* (masculine "you"). With words so similar, the letters are incapable of staying in their place. The *h* has disappeared in the MT, thus inverting the gender of the person addressed in this verse. The coherent male audience slips.

The second case is in verse 27. It reads, with emendation: "See, this I found, said [masculine third-person singular] the Qoheleth." However, it appears in the MT thus: "See, this I found, said [feminine third-person singular] Qoheleth." Again, it is the matter of an *h*. Does the letter belong at the end of the verb, thus rendering it feminine, or does it belong at the beginning of the next word, which would maintain the masculine gender of Qoheleth but turn the proper name into an object with a definite article? The gender of Qoheleth slips.

There are two texts here: the one that appears in the MT and the one that is formed through the emendations of the text critic. In a deconstructive reading, neither of these texts is privileged; rather, they are superimposed upon each other and remain undecidable. From one angle, there is a coherent male speaker and audience. But out of the corner of my eye, I see the text shimmer and shake; bursts of the feminine interrupt its smooth surface.

In addition to these small, although intriguing, textual instabilities, the very word Qoheleth is a feminine form of the root *qhl*. Although all of the verbs, except for the case noted above, are masculine, the form of the name—which is untranslatable and unattested anywhere else—retains its feminine side. The more that Qoheleth attempts to suppress these feminine facets of language and text, the more that feminine breaks out at other textual sites. Who is Qoheleth, and what is Qoheleth trying to hide?

So what do we have? A figure with an untranslatable and femininely formed name and places in the text where feminine forms unexpectedly emerge. The book is a body, the body of Qoheleth. As the language shifts and changes, revealing inconsistencies and instabilities, so the body is unstable too. Marjorie Garber names this type of unstable, boundary-crossing, category- confusing figure "the transvestite." "The transvestite willfully creates a third space beyond the masculine/feminine dichotomy, the homo/hetero binary, the real/artificial antithesis" (Veeser: xxi; see Garber). And this third category is what compels desire. Building on Lacan's dictum that "the object of desire remains potent only when veiled" (Veeser: xxi), a cross-dressing Qoheleth covers and uncovers herself/himself, herself/himself.... A cross-dressing Qoheleth creates the desire that compels the reader.

And desire leads us to the deeper level of the feminine, one that threatens to undermine the entire book. As a text about wisdom, the feminine is the very subject of the text, the feminine structures the text, and the feminine is what is desired above all else. Wisdom is a feminine noun and as such demands feminine pronouns and verbs. Although this is obscured in the English translation, in the Hebrew it is an unavoidable aspect of the text:

"All of this I tested in wisdom; I said, 'I will be wise,' but *she* was far from me" (Qoh 7:23). Qoheleth is searching for this elusive feminine word/concept, and the more he desires and pursues his desire for wisdom, the more he negates women.

Wisdom is personified in Proverbs as a woman, and this woman lurks around the edges of the Qoheleth text. One cannot read the one without the other. Qoheleth's silence on her presence is glaring. Rather than hiding the feminine aspect of wisdom, Qoheleth's silence draws attention to her notable absence. The more he is silent, the more he suppresses, the more he tries to hide the feminine, the more he is betrayed by its insuppressible presence. Qoheleth is full of anxiety because the feminine is there, in the book and in the body.

There is another intertext here: "Love is as strong as death" (Song 8:6). Is the proclamation that "woman is as bitter as death" a response to this climatic moment in the Song of Songs, a text where the narrative voice is female and love and pleasure is lauded? Or vice versa? The texts echo each other, calling each other into question, destabilizing each in a dance between death, love, and women. Because of its character as a general maxim, these verses represent a little piece of wisdom embedded in the love lyrics of the Song. It is wisdom countering wisdom.

Georges Bataille enters the dance with another maxim: "Eroticism ... is assenting to life up to the point of death" (11). Sex, death, and life are intimately bound together because of humanity's ambivalent feelings about our own discontinuous being. It is this desire for and fear of discontinuity that compels our relationships with other bodies. Life begins with the continuity of our being with another body—the maternal body. Birth brings discontinuity, and as the child grows this discontinuity becomes more and more apparent. This discontinuity is not a negative state, for independence of being brings satisfaction and our consciousness of our separate and unique selves is what makes us human. However, there is also profound loneliness at the heart of humanity, and this loneliness results in a nostalgia for the continuous life.

During sex, both individuals "are simultaneously open to continuity. But nothing persists in their imperfect awareness. The crisis over, the discontinuity of each is intact" (Bataille: 103). But sex is more than the hearkening back to the continuity experienced before birth. It is also a drive toward the continuity of death. First of all, reproduction goes hand in hand with death. Life grows out of the decomposition and decay of the deceased. And even with human life, where parents survive the birth of their offspring, "the reprieve is only temporary" (100). Reproduction is super-abundance, excess, and the death of the parents must eventually follow from this excess. Bataille writes:

One need look no further for the cause of the fear associated with sexual activity. Death is exceptional, an extreme case; each loss of normal energy is indeed only a little death [exhaustion following orgasm] ... but whether obscurely or clearly this little death is what is feared. On the other hand it is also desired.... No one could deny that one essential element of excitement is the feeling of being swept off one's feet, of falling headlong. If love exists at all it is, like death, a swift movement of loss within us, quickly slipping into tragedy and stopping only with death. For the truth is that between death and the reeling, heady motion of the little death the distance is hardly noticeable. (239)

Qoheleth desires and fears women, wisdom, and even the feminine inside of Qoheleth's own self. It is in the interplay of desire and fear in the book of Qoheleth that the body of Qoheleth contemplates death. Qoheleth 7:26 is only one instance of a discourse on death that runs from the first chapter to the last. Qoheleth knows that that which he desires most is feminine—women and wisdom contaminate each other and become inextricably bound. The text and its ideology cannot remain stable and contained. Instead, it quickly unravels as Qoheleth frantically grabs at its loose ends.

4.

This is a true story. Once upon a Monday night, I was reading Fernando Segovia's introduction to volume 2 of *Reading from This Place* (1995a). Curled up in bed, I finished the essay. I turned off the light and began to drift to sleep while thinking of Qoheleth and my social location. I began to dream.

What is my social location? What are the components of my identity that read Qoheleth, and why my attraction to this text? I thought of the ways in which my own identity is as contradictory as this text, how I am alienated from parts of my own self, and how these parts shift and change under examination and over time. Neither my class position nor my sexual orientation nor my Jewish identity has remained unproblematic or stable. I have always been a woman, but my understanding of my sex and gender has changed. Who is reading when "I" look at Qoheleth?

Qoheleth rises up before me. It is an architectural structure of words, a building almost but unlike any building I have ever encountered. Its angles are unpredictable; there are places to enter in the most unlikely locations—neither doors nor windows but something else altogether. The spaces between the words are white, and the black lines run in all directions without order. It stretches up vertically further than I can see. I fracture. Different aspects of my identity split off and become independently animated. Like pieces of a jigsaw puzzle they stand before Qoheleth and start to fit themselves into its structure. They scatter up and around the edifice, some disappearing into its strange openings, some climbing further up and on.

Each one is a persona, but not a false front that hides something more authentic or real. Each persona tells part of the story but at the same time obfuscates other identities. Peeling off one only reveals others, never getting closer to some essential core. This is my multifaceted and sometimes contradictory social location. Hélène Cixous writes that "the human subject is not singular, which is why one should never say 'who am I?' but 'who are I?' … We are all the ages we were and will be, all the characters we dream, all of our combinations with others, exchanges between languages and sexes, each one changing us with others" (Sellers: xvii). And finally, we even have the "I who escapes me" (Sellers: xviii)—like those figures in my dream that climb up and on, escaping my gaze to have their own encounters with the body of Qoheleth.

Psalms, Postcolonialism, and the Construction of the Self

Jon L. Berquist

The study of the book of Psalms often proceeds from literary assumptions rather than from the historical and sociological approaches that have become the hallmark of Persian-period studies. Yet Psalms has long been understood as the "songbook of the Second Temple," a phrase attributed to scholars such as Knudson (1918) and Mowinckel (1921) and adopted by many since then. Despite this recognition that the psalms were used in the Second Temple and quite possibly in the Persian period, few scholars have addressed the historical function of the psalms, at least since classic form-critical studies.

An understanding of Psalms within a historical context of the Second Temple must begin with the imperial context of the Persian Empire. In the years between 539 and 333 B.C.E., the land and people who earlier identified as Judah existed as Yehud, a segment of the Persian Empire. Yehud's coloniality manifested itself in the imperial domination of life and culture in Yehud as well as in the imperial use of the colony for the empire's own needs, particularly in terms of economic extraction and military posturing. This coloniality may be described in social terms as a dominating interdependence (Berquist 1995a:243–45) or in spatial terms of core and periphery (245–47). Empires used the subjugated provinces or colonies as sources of local labor, as a tax-base, and as a military outpost. The empire's relationship was often one of intensification, of attempting to maximize the colony's benefits to the empire while maintaining the basis of colonial production and reproduction. In other words, the empire managed its colonies as assets from which the empire should derive benefits as a regular matter of course, but the empire was also interested in its colonies' long-term survival so that it could provide income on an ongoing basis.

Based on this understanding of Persian-period history and imperial/colonial relations, Psalms can be understood within ancient Yehud in terms of how these songs integrated popular religion, personal lived reality, and the empire's domination of individual lives. In other words, the psalms were part of the empire's control of the region through its ideological social control of persons and lives (Berquist 1995a:193–203). Psalms offer words and social spaces that shape individual experiences and emotions into socially accepted expressions, which at least indirectly serve imperial interests. Through the embrace of such permissible emotions within worship, the priests and other forces of culture within this colonized society gained access to the joys and the crises of people's lives.

This analysis concentrates on the function of Psalms within an imperial context. But postcolonial perspectives can enhance the analysis. Instead of examining the sociology of domination as the sole factor in literary production, postcolonialism highlights the interplay of empire and resistance. Literature is not only a product of empire but also a resistance to it. In this sense, Yehud is not only a colony but simultaneously a postcolonial society—not because Yehud existed after empire but because empires are constantly being refashioned.

YEHUD AS A POSTCOLONIAL SOCIETY

During 587–539 B.C.E., Babylonia operated the region as a colony. After 539, Yehud existed as a Persian colony. But after about 450 B.C.E., the Persian Empire decreased its influence in the eastern Mediterranean seaboard, and Yehud exhibited some of the characteristics of a border or frontier as well as continuing its role as a colony (Berquist 1995c). Thus, Yehud functioned as a colony but also in ways that resisted the empire. This interplay of dominance and resistance formed the social context for life in Yehud.

Postcolonialism is a complex set of movements within literary and social fields. Definitions of postcolonialism are varied and wide-ranging (see Adam; Moore; Sugirtharajah 2002; 2005), but two specific dimensions of postcolonial study are relevant for the present argument. First, postcolonialism is the study of cultures and cultural products in periods that follow imperial domination. In such cultures, the marks of the past empire are still present, but the society is investing great energies in emerging patterns of life. Postcolonialism concentrates on these energies and patterns, observing how they bear the marks of empire as well as how they represent social life after empire.

Second, postcolonialism refers to the study of societies with the recognition that hegemonic forces are always limited. Domination of living beings is never complete; there is always at least a remainder. In many cases, the colonial experience is strongly shaped by a colony's resistance and even contradiction of empire. Imperializing forces compete with desires for local autonomy. For instance, empires require colonial leadership that is both local and imperial in orientation and identity. This double-mindedness creates a hybridity and a complex multiplication of loyalties, interests, and alliances. In a sense, this aspect of postcolonialism tends toward a deconstruction of the categories of empire and colony; whereas earlier scholarship saw the colony-empire relationship as thorough if not also total, postcolonialism knows that colony and empire cannot be split into a simple binary of two entities that would each be pure and opposite from the other. Postcolonialism functions as an interpretive strategy to interrogate such categories and to find the cracks in them, or to pursue the exceptions and interruptions that exist within any imperializing control system. Perhaps postcolonialism extends even to the search for knowledges and practices that subvert empire.

Thus, postcolonial investigation is often expressed in terms of finding a voice. That may involve finding the voices of ancient peoples that have been stifled for some time, either buried within or occluded by more dominant literatures. But postcolonialism may also involve our listening attentively to the ways that imperial discourse is lopsided or strained.

Such an understanding of postcolonialism suggests a reading strategy for texts of Yehud, such as the book of Psalms or the prayers in the books of Chronicles. Such reading of Persian Yehudite texts should properly be postexilic, postcolonial, partial, plural, and persuasive.

To say that such a reading is *postexilic* is to root the experience of Yehud and the conditions of Yehud's texts within the time after exile. This goes against much traditional reading of the psalms as relevant to the supposed exilic experiences of landlessness and despair. Even when scholars have dated psalms to the fifth or fourth centuries, many have interpreted such psalms as reactions to exile, as the pain of that sixth-century experience lingers in the emotions and imaginations of the people's cultural memory. To interpret the texts as postexilic requires focusing attention on the problems within the colonized life of Yehud. Psalms respond not so much to the exigencies of sixth-century life in Babylon but to the pains of settled Jerusalem life in the subsequent two centuries. Psalms need to be read in terms of the rhetorical needs of a postexilic community, a culture for whom the questions of exile are mostly in the past.

Second, reading of the Psalms needs to be a *postcolonial* reading, so that interpretation would take into account the colonized nature of Yehud (as well as the colonized nature of much present scholarship). Psalms and Chronicles, like other Persian-period texts, participate in Yehud's complex life as a dominated subculture and as a locally autonomous social unit. The contradictions of postcolonial life must be considered the proper context for interpreting these psalms and prayers. It may well be that scholarly opinions will see traces of older concerns as well and that some psalms fixate on precolonial images such as monarchy. But even while recognizing such topics and tendencies, scholarship must remember that these are anachronistic (at the time of the Psalms' or Chronicles' assemblage, even if not also at the time of the psalm's composition). Instead, attention needs to be given to how such images function in an empire and in a culture that resists empire.

This participation in empire and simultaneous resistance to empire forms at least a dual function of Psalms, but the psalms require a more *plural* perspective. Each text is only one view into a postcolonial mindset; scholarship must attend to the variety of ideas and expressions that coexist within the colony. Just as there is no one imperial domination, there is no singular form of resistance to it. A postcolonial world is pluralistic, in that the society includes multiple positions and positionalities that exist next to each other. To examine only one of these aspects of Persian-period texts is to misinterpret the one, because it refuses the contestedness within the culture.

Thus, such readings must also be *partial*. On the one hand, this requires an admission that all ideologies in Yehudite literature are incomplete. Interpreters must avoid tendencies to find total ideologies or systematic (that is, systematizable) worldviews within Psalms or Chronicles. No ideology in Yehud explained everything, and thus every ideology is one of many minority positions that coexist in a pluralistic society. On the other hand, these ideologies are also partial in the sense that they are partisan. Each reading of each text creates skewed observations that argue for specific aspects of reality. The images and metaphors are used to support social movements of varying kinds. Texts are partial, not neutral.

Reading of the psalms and the prayers of Chronicles, as well as all other Persian-period literature, must attend not only to the reality of such partisanship but also to the strategies employed to advance the partial nature of these texts. This requires understanding the texts as *persuasive*. Yehudite texts are rhetorical devices intended to support certain positions and agendas, but texts must persuade in order to be successful. Texts must be sufficiently persuasive before they will be preserved; there would be no replication of scrolls until and unless a text has proved sufficient value. Since the texts must convince, they must also compel. There will be intellectual and emotional grounds for belief, and the scholar must be attentive to both within the text.

Identity Formation in a Postcolonial World

One of the proper focuses of this reading strategy is a concentration on identity. In a postcolonial context, identity is always contested. Without cultural hegemony, there is no ability to compel a certain identity, so identity of the people cannot be assumed. Instead, psalms communicate the signs of struggle to identify one's self and one's group, and so the reader can begin to see how those identities are constructed, managed, and deployed. This includes corporate identities, such as ethnicity, but also individual identities such as roles and loyalties (see Berquist 2006).

The construction of identity along borders involves the struggle to be one or the other in the midst of social clashes. The people are aware of multiple ethnicities, multiple languages, multiple cultures, and multiple ideologies. From these options, people construct their identities with certain allegiances. But much of the process of identity formation develops into simpler choices: Are you one of those who speak of yourself as Yehudite, Jerusalemite, or Persian? Do you speak Hebrew or Aramaic? The choices one makes in one area may well constrain choices in other areas, or at least subject one's self to social pressures to conform to one specific group or another. Such would be visible, for instance, in the accounts in Ezra and Nehemiah, where the array of plural social options results in a call to join one side or another. But the processes of individual identity formation often disrupt such dichotomies. Even when leaders express a rhetorical either/or, people frequently make their lives into a bricolage of both/and. On a social scale, such individual choices add up to the diversity of a pluralistic culture.

The construction of ethnic identity and group identity becomes, therefore, one of the cultural tasks of postcolonial literature such as Psalms and Chronicles. This occurs in a number of ways.

First, both Psalms and Chronicles develop music. The poetic nature of the book of Psalms, along with the possible ascription of certain tunes, creates a literature to be sung by the people. In Chronicles, the presence of spoken prayers by key figures as well as the frequent mention of Levites who sing combine to create those books' concentration on the use of music. Hymns are a major part of popular culture and its transmission in modern times as well, especially in border situations. Music builds both culture and identity. Examples abound from the modern world as well, whether it is Tejano gospel music, Buddhist chant, the distinctive hymnody of Korean or Ghanaian Christians, African American spirituals, or simply the denominational cultures bound up in hymnals. Through singing familiar songs together, music forms cohesion and identity and builds loyalties, some of which may transcend or transgress other identity issues.

Second, prayers construct an identity that identifies with God. Because these songs, prayers, and poems address God, they build within the one who performs them a sense of God's reality, God's nearness, God's involvement, and also God's relationality. God is the one to whom and of whom the reader sings. Through the music of Psalms and the prayers of Chronicles, one identifies with God, specifically as one of God's people.

Furthermore, both books offer history and tales that narrate a past that validates the present. In this postexilic reading, the purpose of remembering the past is to join together as a meaningful community in the present. More than that, it is a specific kind of community—one based on God, who is the one commonality shared by all the people. Rarely do these books offer the empire as the subject, even though they depict an imperial world. Instead, the emphasis on God operates within a countercultural awareness, pointing not to the realities of daily life but to ideas of how life should be.

IMPERIAL DOMINATION AND RESISTING EMPIRE

Are the songs and prayers in Psalms and Chronicles for or against empire? There are few explicit references to such political questions within these texts, but the assumptions of the books make two things clear. As postcolonial literature, Psalms and Chronicles construct the self in ways that connect to the empire and that resist the empire.

The acts of identity within the Psalms deploy old, previous, or nostalgic identities that have been found useful, reclaimed, and taken over. In this sense, ethnicity has become a consumer good. It is a commodity to be made, exchanged, and acquired. The empire finds ethnicity a way to keep people in their imperial spaces and within their imperial roles.

The acts of identity are also resistances to empire: the invention and celebration of a national history, the establishment of local autonomy, and insistence on God as controlling the empires of the past. God takes the role of the King, both displacing the human king and making sure that the empire does not have to face war against a king who could lead a colony in revolt.

Likewise, the Torah psalms lift up the law both as a distinctively Jewish way of being in the world and as a way to live peaceably with others. The praise of law builds the tradition of autonomy.

Laments call God back to responsibility after abandonment; thus, God saves the people, forming the community of God's saved and thereby granting an identity tied to God, while returning to an older mythic time. The solutions to God's abandonment lie not with the old traditions of Israel's kings but with older notions of God as their King.

CONCLUSION

This postcolonial construction of self and identity suggests new paths forward in the study of the Psalter and the Chronicler as Persian-period literature. First, as popular songs of faith become written texts, they become ever less accessible. The enscrolling creates new identities, such as song leader and scribe. Their job is to construct the identity of the people and to define what it means to be Yehudite. The function of the song and the function of the text are separate, yet issues of identity formation shape them both in related ways.

Most cultures use narratives to tell stories within locales such as campfires and sleepovers (in the modern world). As such, narratives engage the listener (and the reader) to think about another world. Biblical narratives are always in the third person; they are always stories about the other. The listeners and readers reside at some distance from the narrative that they observe. In the modern world, plays function similarly, on the distant side of the breach between audience and performer. But contemporary musicals begin to cross the divide; the audience sings in their minds and sings on the way home. Once they leave the musical, they sing—in first person, having taken on (or having been taken over by?) one of the identities within the play. The performance shifts so that the hearers become participants. The songs of the characters, rendered in first person, become statements that the listeners and readers say about themselves, forming identity.

It may well be that the Persian-period literature of Psalms and Chronicles have an analogous function. Through prayers, Chronicles is a musical; the Levites have become singers in the chorus, and the audience begins to enthrone themselves in the title roles of David, Solomon, Hezekiah, and so forth. With the sundering of the objective/subjective dichotomy, the audience becomes kings and queens, in a world without a monarchy. In the Psalms, the frequent use of the first person echoes this, and the speech of the psalmist becomes the common speech of the Yehudite worshipers. From this discursive point, they learn the words and the tunes that will build temples and inhabit God's courts. Their words build the temple, and God sits enthroned on the prayers of God's people. Identity builds itself with discourse, and so identity builds itself up into religion.

But such psalms, songs, and prayers do more than create identity. They also construct the self, in the sense of individual as community member, as faithful follower, as heir of history, as object of priestly and scribal attention. But the psalms also construct the self as one who worships, as one who gives voice to ancient and new sensibilities, as one who is positioned around the temple, as one whose voice rises to Yahweh, and one who is subject with Yahweh to creating the self and the world.

Jacques Lacan (1982) writes of the law, the phallus, and the father. But in Psalms comes a self who ventures out of the shadow of law and begins to explore *jouissance*. When they sing, dance, celebrate, laugh, and cry, they are part of something other than a dour legalism (if such ever existed) and a cold intellect. These are perhaps not so much analogous to songs of bards or campfire tales but instead similar to chants, drinking songs, marching songs, and so forth. They build solidarity by sharing voice and embodying faith.

Psalms creates a world where those whom God loves always vanquish their enemies and where faith and politics always move in the same direction. This is a utopia, a place that is no place, but it lives within the mind and constructs the individual and communal identity. Before the Yehudites say "amen," they have learned to say "I." After they say "amen," they do not stop humming the tune nor do their feet forget the steps.

RESPONSE: IN THE BEGINNING—AGAIN

Alice W. Hunt

That this volume is possible speaks to the changing landscape of biblical studies. (By "biblical studies," I am referring primarily to the Hebrew Bible with the hope that there may be relevance for wider notions of biblical studies.) Long considered the most obscure period, the ignored stepchild of the biblical periods, and the eccentric uncle of New Testament studies, the Second Temple period now finds itself front and center as a focus for biblical scholars and historians. Instead of adopting a single, linear approach to the Persian period beginning with the ancestors, moving through the tribes, driving up the fortified mountain of the united monarchy and among the hills of the divided monarchy through the barrenness of the exile into the dimly lit tunnel of the Persian period, biblical scholars now approach the Second Temple period from many angles. Transitioning from the well-traveled, pothole-filled road that used to dominate access to the Persian period to multiple avenues of entrance is teaching us many lessons. Assumptions once recognized as pillars have been reshaped by new understandings. Biblical studies can no longer operate under the presupposition of a monolithic, linear development of ancient Israel's political and religious life resulting in a unique, singular, and pure Judaism. In its place, we find a growing understanding of Judaisms developing in a vibrantly organic cultural, political, economic, social, and religious milieu. Concurrently, biblical scholars must question the Wellhausenian notion of a tripartite division for the history of ancient Israel, beginning with the naïve innocence of the tribal period, followed by the glorious days of the monarchy, and ending with the diminished period controlled by legalistic priests (1973). Likewise, notions of a single, pure Judaism standing firm in the face of an encroaching, evil Hellenism have given way to nuanced discussions about Hellenistic Judaisms; suggestions of obtaining a scientifically objective history are being replaced with articulations of historiographic method and starting points; conceptualizations of biblical theology have been challenged by dialogical notions of biblical theologies; ideas of an exilic empty land have given way to understandings of the complicated lives of many groups of people. Where biblical studies once served as the center, providing the grounding questions and assumptions for other disciplines of inquiry (such as archaeology, historiography, and demography), biblical studies now stands alongside other disciplines in rich, interdisciplinary studies. Homogeneity in biblical studies has opened to diversity and multiple approaches.

The essays in this volume speak to the depth and breadth of possibilities for biblical studies. For me, they accentuate two trends in biblical studies and raise one area of concern.

Two Trends

Trend 1: The productivity and creativity of biblical scholarship rests squarely on its ability both to recognize the multivalent nature of the work at hand and to engage the theoretical framework of related disciplines.

In 1985, William G. Dever published "Syro-Palestinian and Biblical Archaeology" in *The Hebrew Bible and Its Modern Interpreters*, situating biblical archaeology in the history of American biblical studies as a discipline of a day gone by. For Dever, the role of biblical archaeology as a discipline had subsided with the necessarily diminishing influence of colonialism, the increasing sophistication in archaeological field methods, and the pragmatic need for funds and workers in the fields. He chastised biblical studies for living in a passé world, for assuming the subservience of all other disciplines to itself. While Dever himself has been unable to follow his own counsel, he provided leadership on the cutting edge of biblical studies scholarship. Biblical studies is enhanced, then, by standing alongside Syro-Palestinian archaeologists, who in turn stand alongside other experts such as demographers, archaeozoologists, statisticians, gemologists, surveyors, and engineers. Likewise, biblical scholars engage the theoretical frameworks of other disciplines.

Several of the essays in this volume make just such an effort. In his review essay, Bautch appeals to theories of intertextuality and suggests that intertextuality may be used to shed light on the Persian period. Although some scholars question the value of intertextual studies, Bautch shows that these issues become essential as traditional historical timelines and their associations with particular collections of biblical texts become less defensible. As biblical scholars seek to propose meaning using available data and theoretical approaches, intertextuality studies will provide an essential piece of the framework. Polaski sociologically investigates issues of power and legitimation resident in textuality to focus on community formation and canonization. Polaski's engagement of the book of Joshua fits nicely with the Persian-period analysis suggested by Douglas A. Knight (2002). However, I find Polaski's understanding of canonization in the Persian period problematic as well as anachronistic. I take issue in particular with his assumption of a singular (Torah) set of authoritative texts. The Dead Sea Scroll material seems to indicate that each of many groups may have had its own set of authoritative texts. Janzen uses anthropological theory along with a bit of sociology to add to understandings of the separatist rhetoric of Ezra 9–10. Janzen raises issues of other-ness that should become increasingly important as biblical interpreters, both from academia and communities of faith, relate biblical material to contemporary issues of justice. Janzen falls prey to the trap of looking for a singular cause instead of seeing the multivalent nature of the work (cf. Marbury 2003). Furthermore, as biblical studies moves toward a focus on the Persian period, translation issues, such as the translation of "strange" woman, will require additional analysis.

Mitchell appeals to philosophy of history in searching for the origins of historiography in ancient Israel. While scholars such as William Dever, Philip Davies, Neils Peter Lemche, and Baruch Halpern have long advocated an appeal to historiography and the philosophy of history, biblical scholarship has been slow to move from traditional starting points. Second Temple studies will lead the way to a new level of historiography in biblical studies. Strawn demonstrates the efficacy of contemporary biblical studies, suggesting that both Isa 60 and the Persepolis Apadana reliefs are products of Persian imperial propaganda. His work dovetails nicely with the work of Berquist, Knight, and Marbury in examining how empires form society and culture, yet another leading edge for Second Temple studies. Marbury provides an inspiring example of the integration of multivalent scholarship, noting the political, economic, cultural, and cultic aspects of biblical rhetoric while focusing on the strange woman of Prov 7. Marbury's essay, accompanied by Janzen's essay, sets a benchmark for Second Temple studies, as he develops previous scholarship and avails himself of the theoretical underpinnings of related disciplines. The implication of the essays in this volume for biblical scholarship is a clarion call to integration, to engagement with the theoretical underpinnings of other disciplines that will result in mutual transformation.

Trend 2: The ethical urgency of attending to multiple and often other-ed and/or silenced voices is a primary responsibility of biblical scholars today.

Even a cursory survey of the sessions offered at a Society of Biblical Literature Annual Meeting both elicits amazement at the variety of offerings and raises concerns about significations and perceived identities. A simple examination of the names of the program units yields a subtle yet plaguing concern about who is "in" and who is "out" in biblical studies. Some program units are named by the biblical books upon which they focus, some are named for a particular topic, some are named for a particular period, and some are named with labels for their methodological approach. One might observe that some arenas of biblical scholarship acquire a certain type of other-labeling, while other areas of biblical scholarship carry no such label. For example, we hear of feminist biblical studies, African American biblical hermeneutics, womanist biblical studies, liberation biblical studies, postcolonial biblical studies, LGBT/queer biblical studies, African biblical hermeneutics, ecological hermeneutics, Asian and Asian American biblical hermeneutics, and contextual biblical interpretation. That some groups have no such labels and others carry identifying labels implies not so subtly that the labeled groups are "other," or extra; they are nice to have around but are not necessary; they are helpful to biblical studies but do not function as hard-core biblical scholarship. That the labeled groups are self-labeled indicates how difficult it has been in the field of biblical studies even to get a place at the table.

The essays in this volume invite biblical scholarship to value those, ancient and contemporary, who traditionally have been other-ed. Kessler broadens discussions of identity and raises inclusion/exclusion issues that must have been prominent and formative in the Second Temple period. Koosed reminds biblical scholars of the centrality of embodied readers. Marbury calls on scholars to ferret out how seemingly subtle cultural socialization propagates oppression. Berquist complexifies our understanding of the impact of imperialism, elaborating on texts as means of resistance and identity formation. Ruiz reflects on the continuing and devastating effects of imperialism when thrust upon the lives of immigrants. His work on immigration issues brings the Second Temple period once again to the forefront; for scholars, as notions of migration become increasingly interesting, and for biblical interpreters in communities of faith, in the United States particularly, as immigration debates remain central on the social, cultural, and political landscape. These essays demonstrate how biblical scholarship may be made relevant to today's globalized and diverse world.

A Concern: The Danger of Throwing the Baby Out with the Bathwater

In finding new avenues of approach, scholars may be tempted to abandon the old, now-bumpy road that used to be the only highway in and out of the Persian period. In particular, my concern focuses on the creation and use of history. Biblical scholarship must not see itself faced with an either/or situation of discarding old and traditional scholarship for new scholarship. Instead, biblical scholarship must live in a both/and world. Specifically, history cannot be ignored. Whether scholars admit it or not, all biblical scholarship uses history—either good history or bad history. It is incumbent on biblical scholars, then, to attend to issues of historiography.

The essays in this volume face this challenge. Melody Knowles's essay demonstrates scholarship's struggle with incorporating historical understanding into a study of religious practice. Richard Bautch's essay reminds us that, while work on intertextuality appears at first glance to extend beyond the historical-critical work of source, redaction, and tradition criticisms, intertextuality studies still rely on the quality of historical work and so cannot ignore issues of historiography, particularly as they place texts in specific, historical contexts. Donald Polaski's work depends heavily on the historical dating of texts, and David Janzen's study affirms Wellhausen's contribution that texts reflect issues contemporaneous with the times in which they were written. Berquist places Psalms and Chronicles in the Persian period. Ruiz depends on an exilic date for Ezek 20.

A challenge facing biblical scholars, and Second Temple scholars in particular, is the increasingly apparent need for a rigorous and exhaustive sense of history that will provide a foundation for analysis of how the biblical texts fit together with the social, political, and cultural history of ancient Israel. Biblical studies both creates and uses history. Responsibility to scholarship demands the use of the best possible history.

From Exile to Empire: A Response

Julia M. O'Brien

I

I would like to believe that, after two decades of important new scholarship on the Persian period, no one is still teaching what older Hebrew Bible/Old Testament textbooks claimed: that the Persian period is a "dark age" in Israel's history, one for which we have limited sources beyond the biblical texts themselves, and that this period reveals the ossification of Israelite religion into a "incrusted" *Spätjudentum* (as in Wellhausen 1973: 497) or, to use Bernhard Anderson's only slightly less derogatory label, "the weaknesses of Judaism" (1986: 538). I would like to believe that these broad, generic, ideologically driven portrayals have given way to more rich context-specific treatments of this widely studied period.

But I know better.

A random survey of recent textbooks suggests that, while they may avoid the anti-Judaism of earlier generations, they are similarly lacking in significant detail about the Persian period. For example, Michael Coogan's treatment of "The Early Restoration" and "Judah in the Fifth Century BCE" in his 2006 volume does mention that those who returned from Babylon to Yehud lived under Persian governance and even debates under which Persian king Ezra returned, but it does not engage the question of how the sociopolitical reality of Achaemenid rule might inform texts such as Ezra, Nehemiah, Haggai, Zechariah, and Third Isaiah and the community/ies from which they derive. The Ezra-Nehemiah reforms, the politics of the Second Temple, the arguments over the boundaries of the community—indeed, all the dominant concerns of Persian-period biblical texts—are treated as heady theological concerns or indications of intra-Jewish conflict, the evidence for which can be found in other Persian-period biblical texts.

Clearly, if nothing else, we need volumes like the present one to give the sophisticated work being done in Persian-period studies a wider press, better

PR, another shot at getting on the radar of academics who teach and write about the period.

But this volume is not a primer on the Persian period. It does not rehash the debates about the economic and political functions of the Second Temple or explain, again, that we do indeed have extrabiblical documents for the period. Rather, these essays engage the Persian period from particular angles of vision—or, really, from one predominant angle of vision. The large majority of essays take up understandings about empire as a lens through which to read texts, even texts that do not clearly derive from the Persian period. While Berquist's introduction claims that the essays offer diverse perspectives on the Persian period, the volume could just as well be cast as a "Reader in Empire."

The essays reveal that the concept of empire is indeed a fruitful way to engage the literary productions of Persian Yehud. All the authors (in varying degrees) underscore that a dominant external power shaped the politics, economies, and indeed the very contours of the life in Yehud and that, in turn, texts from the period do not debate transhistorical theological issues but instead are embroiled in the human struggle for power and dignity under empire. These essays appropriately challenge the willingness of earlier generations of scholars naïvely to parrot Ezra's and Second Isaiah's description of benevolent Persians kindly allowing exiles to return home. Along with other Persian-period scholarship, they remind us that the Ezra-Nehemiah reforms cannot be nationalistic in the true sense of the term and that Second Isaiah's powerful insistence on monotheism and Yahweh's universal power carry not just theological but also political import.

Yet many of the essays reveal that, in biblical studies as elsewhere in the humanities, the concept of empire itself runs the risk of being broad, generic, and ideologically driven. Once invoked, the label "empire" can become a buzzword, a posture. The Achaemenid regime and the Yehud that it controlled can lose their particularities, giving up their distinctive voices to mouth the scripted lines of the grand imperial narrative.

As others inside and outside the academy have insisted, not all empires are the same. Not all responses to imperial domination are the same—or equally effective. Writing back to the empire is not always the most effective or even the most courageous act of resistance.

A famous example of how opposition to empire is itself contextually specific can be found in the personal correspondence between Mahatma Gandhi and Martin Buber. When Gandhi claimed that the passive resistance strategies used against the British colonizers in India could provide a model for other anticolonial movements, including that of Nazi Germany, Buber protested:

Now, do you know or do you not know, Mahatma, what a concentration camp is like and what goes on there? ... And do you think perhaps that a Jew in Germany could pronounce in public one single sentence of a speech such as yours without being knocked down? ... In the five years which I myself spent under the present régime, I observed many instances of genuine *satyagraha* among the Jews.... Such actions, however, apparently exerted not the slightest influence on their opponents.... A diabolic universal steam-roller cannot thus be withstood.... Testimony without acknowledgement, ineffective, unobserved martyrdom, a martyrdom cast to the winds—that is the fate of innumerable Jews in Germany. (personal response dated 24 February 1939, http://www.gandhiserve.org)

According to Buber, Gandhi's failure to recognize the difference between British and Nazi imperialism rendered his proposal for a "universal" response to empire invalid.

By invoking Buber, I do not imply that his own claims are self-evident or pure. For Buber, the uniqueness of the Nazi horror justified a unique response: the remaking of Palestine into a Jewish homeland. His response to empire was no less ethically complex than that of other postcolonial responses, but, to underscore my point, it *was* contextually specific.

Reading many of the essays in this volume left me wondering what distinguishes "empire" in a Persian context from that of Neo-Babylonian or Neo-Assyrian contexts. How did the responses to empire in Persian texts compare with previous anti-imperial responses in the people's past? I was puzzled, too, when the experience of living in Babylon as an exile was conflated with living in Yehud under Persian overlords. Surely the situations share important elements, but if the information we have about the Persian period is to be taken seriously, then the difference between Neo-Babylonian policy and that of the Achaemenids warrants attention.

II

For this reason, I find most interesting and convincing those essays that are rich in detail and focused on particularities, ones that attempt to distinguish the Persian Empire from others while still reaping the fruits of this overall approach.

Strawn's treatment of Isa 60 is particularly successful in this regard. His analysis of the iconography of imperial propaganda on the Apadana reliefs at Persepolis is attentive to detail—to the position of the reliefs in space, to their use of symbols, to the artist's technique for directing our eye, and to the parallels between the reliefs and Persian documentary evidence. Key to his argument, however, are the details of the postures of the subjects portrayed in the act of bearing tribute to the king. By contrasting the poses on the Adapana reliefs with the poses of subject peoples on Neo-Assyrian imperial products such as the Black Obelisk, Strawn is able to show the *distinctively Persian* ideology of the grateful, willing subject. Moreover, once he establishes that the willing, joyful acceptance of the empire was a propagandistic motif of the Persians *in contrast to that of other empires*, Strawn can demonstrate that the depiction of Yahweh as a willingly embraced cosmic ruler in Isa 60 responds specifically to *Persian* imperial claims. Strawn's claim could be corroborated further by comparing his treatment of the Persian reliefs with Cynthia Chapman's work on Neo-Assyrian imperial iconography and its adoption/adaptation in the biblical prophetic literature (2004). Both Strawn and Chapman show biblical writers riffing on the iconography of empire—but in different ways due to the differences in empire, or at least in that empire's public face.

Although her use of poststructural intertextuality is puzzling given her historical project, Mitchell is also context-specific when she traces the rise of historiography in Persian colonies. Both in Yehud and in Greece via Herodotus, she maintains, national narratives were a means of "writing back to empire." Mitchell's acknowledgement that an identity-forming national narrative of the oppressed can also be adopted by the oppressor for nationalistic purposes is an important one, but also one that is left unmined for its significance. In reading "nationalistic" texts, how do we know which are from empire and which are in opposition to empire?

III

Several essays are evocative and engaging but could benefit from more of the detail I have discussed. Berquist's suggestion that the Psalms (indirectly) serve imperial interests by shaping "individual experiences and emotions into socially accepted expressions" intriguingly challenges the common assumption that the religious expression of the psalms is somehow removed from the political realities in which that religiosity was expressed. But, especially because the thesis seems fruitful, I want details. I want close readings of texts. I want to know how Berquist's claim that Psalms portrays Yahweh as king relates to other studies, such as that by Gerald Wilson (1993), who argues that the Psalter has been thoroughly and consciously edited into a book that walks a sequential reader from allegiance to a human king to acceptance of a divine king. I want more discussion of the diverse political functions that utopian visions like that of the Psalms can perform.

Janzen appropriately focuses on Ezra 9–10, a key text in the history of the interpretation of the Persian period. In a bad paraphrase of William

Carlos Williams, everything depends on the Ezra-Nehemiah reforms. Are they evidence that the postexilic community became narrow and exclusivistic, or perhaps more sexist or racist? Are they the direct response to Persian mandates? Are they a response to the challenge that foreigners posed to the returnees' land rights? Jansen's argument is that the reforms parallel the witchcraft crazes of other cultures, in which women are scapegoated when the community believes that its social norms are being violated. While this line of thought takes the text's purity language more seriously than do other interpreters, Jansen does not go far enough to name just which social norms were under threat or who the "foreign" women were.

Other essays are interesting on methodological grounds but reveal little about the Persian period. For example, Ruiz uses postcolonial theory thoughtfully, distinguishing between different types of empire while still illuminating Ezekiel through discussion with contemporary experiences of colonialization. Following Daniel Smith-Christopher in relying on the work of Frantz Fanon, he argues passionately and persuasively against biblical interpreters who downplay the trauma of exile on the Judahite community. I find his description of exile and colonialization moving, but I remain unclear about how he would apply these observations to the Persian period in the kind of specific, detailed way that he claims is necessary for good postcolonial theory.

In those essays that foreground other methodological approaches, the "Persian-ness" of the texts also frequently fades from view. Koosed's autobiographical feminist reading of Qoheleth was playful and engaging, destabilizing the androcentrism of the text. Is Qoheleth, however, a Persian-period text? And would that even matter to her analysis? If not, how is hers a new perspective on the Persian period?

I expect a Semeia Studies essay to differ from a standard *JBL* article, to speak with a distinctive voice, to do something new—whatever that may be. I expect something "fresher" than the standard academic formula of outlining the state of the question, critiquing previous commentators, and then offering an alternative hypothesis. For that reason, some essays educated me but did not feel "experimental." Knowles faithfully catalogued attitudes toward pilgrimage in various Persian-period texts, and Bautch surveyed the different ways in which scholars read Persian-period texts intertextually, but neither prompted new insights into the period or the method at hand.

IV

There is much here to suggest alternatives to common understandings of individual texts. Kessler's claim that Zech 1–8 is inclusivistic, nonpolemical, and nonexclusionary runs counter to those who would peg the book's interest in the temple as elitist and hierarchical; Marbury's treatment of the אשה זרה in Prov 7 challenges the assumption that all women fared the same in ancient Yehud; and Polaski engages the debate about the role of texts in Yehud by arguing that in Joshua, as in the Achaemenid documentary evidence, authority is granted to textuality itself rather than to the actual content of texts.

But the importance of this volume derives less from the merits of individual essays than from the repeated, dogged insistence that Persian-period texts cannot be read apart from the ideological and material dimensions of the empire in which they were created. At least here, it is clear that Berquist is right that our paradigm for interpreting this period has shifted from that of exile-to-restoration to life under/with empire.

BIBLIOGRAPHY

Ackerman, Susan. 1991. The Deception of Isaac, Jacob's Dream at Bethel and Incubation on an Animal Skin. Pages 92–120 in *Priesthood and Cult in Ancient Israel*. Edited by Gary A. Anderson and Saul M. Olyan. JSOTSup 125. Sheffield: JSOT Press.

Ackroyd, Peter R. 1968. *Exile and Restoration: A Study of Hebrew Thought of the Sixth Century B.C.* OTL. Philadelphia: Westminster.

———. 1973. *I and II Chronicles, Ezra, Nehemiah*. TBC. London: SCM.

———. 1990. The Biblical Portrayal of Achaemenid Rulers. Pages 1–16 in *Achaemenid History V*. Edited by H. Sancisi-Weerdenburg and J. W. Drijvers. Leiden: Nederlands Instituut voor het Nabije Oosten.

Adam, A. K. M., ed. 2001. *Handbook of Postmodern Biblical Interpretation*. St. Louis: Chalice.

Ahlström, Gösta W. 1993. *The History of Ancient Palestine from the Palaeolithic Period to Alexander's Conquest*. Sheffield: JSOT Press.

Ahn, Gregor. 1992. *Religiöse Herrscherlegitimation im achämenidischen Iran: Die Voraussetzungen und die Struktur ihrer Argumentation*. Acta Iranica 31. Leiden: Brill.

Aichele, George, and Gary A. Phillips, eds. 1995. *Intertextuality and the Bible*. Semeia 69/70. Atlanta: Scholars Press.

Albertz, Rainer. 1994. *From the Exile to the Maccabees*. Vol. 2 of *A History of Israelite Religion in the Old Testament Period*. OTL. Louisville: Westminster John Knox.

Albright, W. F. 1963. *The Biblical Period from Abraham to Ezra*. New York: Harper & Row.

Alexander, P. S. 1978. Remarks on Aramaic Epistolography in the Persian Period. *JSS* 23:158–59.

Allen, Leslie C. 1990. *Ezekiel 20–48*. WBC 29. Dallas: Word.

———. 1994. *Ezekiel 1–19*. WBC 28. Dallas: Word.

Alt, A. 1953. Die Rolle Samarias bei der Entstehung des Judentums. Pages 313–37 in idem, *Kleine Schriften II*. Munich: Beck.

Amiet, Pierre. 1974. L'art achéménide. Pages 163–70 in vol. 1 of *Commémoration Cyrus: Actes du Congrès de Shiraz 1971 et autres études rédigées à l'occasion du 2500e anniversaire de la fondation de l'Empire perse*. Leiden: Brill.

————. 1980. *Art of the Ancient Near East.* New York: Abrams.

Amsler, Samuel, André Lacoque, and René Vuilleumier. 1988. *Aggée-Zacharie 1–8, Zacharie 9–14, Malachi.* Geneva: Labor et Fides.

Anbar, Moshé. 1992. *Josue et l'alliance de Sichem (Josue 24:1–28).* BBET 25. Frankfurt: Lang.

Anderson, Bernhard W. 1986. *Understanding the Old Testament.* 4th ed. Englewood Cliffs, N.J.: Prentice-Hall.

Anderson, Francis I., and A. Dean Forbes. 1986. *Spelling in the Hebrew Bible.* BO 41. Rome: Biblical Institute Press.

Ariel, Donald T., Hannah Hirschfeld, and Neta Savir. 2000. Area D1: Stratigraphic Report. Pages 59–62 in *Excavations at the City of David.* Edited by Donald T. Ariel. Qedem 40. Jerusalem: The Hebrew University of Jerusalem, 2000.

Ashcroft, Bill, Gareth Griffiths, and Helen Tiffin, eds. 1989. *The Empire Writes Back: Theory and Practice in Postcolonial Literatures.* London: Routledge.

Astour, Michael C. 1995. Overland Trade Routes in Ancient Western Asia. *CANE* 3:1417–18.

Auld, A. Graeme. 1999. What Was the Main Source of the Books of Chronicles? Pages 91–99 in *The Chronicler as Author: Studies in Text and Texture.* Edited by M. Patrick Graham and Steven L. McKenzie. JSOTSup 263. Sheffield: Sheffield Academic Press.

Avigad, Nahman. 1976. *Bullae and Seals from a Post-Exilic Judean Archive.* Translated by R. Grafman. Qedem 4. Jerusalem: Institute of Archaeology, The Hebrew University of Jerusalem.

Bailey, Randall. 1991. Beyond Identification: The Use of Africans in Old Testament Poetry and Narratives. Pages 165–85 in *Stony the Road We Trod: African American Biblical Interpretation.* Edited by Cain Hope Felder. Minneapolis: Fortress.

Bakhtin, Mikhail M. 1981. Discourse in the Novel. Pages 259–422 in *The Dialogic Imagination: Four Essays.* Edited by Michael Holquist. Translated by Michael Holquist and Caryl Emerson. Austin: University of Texas Press.

————. 1984. *Problems of Dostoevsky's Poetics.* Translated by Caryl Emerson. Minneapolis: University of Minnesota Press.

————. 1986. The Problem of Speech Genres. Pages 60–102 in *Speech Genres and Other Late Essays.* Edited by Caryl Emerson and Michael Holquist. Translated by Vern W. McGee. Austin: University of Texas Press.

Baldwin, Joyce G. 1972. *Haggai, Zechariah, Malachi.* Rochester, Kent: Inter-Varsity Press.

Bar-Kochva, Bezalel. 1996. *Pseudo-Hecataeus, On the Jews: Legitimizing the Jewish Diaspora.* Berkeley and Los Angeles: University of California Press.

Barstad, Hans M. 1996. *The Myth of the Empty Land: A Study in the History and Archaeology of Judah during the "Exilic" Period.* Symbolae Osloenses Fasc. Suppl. 28. Oslo: Scandinavian University Press.

Barth, Frederik. 1969. *Ethnic Groups and Boundaries: The Social Organization of Culture Difference.* Boston: Little & Brown.

Barthélemy, Dominique. 1992. *Ezéchiel, Daniel et les 12 prophètes.* Vol. 3 of *Critique textuelle de l'Ancien Testament.* Fribourg: Editions Universitaires; Göttingen: Vandenhoeck & Ruprecht.

Barthes, Roland. 1983. *Mythologies.* Translated by Annette Lavers. New York: Hill & Wang.

Bastiaens, Jean, Wim Beuken, and Ferenc Postma. 1984. *Trito-Isaiah: An Exhaustive Concordance of Isa 56–66, Especially with Reference to Deutero-Isaiah: An Example of Computer Assisted Research.* Amsterdam: Free University Press.

Bataille, Georges. 1986. *Eroticism: Death and Sensuality.* San Francisco: City Lights.

Batto, Bernard Frank. 1974. *Studies on Women at Mari.* Johns Hopkins Near Eastern Studies. Baltimore: Johns Hopkins University Press.

Bauer, Lutz. 1992. *Zeit des Zweiten Tempels, Zeit der Gerechtigkeit: Zur sozio-ökonomischen Konzeption in Haggai-Sacharja-Maleachi-Korpus.* BEATAJ 31. Frankfurt am Main: Lang.

Bauer-Kayatz, Christa. 1966. *Studien zu Proverbien 1–9: Eine Form- und Motivgeschichtliche Untersuchung unter Einbeziehung ägyptischen Vergleichsmaterial.* WMANT 22. Neukirchen-Vluyn: Neukirchener.

Beal, Timothy K. 1992a. Glossary. Pages 21–24 in Fewell 1992.

———. 1992b. Intertextuality and Ideology: Surplus of Meaning and Controlling the Means of Production. Pages 27–39 in Fewell 1992.

———. 1994. The System and the Speaking Subject in the Hebrew Bible: Reading for Divine Abjection. *BibInt* 2:171–89.

Bedford, Peter R. 2002. Diaspora: Homeland Relations in Ezra-Nehemiah. *VT* 52:147–65.

Behar, Ruth. 1996. *The Vulnerable Observer: Anthropology That Breaks Your Heart.* Boston: Beacon.

Ben Zvi, Ehud. 1995. Inclusion in and Exclusion from "Israel" in Post-monarchic Biblical Texts. Pages 95–149 in *The Pitcher Is Broken: Memorial Essays for Gösta W. Ahlström.* Edited by Steven W. Holloway and Lowell K. Handy. JSOTSup 190. Sheffield: JSOT Press.

———. 1996. Studying Prophetic Texts against Their Original Backgrounds: Preordained Scripts and Alternative Horizons of Research. Pages 125–35 in *Prophets and Paradigms: Essays in Honor of Gene M. Tucker.* Edited by Stephen Breck Reid. JSOTSup 229. Sheffield: JSOT Press.

———. 1998. Looking at the Primary History and the Prophetic Books as Literary/Theological Units within the Frame of the Early Second Temple: Some Considerations. *SJOT* 12:26–43.

Berquist, Jon L. 1995a. *Judaism in Persia's Shadow: A Social and Historical Approach.* Minneapolis: Fortress.

————. 1995b. Reading Difference in Isaiah 56–66: The Interplay of Literary and Sociological Strategies. *Method and Theory in the Study of Religion* 7:23–42.

————. 1995c. The Shifting Frontier: The Achaemenid Empire's Treatment of Western Colonies. *Journal of World-Systems Research* 1/17:1–38.

————. 2006. Constructions of Identity in Postcolonial Yehud. Pages 53–66 in Lipschits and Oeming 2006.

Bertheau, Ernst. 1862. *Die Bücher Esra, Nehemia und Ester.* KeH. Leipzig: Hinzel.

Beuken, Wim A. M. 1967. *Haggai–Sacharja 1–8: Studien zur Überlieferungsgeschichte der frühnachexilischen Prophetie.* SSN 10. Assen: Van Gorcum.

————. 1989. *Jesaja, deel III.* De Prediking van het Oude Testament. Nijkerk: Callenbach.

Beyerlin, Walter. 1977. *"Wir sind wie Träumende": Studien zum 126. Psalm.* SBS 89. Stuttgart: Catholisches Bibelwerk.

————. 1982. *We Are Like Dreamers: Studies in Psalm 126.* Translated by Dinah Livingstone. Edinburgh: T&T Clark.

Bhabha, Homi K. 1994. *The Location of Culture.* New York: Routledge.

Bianchi, F. 1994. Le rôle de Zorobabel et la dynastie davidique en Judée du VIe siècle au IIe siècle av. J.-C. *Transeu* 7:153–65.

Bible and Culture Collective. 1995. *The Postmodern Bible.* New Haven: Yale University Press.

Bird, Phyllis. 1997. *Missing Persons and Mistaken Identities: Women and Gender in Ancient Israel.* OBT. Minneapolis: Fortress.

Bivar, A. D. H. 1975. Document and Symbol in the Art of the Achaemenids. Pages 49–67 in *Monumentum H. S. Nyberg.* Acta Iranica 4. Leiden: Brill.

Black, Jeremy, and Anthony Green. 1992. *Gods, Demons and Symbols of Ancient Mesopotamia: An Illustrated Dictionary.* Austin: University of Texas Press.

Blenkinsopp, Joseph. 1988. *Ezra-Nehemiah: A Commentary.* OTL. Philadelphia: Westminster.

————. 1991. The Social Context of the "Outsider Woman" in Proverbs 1–9. *Bib* 72:457–73.

————. 1996. *A History of Prophecy in Israel.* Rev. ed. Louisville: Westminster John Knox.

————. 1998. The Judaean Priesthood during the Neo-Babylonian and Achaemenid Periods: A Hypothetical Reconstruction. *CBQ* 60:25–43.

————. 2000. A Case of Benign Imperial Neglect and its Consequences. *BibInt* 8:129–36.

Bloch, Renée. 1978. Midrash. Translated by M. H. Callaway. Pages 29–50 in *Approaches to Ancient Judaism: Theory and Practice.* Edited by William Scott Green. BJS 1. Missoula, Mont.: Scholars Press.

Block, Daniel I. 1997. *The Book of Ezekiel Chapters 1–14.* NICOT. Grand Rapids: Eerdmans.

Boda, Mark J. 2003a. From Fasts to Feasts: The Literary Function of Zechariah 7–8. *CBQ* 65:390–407.

———. 2003b. Zechariah: Master Mason or Penitential Prophet. Pages 49–69 in *Yahwism after the Exile: Perspectives on Israelite Religion in the Persian Period.* Edited by Bob Becking and Rainer Albertz. Assen: Van Gorcum.

———. 2005. Terrifying the Horns: Persia and Babylon in Zech 1–6. *CBQ* 67:22–41.

Bodi, Daniel. 2002. *Jérusalem à l'époque perse: "Levons-nous et bâtissons" (Néhémie 2, 18).* Paris: Geuthner.

Boer, Roland, ed. 2001. *A Vanishing Mediator? The Presence/Absence of the Bible in Postcolonialism. Semeia* 88. Atlanta: Society of Biblical Literature.

Boström, Gustav. 1935. *Proverbiastudien: Die Weisheit und das fremde Weib in Sprüche 1–9.* Lunds Universitets Arsskrift 30.3. Lund: Gleerup.

Bowersock, Glen W. 1994. *Fiction as History: Nero to Julian.* Berkeley and Los Angeles: University of California Press.

Boyce, Mary. 1984. Persian Religion in the Achemenid Age. Pages 279–307 in *Introduction; The Persian Period.* Vol. 1. of *The Cambridge History of Judaism.* Edited by W. D. Davies and Louis Finkelstein. Cambridge: Cambridge University Press.

———. 1992. Ahuramazda. *ABD* 1:124–25.

Braun, Roddy L. 1977. A Reconsideration of the Chronicler's Attitude toward the North. *JBL* 96:59–62.

Brayley, I. F. M. 1960. "Yahweh is the Guardian of His Plantation": A Note on Is. 60,21. *Bib* 41:275–86.

Brenner, Athalya. 1995. Some Observations on the Figurations of Woman in Wisdom Literature. Pages 59–61 in *A Feminist Companion to Wisdom Literature.* Edited by Athalya Brenner. FCB 9. Sheffield: Sheffield Academic Press.

Brettler, Marc Zvi. 1995. *The Creation of History in Ancient Israel.* London: Routledge.

Briant, Pierre. 1992. Persian Empire. Translated by Stephen Rosoff. *ABD* 5:236–44.

———. 2002. *From Cyrus to Alexander: A History of the Persian Empire.* Translated by Peter D. Daniels. Winona Lake, Ind.: Eisenbrauns.

Briggs, Charles Augustus, and Emilie Grace Briggs. 1907. *A Critical and Exegetical Commentary on the Book of Psalms.* ICC 13.2. Edinburgh: T&T Clark.

Broome, Edwin C. 1946. Ezekiel's Abnormal Personality. *JBL* 65:277–92.

Brosius, Maria. 1996. *Women in Ancient Persia, 559–331 BC.* Oxford Classical Monographs. Oxford: Oxford University Press.

Brueggemann, Walter. 1984. Unity and Dynamic in the Isaiah Tradition. *JSOT* 29:89–107.

———. 1992. *Old Testament Theology: Essays on Structure, Theme, and Text.* Edited by Patrick D. Miller. Minneapolis: Fortress.

Bulhan, Hussein Abdilahi. 1985. *Frantz Fanon and the Psychology of Oppression.* New York: Plenum

Burghardt, Walter J. 1990. Isaiah 60:1–7. *Int* 44:396–400.

Callenbach, G. F. 1990. The Main Theme of Trito-Isaiah: "The Servants of YHWH." *JSOT* 47:67–87.

Calmeyer, Peter. 1979. Fortuna-Tyche-Khvarnah. *Jahrbuch des Deutschen Archäol. Instituts* 94:347–65.

———. 1987. Greek Historiography and Achaemenid Reliefs. Pages 11–26 in *Achaemenid History II*. Edited by Heleen Sancisi-Weerdenburg and Amélie Kuhrt. Leiden: Nederlands Instituut voor het Nabije Oosten.

———. 1990. Das Persepolis der Spätzeit. Pages 7–36 in *Achaemenid History IV*. Edited by Heleen Sancisi-Weerdenburg and Amélie Kuhrt. Leiden: Nederlands Instituut voor het Nabije Oosten.

———. 1991. Ägyptischer Stil und reichsachaimenidische Inhalte auf dem Sockel der Dareios-Statue aus Susa/Heliopolis. Pages 25–33 in *Achemenid History VI*. Edited by Heleen Sancisi-Weerdenburg and Amélie Kuhrt. Leiden: Nederlands Instituut voor het Nabije Oosten.

———. 1994. Babylonische und assyrische Elemente in der achaimenidischen Kunst. Pages 131–47 in *Achaemenid History VIII*. Edited by Heleen Sancisi-Weerdenburg, Amélie Kuhrt, and Margaret Cool Root. Leiden: Nederlands Instituut voor het Nabije Oosten.

Cameron, George G. 1948. *Persepolis Treasury Tablets*. University of Chicago Oriental Institute Publications 65. Chicago: University of Chicago Press.

Camp, Claudia V. 1985. *Wisdom and the Feminine in the Book of Proverbs*. Bible and Literature Series 11. Sheffield: JSOT Press.

———. 1995. Wise and Strange: An Interpretation of the Female Imagery in Proverbs in Light of Trickster Mythology. Pages 131–56 in *A Feminist Companion to Wisdom Literature*. Edited by Athalya Brenner. FCB 9. Sheffield: Sheffield Academic Press.

Campbell, Anthony F., and Mark A. O'Brien. 2000. *Unfolding the Deuteronomistic History: Origins, Upgrades, Present Text*. Minneapolis: Fortress.

Cardascia, Guillaume. 1951. *Les Archives des Murašû, une famille d'hommes d'affaires babyloniens á l'époque perse (455–403 av. J.-C.)* Paris: Imprimerie Nationale.

Carroll, Robert P. 1986. *Jeremiah: A Commentary*. Philadelphia: Westminster.

———. 1992. The Myth of the Empty Land. *Semeia* 59:79–93.

Carter, Charles E. 1996. A Discipline in Transition: The Contributions of the Social Sciences to the Study of the Hebrew Bible. Pages 3–36 in *Community, Identity, and Ideology: Social Science Approaches to the Hebrew Bible*. Edited by Charles E. Carter and Carol Meyers. Winona Lake, Ind.: Eisenbrauns.

———. 1999. *The Emergence of Yehud in the Persian Period: A Social and Demographic Study*. JSOTSup 294. Sheffield: Sheffield Academic Press.

Causse, Antonin. 1937. *Du groupe ethnique à la communauté religieuse*. Paris: Félix Alcan.

Ceresko, Anthony R. 1982. The Function of *Antanaclasis* (*mṣ'* "Find" // *mṣ'* "to

Reach, Overtake, Grasp") in Hebrew Poetry, Especially in the Book of Qoheleth. *CBQ* 44:551–69.

Chapman, Cynthia. 2004. *The Gendered Language of Warfare in the Israelite-
Assyrian Encounter.* HSM 62. Winona Lake, Ind.: Eisenbrauns.

Charlesworth, James H. 1997. Intertextuality: Isaiah 40:3 and the Serek ha-Yahad.
Pages 97–224 in *The Quest for Context and Meaning: Studies in Biblical
Intertextuality in Honor of James A. Sanders.* Edited by Craig A. Evans and
Shemaryahu Talmon. BibInt 28. Leiden: Brill.

Chary, Theophane. 1969. *Aggée, Zacharie, Malachie.* SB. Paris: Gabalda.

Childs, Brevard. 1979. *Introduction to the Old Testament as Scripture.* Philadelphia: Fortress.

Clements, Ronald E. 1983. *A Century of Old Testament Study.* Rev. ed. Guildford:
Lutterworth.

———. 1996. *Ezekiel.* Westminster Bible Companion. Louisville: Westminster
John Knox.

———. 1997. "Arise, Shine; For Your Light Has Come": A Basic Theme of the
Isaianic Tradition. Pages 441–54 in vol. 1 of *Writing and Reading the Scroll
of Isaiah: Studies of an Interpretive Tradition.* Edited by Craig C. Broyles and
Craig A. Evans. VTSup 70. Leiden: Brill.

Clifford, Richard J. 1993. Woman Wisdom in the Book of Proverbs. Pages 61–
72 in *Biblische Theologie und gesellschaftlicher Wandel für Norbert Lohfink,
S.J.* Edited by Georg Braulik, Walter Groß, and Sean McEvenue. Freiburg:
Herder.

———. 1998. *The Wisdom Literature.* IBT. Nashville: Abingdon.

———. 1999. *Proverbs: A Commentary.* OTL. Louisville: Westminster John Knox.

Clines, David J. A. 1984. *Ezra, Nehemiah, Esther.* NCBC 15. Grand Rapids: Eerdmans.

Coggins, R. J. 1987. *Haggai, Zechariah, Malachi.* OTG. Sheffield: JSOT Press.

Cohen, Shaye J. D. 1999. *The Beginnings of Jewishness: Boundaries, Varieties,
Uncertainties.* Berkeley and Los Angeles: University of California Press.

Collins, John J. 1997. Marriage, Divorce, and Family in Second Temple Judaism.
Pages in *Families in Ancient Israel.* Edited by Leo G. Perdue, Joseph Blenkin-
sopp, John J. Collins, and Carol Meyers. The Family, Religion, and Culture.
Louisville: Westminster John Knox.

Collon, Dominique. 1987. *First Impressions: Cylinder Seals in the Ancient Near
East.* Chicago: University of Chicago.

———. 1995. *Ancient Near Eastern Art.* Berkeley and Los Angeles: University of
California.

Conrad, Edgar W. 1999. *Zechariah.* Readings, a New Biblical Commentary. Sheffield: Sheffield Academic Press.

Coogan, Michael D. 1987. Canaanite Origins and Lineage: Reflections on the
Religion of Ancient Israel. Pages 115–24 in *Ancient Israelite Religion: Essays*

in Honor of Frank Moore Cross. Edited by Patrick D. Miller Jr., Paul D. Hanson, and S. Dean McBride. Philadelphia: Fortress.

———. 2006. *The Old Testament: A Historical and Literary Introduction to the Hebrew Scriptures.* New York: Oxford University Press.

Cook, John M. 1983. *The Persian Empire.* New York: Schocken.

Cowley, Arthur E. 1923. *Aramaic Papyri of the Fifth Century B.C.* Oxford: Oxford University Press.

Crenshaw, James L. 1985. Education in Ancient Israel. *JBL* 104:601–15.

———. 1987. *Ecclesiastes.* OTL. Philadelphia: Westminster.

———. 1990. The Sage in Proverbs. Pages 205–16 in *The Sage in Israel and the Ancient Near East.* Edited by John G. Gammie and Leo G. Perdue. Winona Lake, Ind.: Eisenbrauns.

Cross, Frank Moore. 1973. *Canaanite Myth and Hebrew Epic: Essays in the History of the Religion of Israel.* Cambridge: Harvard University Press.

Crow, Loren D. 1996. *The Songs of Ascents (Psalms 120–134): Their Place in Israelite History and Religion.* SBLDS 148. Atlanta: Scholars Press.

Culler, Jonathan. 1981. *The Pursuit of Signs: Semiotics, Literature, Deconstruction.* Ithaca, N.Y.: Cornell University Press.

Curtis, John. 1989. *Ancient Persia.* London: British Museum Publications.

Dahood, Mitchell. 1965–70. *Psalms.* 3 vols. AB 16–17A. Garden City, N.Y.: Doubleday.

———. 1975. The Aleph in Psalm CXXVII 2. *Or* 44:103–5.

Danby, Herbert. 1933. *The Mishnah: Translated from the Hebrew with Introduction and Brief Explanatory Notes.* Oxford: Oxford University Press.

Dandamayev, Muhammad A. 1984a. Royal *Paradeisoi* in Babylonia. Pages 113–17 in *Orientalia J. Duchesne-Guillemin Emerito Oblata.* Acta Iranica 23. Leiden: Brill.

———. 1984b. *Slavery in Babylonia: From Nabopolassar to Alexander the Great (621–331 B.C.).* Translated by V. A. Powell. Dekalb: North Illinois University Press.

Dandamayev, Muhammad A., and Vladimir G. Lukonin. 1989. *The Culture and Social Institutions of Ancient Iran.* Cambridge: Cambridge University Press.

Davies, Graham I. 1991. *Ancient Hebrew Inscriptions: Corpus and Concordance.* Cambridge: Cambridge University Press.

Davies, Philip R. 1992. *In Search of "Ancient Israel."* JSOTSup 148. Sheffield: JSOT Press.

———. 1995. *In Search of "Ancient Israel."* Rev. ed. JSOTSup 148. Sheffield: Sheffield Academic Press.

———. 1998. *Scribes and Schools: The Canonization of the Hebrew Scriptures.* Library of Ancient Israel. Louisville: Westminster John Knox.

De Groot, Alon, and Donald T. Ariel. 2000. Ceramic Report. Page 98 in *Excavations at the City of David.* Edited by Donald T. Ariel. Qedem 40. Jerusalem: The Hebrew University of Jerusalem.

Delitzsch, Franz. 1898. *A Biblical Commentary on the Psalms.* Translated by Francis Bolton. Edinburgh: T&T Clark.

Delitzsch, Franz. 1966. *Biblical Commentary on the Old Testament: Proverbs, Ecclesiastes, Song of Songs.* Peabody, Mass.: Hendrickson. [orig. 1875]

Demsky, Aaron. 1999. Double Names in the Babylonian Exile and the Identity of Sheshbazzar. Pages 23–39 in *These Are the Names.* Edited by Aaron Demsky. Ramat Gan: Bar Ilan University Press.

Depla, A. 1994. Women in Ancient Egyptian Wisdom Literature. Pages 24–52 in *Women in Ancient Societies: An Illusion of the Night.* Edited by Léonie J. Archer, Susan Fischler and Maria Wyke.. London: Macmillan.

Dever, William G. 1985. Syro-Palestinian and Biblical Archaeology. Pages 31–74 in *The Hebrew Bible and Its Modern Interpreters.* Edited by Douglas A. Knight and Gene M. Tucker. Minneapolis: Fortress.

Diebner, Bernd-Jörg. 1992. Entre Israël et Israël, le Canon. Pages 101–12 in *Le livre de traverse: De l'exégèse biblique a l'anthropologie.* Edited by Olivier Abel and Françoise Smyth. Paris: Cerf.

Dietrich, Ernst Ludwig. 1925. *Die endzeitliche Wiederherstellung bei den Propheten.* BZAW 40. Giessen: Töpelmann.

Dillon, Matthew. 1997. *Pilgrims and Pilgrimage in Ancient Greece.* London: Routledge.

Dirlik, Arif. 1997. *The Postcolonial Aura: Third World Criticism in the Age of Global Capitalism.* Boulder, Colo.: Westview.

Dobbs-Allsopp, F. W. 1998. Linguistic Evidence for the Date of Lamentations. *JANESCU* 26:1–36.

Dombrowski, Bruno. W. W. 1997. Socio-religious Implications of Foreign Impact on Palestinian Jewry under Achaemenid Rule. *Transeu* 13: 65–89.

Donaldson, Laura E., ed. 1996. *Postcolonialism and Scriptural Reading. Semeia* 75. Atlanta: Scholars Press.

Donner, Herbert. 1988. Psalm 122. Pages 86–89 in *Text and Context: Old Testament and Semitic Studies for F. C. Fensham.* Edited by Walter Claassen. JSOTSup 48. Sheffield: Sheffield Academic Press.

Douglas, Mary. 1966. *Purity and Danger: An Analysis of the Concepts of Pollution and Taboo.* London: Routledge.

———. 1973. *Natural Symbols: Explorations in Cosmology.* New York: Vintage.

Driver, Samuel R. 1960. *An Introduction to the Literature of the Old Testament.* 9th ed. New York: Meridian.

Duggan, Michael W. 2001. *The Covenant Renewal in Ezra-Nehemiah (Neh 7:72b–10:40): An Exegetical, Literary, and Theological Study.* SBLDS 164. Atlanta: Society of Biblical Literature.

Duguid, Ian M. 1994. *Ezekiel and the Leaders of Israel.* VTSup 56. Leiden: Brill

Duhm, Bernard. 1968. *Das Buch Jesaja.* 5th ed. HKAT 3.1. Göttingen: Vandenhoeck & Ruprecht. (orig. 1892)

Dupont-Sommer, André, and Jean Starcky. 1958. *Les Inscriptions Araméennes de Sfiré*. Paris: Imprimerie Nationale.

Dyck, Jonathan E. 1998. *The Theocratic Ideology of the Chronicler*. BIS 33. Leiden: Brill.

———. 2000. Ezra 2 in Ideological Critical Perspective. Pages 129–45 in *Rethinking Contexts, Rereading Texts*. Edited by M. Daniel Carroll R. JSOTSup 299. Sheffield: Sheffield Academic Press.

Eagleton, Terry. 1998. Postcolonialism and "Postcolonialism." *Interventions: International Journal of Postcolonial Studies* 1/1:24–26.

———. 1999. In the Gaudy Supermarket. *London Review of Books* 21:10 (13 May). Online: http://www.lrb.co.uk/v21/n10/eagl01_.html.

Eichrodt, Walther. 1968. *Der Prophet Hesekiel*. ATD 22. Göttingen: Vandenhoeck & Ruprecht.

Eissfeldt, Otto. 1965. *The Old Testament: An Introduction*. Translated by Peter R. Ackroyd. New York: Harper & Row.

Elgavish, Joseph. 1993. Shiqmona. *NEAEHL* 4:1375.

Eliade, Mircea. 1958. *Patterns in Comparative Religion*. Translated by Rosemary Sheed. New York: Sheed & Ward.

Elliger, Karl. 1928. *Die Einheit des Tritojesaia, Jesaia 56–66*. BWANT 3/9. Stuttgart: Kohlhammer.

Emerton, John A. 1974. The Meaning of šēnā' in Psalm CXXVII 2. *VT* 24:15–31.

Eskenazi, Tamara Cohn. 1992. Out from the Shadows: Biblical Women in the Post-exilic Era. *JSOT* 54:25–43.

Falkenstein, Adam, and Wolfram von Soden. 1953. *Sumerische und akkadische Hymnen und Gebete*. Zurich: Artemis.

Fanon, Frantz. 1952. *Peau Noire, Masques Blancs*. Points 26. Paris: Seuil.

———. 1959. *L'an V de la Révolution Algérienne*. Cahiers libres 3. Paris: Maspero.

———. 1961. *Les Damnés de la Terre*. Cahiers libres 27–28. Paris: Maspero.

———. 1963. *The Wretched of the Earth*. Translated by Constance Farrington. New York: Grove.

———. 1965. *A Dying Colonialism*. Translated by Haakon Chevalier. New York: Grove.

———. 1967. *Black Skin, White Masks*. Translated by Charles L. Markmann. New York: Grove.

Fantalkin, Alexander, and Oren Tal. 2006. Redating Lachish Level 1: Identifying Achaemienid Imperial Policy at the Southern End of the Fifth Satrapy. Pages 167–97 in Lipschits and Oeming 2006.

Farkas, Ann E. 1974. *Achaemenid Sculpture*. Istanbul: Nederlands Historisch-Archaeologisch Instituut in het Nabije Oosten.

Fenn, Richard. 1997. *The End of Time: Religion, Ritual, and the Forging of the Soul*. Cleveland: Pilgrim.

Fetterly, Judith. 1978. *The Resisting Reader: A Feminist Approach to American Fiction*. Bloomington: Indiana University Press.

Fewell, Danna Nolan, ed. 1992. *Reading between Texts: Intertextuality and the Hebrew Bible.* LCBI. Louisville: Westminster John Knox.

Fishbane, Michael. 1985. *Biblical Interpretation in Ancient Israel.* Oxford: Clarendon.

Fitzmyer, Joseph A. 1995. *The Aramaic Inscription of Sefire.* Rev. ed. BO 19A. Rome: Pontifical Biblical Institute.

Floyd, Michael H. 1997. Cosmos and History in Zechariah's View of the Restoration (Zechariah 1:7–6:15). Pages 125–44 in *Problems in Biblical Theology: Essays in Honor of Rolf Knierim.* Edited by Henry T. C. Sun and Keith L. Eades. Grand Rapids: Eerdmans.

———. 2000. *Minor Prophets.* FOTL 22. Grand Rapids: Eerdmans.

Fontaine, Carole R. 1992. Ecclesiastes. Pages 153–55 in *The Women's Bible Commentary.* Edited by Carol A. Newsom and Sharon H. Ringe. Louisville: Westminster John Knox.

———. 1995. The Social Roles of Women in the World of Wisdom. Pages 24–49 in *A Feminist Companion to Wisdom Literature.* Edited by Athalya Brenner. FCB 9. Sheffield: Sheffield Academic.

Fornara, Charles William. 1983. *The Nature of History in Ancient Greece and Rome.* Berkeley and Los Angeles: University of California Press.

Fox, Michael V. 1995. World Order and Ma'at: A Crooked Parallel. *JANESCU* 23:37–48.

———. 1997. Ideas of Wisdom in Proverbs 1–9. *JBL* 116: 613–33.

Frankfort, Henri. 1996. *The Art and Architecture of the Ancient Orient.* 5th ed. Pelican History of Art. New Haven: Yale University Press.

Freedman, David N. 1983. The Spelling of the Name "David" in the Hebrew Bible. *HAR* 7:89–102.

Freedy, K. S., and Donald B. Redford. 1970. The Dates in Ezekiel in Relation to Biblical, Babylonian and Egyptian Sources. *JAOS* 90:462–85.

Frei, Peter. 2001. Persian Imperial Authorization: A Summary. Translated by James W. Watts. Pages 5–40 in *Persia and Torah: The Theory of Imperial Authorization of the Pentateuch.* Edited by James W. Watts. SBLSymS 17. Atlanta: Society of Biblical Literature.

Frei, Peter, and Klaus Koch. 1996. *Reichsidee und Reichsorganisation im Perserreich.* 2d ed. OBO 55. Fribourg: Universitätsverlag.

Fried, Lisbeth S. 2002. The Political Struggle of Fifth Century Judah. *Transeu* 24:9–21.

Friedberg, A. D. 2000. A New Clue in the Dating of the Composition of the Book of Esther. *VT* 50:561–65.

Frymer-Kensky, Tikva. 1992. *In the Wake of the Goddesses: Women, Culture and the Biblical Transformation of Pagan Myth.* New York: Ballantine.

Galling, Kurt. 1952. Die Exilswende in der Sicht des Propheten Sacharja. *VT* 2:18–36.

———. 1954. *Die Bücher der Chronik, Esra, Nehemia.* ATD 12. Göttingen: Vandenhoeck & Ruprecht.

———. 1964. *Studien zur Geschichte Israels im persichen Zeitalter.* Tübingen: Mohr Siebeck.

Gandhi, Leela. 1998. *Postcolonial Theory: A Critical Introduction.* New York: Columbia University Press.

Gangloff, Frédéric. 2002. Le pays dévasté et dépeuplé: Genèse d'une idéologie biblique et d'un concepte sioniste: Ene esquisse. *BN* 113:39–50.

Garber, Marjorie. 1996. Overcoming "Auction Block": Stories Masquerading as Objects. Pages 110–20 in *Confessions of the Critics: North American Critics' Autobiographical Moves.* Edited H. Aram Veeser. New York: Routledge.

Garbini, Giovanni. 1988. *History and Ideology in Ancient Israel.* Translated by John Bowden. New York: Crossroad.

García-Treto, Francisco. 2000. Hyphenating Joseph: A View of Genesis 39–41 from the Cuban Diaspora. Pages 134–45 in *Interpreting Beyond Borders.* Edited by Fernando F. Segovia. The Bible and Postcolonialism 3. Sheffield: Sheffield Academic Press.

Garelli, P. 1995. Les déplacements de personnes dans l'empire assyrien. Pages 79–82 in *Immigration and Emigration within the Ancient Near East: Festschrift E. Lipiński:* Edited by Karel van Lerberghe and Antoon Schoors. Leuven: Uitgeverij Peeters en Department Oriëntalistiek.

Garrison, Mark B., and Margaret Cool Root, eds. 1996. *Achaemenid History IX: Persepolis Seal Studies.* Leiden: Nederlands Instituut voor het Nabije Oosten.

Gaster, Theodor H. 1969. *Myth, Legend, and Custom in the Old Testament: A Comparative Study with Chapters from Sir James G. Frazer's Folklore in the Old Testament.* 2 vols. New York: Harper & Row.

Geertz, Clifford. 1973. Ideology as a Cultural System. Pages 193–233 in idem, *The Interpretation of Cultures: Selected Essays.* New York: HarperCollins.

Gershevitch, Ilya. 1979. The Alloglottography of Old Persian. Pages 114–90 in *Transactions of the Philological Society: 1979.* Oxford: Blackwell.

Gesenius, Wilhelm. 1839. *Thesaurus Philologicus Criticus Linguae Hebrae et Chaldae Veteris Testamenti.* 2d ed. Leipzig: Vogelius.

Geuss, Raymond. 1981. *The Idea of a Critical Theory: Habermas and the Frankfurt School.* New York: Cambridge University Press.

Ghirshman, Roman. 1962. *Arte Persiana: Proto-Iranici, Medi e Achemenidi.* Milan: Feltrinelli.

Glueck, Nelson. 1959. *Rivers in the Desert: A History of the Negev.* New York: Farrar, Straus & Cudahy.

Gnoli, Gherardo. 1974. Politique religieuse et conception de la royauté sous les Achemenides. *Acta Iranica* 2:117–90.

González, Justo L. 1996. *Santa Biblia: The Bible through Hispanic Eyes.* Nashville: Abingdon.

Gordon, Lewis R., T. Denean Sharpley-Whiting, and Renee T. White, eds. 1996. *Fanon: A Critical Reader*. London: Blackwell.

Gottwald, Norman K. 1992. Social Class and Ideology in Isaiah 40–55: An Eagletonian Reading. *Semeia* 59:43–57.

Grabbe, Lester L. 1992. *The Persian and Greek Periods*. Vol. 1 of *Judaism from Cyrus to Hadrian*. Minneapolis: Fortress.

———. 1998a. *Ezra-Nehemiah*. Old Testament Readings. London: Routledge.

———, ed. 1998b. *Leading Captivity Captive: "The Exile" as History and Ideology*. JSOTSup 278. Sheffield: Sheffield Academic Press.

———. 2001. The Law of Moses in the Ezra Tradition: More Virtual Than Real? Pages 91–113 in *Persia and Torah: The Theory of Imperial Authorization of the Pentateuch*. Edited by James W. Watts. SBLSymS 17. Atlanta: Society of Biblical Literature.

Graf, D. F. 1993. The Persian Royal Road System in Syria-Palestine. *Transeu* 6:149–67.

———. 1994. The Persian Royal Road System. Pages 167–89 in *Achaemenid History VIII: Continuity and Change*. Edited by H. Sancisi-Weerdenburg, A. Kuhrt, and M. C. Root. Leiden: Nederlands Instituut voor het Nabije Oosten.

Graffy, Adrian. 1984. *A Prophet Confronts His People: The Disputation Speech in the Prophets*. AnBib 104. Rome: Pontifical Biblical Institute.

Green, Barbara. 2000. *Mikhail Bakhtin and Biblical Scholarship: An Introduction*. SemeiaSt 38. Atlanta: Society of Biblical Literature.

Greenberg, Moshe. 1983. *Ezekiel 1–20: A New Translation with Introduction and Commentary*. AB 22. Garden City, N.Y.: Doubleday.

———. 1990. Biblical Attitudes toward Power: Ideal and Reality in Law and Prophets. Pages 101–12, 120–25 in *Religion and Law*. Edited by Edwin B. Firmage, Bernard G. Weiss, and John W. Welch. Winona Lake, Ind.: Eisenbrauns.

Greenfield, Jonas C., and Bezalel Porten. 1982. *The Bisitun Inscription of Darius the Great: Aramaic Version*. London: Lund Humphries.

Gressman, Hugo, ed. 1927. *Altorientalische Bilder zum Alten Testament*. 2d ed. Berlin: de Gruyter.

Grossberg, Daniel G. 1989. *Centripetal and Centrifugal Structures in Biblical Poetry*. SBLMS 39. Atlanta: Scholars Press.

Gunneweg, Antonius H. J. 1983. ʿm hʾrṣ—A Semantic Revolution. *ZAW* 95: 437–40.

Gunter, Ann C. 1990. Models of the Orient in the Art History of the Orientalizing Period. Pages 130–47 in *Achaemenid History V*. Edited by H. Sancisi-Weerdenburg and J. W. Drijvers. Leiden: Nederlands Instituut voor het Nabije Oosten.

Habel, Norman C. 1972. "Yahweh, Maker of Heaven and Earth": A Study in Tradition Criticism. *JBL* 91:321–37.

Hall, Jonathan. 1997. *Ethnic Identity in Greek Antiquity.* Cambridge: Cambridge University Press.

Hallock, Richard T. 1969. *Persepolis Fortification Tablets.* University of Chicago Oriental Institute Publications 92. Chicago: University of Chicago Press.

———. 1985. The Evidence of the Persepolis Tablets. Pages 588–609 in *The Median and Achaemenian Periods.* Vol. 2 of *The Cambridge History of Iran.* Edited by Ilya Gershevitch. Cambridge: Cambridge University Press.

Halperin, David J. 1993. *Seeking Ezekiel: Text and Psychology.* University Park: Pennsylvania State University Press.

Halpern, Baruch. 1988. *The First Historians: The Hebrew Bible and History.* San Francisco: Harper & Row.

———. 1998. The New Names of Isaiah 62:4: Jeremiah's Reception in the Restoration and the Politics of "Third Isaiah." *JBL* 117:623–43.

Hamilton, Mark W. 1995. Who Was a Jew? Jewish Ethnicity during the Achaemenid Period. *ResQ* 37:102–17.

Hanson, Paul D. 1979. *The Dawn of Apocalyptic: The Historical and Sociological Roots of Jewish Apocalyptic Eschatology.* Philadelphia: Fortress.

———. 1995. *Isaiah 40–66.* IBC. Louisville: John Knox.

Hartog, Francois. 1988. *The Mirror of Herodotus: The Representation of the Other in the Writing of History.* Translated by Janet Lloyd. Berkeley and Los Angeles: University of California Press.

Hawk, L. Daniel. 1991. *Every Promise Fulfilled: Contesting Plots in Joshua.* LCBI. Louisville: Westminster John Knox.

Herrenschmidt, Clarisse. 1987. Notes sur la parente chez les Perses au debut de l'empire Achemenide. Pages 53–67 in *Achaemenid History II: The Greek Sources.* Edited by Heleen Sancisi-Weerdenburg and Amélie Kuhrt. Leiden: Nederlands Instituut voor het Nabije Oosten.

Herzfeld, Ernst Emil. 1941. *Iran in the Ancient Near East.* London: Oxford University Press.

Hiebert, Theodore. 1992. Theophany in the OT. *ABD* 6:505–11.

Hill, Andrew E. 1981. The Book of Malachi: Its Place in Post-exilic Chronology Linguistically Reconsidered. Ph.D. diss. University of Michigan.

———. 1983. Dating the Book of Malachi: A Linguistic Reexamination. Pages 77–89 in *The Word of the Lord Shall Go Forth: Essays in Honor of David Noel Freedman in Celebration of His Sixtieth Birthday.* Edited by Carol L. Meyers and Michael O'Connor. Winona Lake, Ind.: Eisenbrauns.

———. 1998. *Malachi: A New Translation with Introduction and Commentary.* AB 25D. New York: Doubleday.

Hinnells, John R. 1973. *Persian Mythology.* London: Hamlyn.

Hinz, Walther. 1971. Achämenidische Hofverwaltung. *ZA* 61260–311.

———. 1976. *Darius und die Perser: Eine Kulturgeschichte der Archämeniden.* Baden-Baden: Holle.

Hoglund, Kenneth. 1991. The Achaemenid Context. Pages 54–72 in *Second Temple Studies 1. The Persian Period*. Edited by Philip R. Davies. JSOTSup 117. Sheffield: Sheffield Academic Press.

———. 1992. *Achaemenid Imperial Administration in Syria-Palestine and the Missions of Ezra and Nehemiah*. SBLDS 125. Atlanta: Scholars Press.

Hopkins, David. 1996. Farmsteads. *OEAANE* 2:306–7.

Hornblower, Simon. 1994. Introduction: Summary of Papers; The Story of Greek Historiography; Intertextuality and the Greek Historians. Pages 1–72 in *Greek Historiography*. Edited by Simon Hornblower. Oxford: Clarendon.

Humbert, P. 1937. La 'femme étrangère' du livre des Proverbs. *RES* 2:49–64.

Hurvitz, Avi. 1968. The Chronological Significance of "Aramaisms" in Biblical Hebrew. *IEJ* 18:234–40.

———. 1972. *The Transition Period in Biblical Hebrew: A Study in Post-Exilic Hebrew and Its Implications for the Dating of Psalms* [Hebrew]. Jerusalem: Bialik Institute.

———. 1995. Continuity and Innovation in Biblical Hebrew—The Case of "Semantic Change" in Post-Biblical Hebrew. Pages 1–10 in *Studies in Ancient Hebrew Semantics*. Edited by T. Muraoka. Abr-Nahrain Sup 4. Leuven: Peeters.

Hutton, Rodney R. 1992. Korah. *ABD* 4:100–101.

Ibarra, Ignacio. 2003. Border Deaths Now Total 100. *Arizona Daily Star*, 22 July 2003. Online: http://www.azstarnet.com/star/tue/30722CrossingDeaths.html.

Isasi-Díaz, Ada María. 1995. "By the Rivers of Babylon": Exile as a Way of Life. Pages 149–64 in *Social Location and Biblical Interpretation in the United States*. Vol. 1 of *Reading from This Place*. Edited by Fernando F. Segovia and Mary Ann Tolbert. Minneapolis: Fortress.

Jacoby, Russell. 1995. Marginal Returns: The Trouble with Post-colonial Theory. *Lingua Franca* 5/6 (September/October): 30–37.

Janzen, David. 2002. *Witch-Hunts, Purity and Social Boundaries: The Expulsion of the Foreign Women in Ezra 9–10*. JSOTSup 350. New York: Continuum.

Japhet, Sara. 1983. People and Land in the Restoration Period. Pages 103–25 in *Das Land Israel in biblischer Zeit*. Edited by Georg Strecker. Göttingen: Vandenhoeck and Ruprecht.

———. 1989. *The Ideology of the Book of Chronicles and Its Place in Biblical Thought*. Translated by Anna Barber. BEATAJ 9. Frankfurt am Main: Lang.

———. 1991. "History" and "Literature" in the Persian Period: The Restoration of the Temple. Pages 174–88 in *Ah, Assyria…: Studies in Assyrian History and Ancient Near Eastern Historiography Presented to Hayim Tadmor*. Edited by Mordechai Cogan and Israel Eph'al. Jerusalem: Magnes.

———. 2003. Periodization: Between History and Ideology—The Neo-Babylonian Period in Biblical Historiography. Pages 75–89 in Lipschits and Blenkinsopp 2003.

Jeremias, Jörg. 1977. *Theophanie: Die Geschichte einer alttestamentlichen Gattung.* 2d ed. Neukirchen-Vluyn: Neukirchener.

Joosten, Jan. 1996. *People and Land in the Holiness Code: An Exegetical Study of the Law in Leviticus 17–26.* VTSup 67. Leiden: Brill.

Keel, Othmar. 1997. *The Symbolism of the Biblical World: Ancient Near Eastern Iconography and the Book of Psalms.* Winona Lake, Ind.: Eisenbrauns.

Keel, Othmar, and Christoph Uehlinger. 1994a. Der Assyrerkönig Salmanassar III. und Jehu von Israel auf dem Schwarzen Obelisken aus Nimrud. *ZTK* 116:391–420.

———. 1994b. Jahwe und die Sonnengottheit von Jerusalem. Pages 269–306 in *Ein Gott allein? JHWH-Verehrung und biblischer Monotheismus im Kontext der israelitischen und altorientalischen Religionsgeschichte.* Edited by Walter Dietrich and Martin A. Klopfenstein. OBO 139. Fribourg: Universitätsverlag; Göttingen: Vandenhoeck & Ruprecht.

———. 1998. *Gods, Goddesses, and Images of God in Ancient Israel.* Minneapolis: Fortress.

Keet, Cuthbert C. 1967. *A Study of the Psalms of Ascents: A Critical and Exegetical Commentary upon Psalms CXX to CXXXIV.* London: Mitre.

Keil, C. F. 1888. *The Books of Ezra, Nehemiah, and Esther.* Translated by Sophia Taylor. Clark's Foreign Theological Library 4/38. Edinburgh: T&T Clark.

Kelly, Brian E. 1996. *Retribution and Eschatology in Chronicles.* JSOTSup 211. Sheffield: Sheffield Academic Press.

Kent, Roland G. 1953. *Old Persian: Grammar, Texts, Lexicon.* 2d ed. AOS 33. New Haven: American Oriental Society.

Kessler, John. 1992. The Second Year of Darius and the Prophet Haggai. *Transeu* 5:63–84.

———. 2001. Reconstructing Haggai's Jerusalem: Demographic and Sociological Considerations and the Quest for an Adequate Methodological Point of Departure. Pages 137–58 in *Every City Shall Be Forsaken: Urbanism and Prophecy in Ancient Israel and the Near East.* Edited by Lester L. Grabbe and Robert D. Haak. JSOTSup 330. Sheffield: Sheffield University Press.

———. 2002. *The Book of Haggai: Prophecy and Society in Early Persian Yehud.* Leiden: Brill.

———. 2006. Persia's Loyal Yahwists: Power, Identity and Ethnicity in Achaemenid Yehud. Pages 91–121 in Lipschits and Oeming 2006.

Knauf, E. A. 2002. Elephantine und das vor-biblische Judentum. *Religion und Religionskontakte im Zeitaler der Achämeniden.* Edited by R. G. Kratz. Gütersloh: Chr. Kaiser.

Knight, Douglas A. 2002. Joshua 22 and Ideology of Space. Pages 51–63 in *'Imagining' Biblical Worlds: Studies in Spatial, Social and Historical Constructs in Honor of James W. Flanagan.* Edited by David M. Gunn and Paula M. McNutt. Sheffield: Sheffield Academic Press.

Knoppers, Gary N. 2006. Revisiting the Samarian Question in the Persian Period. Pages 265–89 in Lipschits and Oeming 2006.

Knowles, Melody D. 2004. Pilgrimage Imagery in the Returns in Ezra. *JBL* 123:57–74.

Knudson, Albert C. 1918. *The Religious Teaching of the Old Testament.* Cincinnati: Abingdon.

Koch, Heidemarie. 1988. *Persien zur Zeit des Dareios: Das Achämenidenreich im Lichte neuer Quellen.* Marburg: Philipps-Universität.

———. 1992. *Es kündet Dareios der König: Vom Leben im persischen Großreich.* Mainz: Zabern.

———. 1993. Zum Programm der Adapna-Treppen in Persepolis. Pages 93–116 in idem, *Achämeniden-Studien.* Wiesbaden: Harassowitz.

Koch, Klaus. 1982. *The Babylonian and Persian Periods* Vol. 2 of *The Prophets.* Philadelphia: Fortress.

Kohn, Risa Levitt. 2002. *A New Heart and a New Soul: Ezekiel, the Exile and the Torah.* JSOTSup 358. London: Sheffield Academic Press.

Kraus, Hans-Joachim. 1989. *Psalms 60–150: A Commentary.* Translated by Hilton C. Oswald. Minneapolis: Augsburg.

Krefter, Friedrich. 1971. *Persepolis Rekonstruktionen.* Teheraner Forschungen 3. Berlin: Deutsches archäologisches Institut.

Kreissig, H. 1973. *Die sozialökonomische Situation in Juda zur Achämenidenzeit.* Schriften Geschichte und Kultur des Alten Orients 7. Berlin: Akademie.

Kristeva, Julia. 1986. Word, Dialogue and Novel. Pages 34–61 in *The Kristeva Reader.* Edited by Toril Moi. New York: Columbia University Press.

Kuhrt, Amélie. 1990. Achaemenid Babylonia: Sources and Problems. Pages 184–86 in *Achaemenid History IV: Centre and Periphery.* Edited by Heleen Sancisi-Weerdenburg and Amélie Kuhrt. Leiden: Nederlands Instituut voor het Nabije Oosten.

———. 1995. *The Ancient Near East c. 3000–330 BC.* Volume 2. Routledge History of the Ancient World. London: Routledge.

Kutscher, Eduard Yechezkel. 1984. *A History of the Hebrew Language.* Jerusalem: Magnes.

Lacan, Jacques. 1982. *Écrits: A Selection.* New York: Norton.

Lambert, Wilfred G. 1960. *Babylonian Wisdom Literature.* Oxford: Clarendon.

Lang, Bernhard. 1986. *Wisdom and the Book of Proverbs: An Israelite Goddess Redefined.* New York: Pilgrim.

Langer, Birgit. 1989. *Gott als Licht in Israel und Mesopotamien: Eine Studie zu Jes 60,1–3.19f.* Kosterneuburg: Österreichisches Katholisches Bibelwerk.

Lecoq, P. 1984. Un problème de religion achéménide: Ahura Mazda ou Xvarnah? Pages 301–26 in *Orientalia J. Duchesne-Guillemin Emerito Oblata.* Acta Iranica 23. Leiden: Brill.

Lemaire, André. 1994. Histoire et Administration de la Palestine à l'époque Perse.

Pages 11–53 in *La Palestine à l'époque Perse*. Edited by Ernest-Marie Laper-rousaz et André Lemaire. Paris: Cerf.

———. 1996. Zorobabel et la Judée à la lumière de l'épigraphie (fin du VIe s. av. J.-C.). *RB* 103:48–57.

———. 2003. Nabonidus in Arabia and Judah in the Neo-Babylonian Period. Pages 285–98 in Lipschits and Blenkinsopp 2003.

Lemche, Niels Peter. 1988. *Ancient Israel: A New History of Israelite Society*. Biblical Seminar 5. Sheffield: Sheffield Academic Press.

Lerner, Judith A. 1977. *Christian Seals of the Sasanian Period*. Leiden: Nederlands Instituut voor het Nabije Oosten.

Lewis, David M. 1990. The Persepolis Fortification Texts. Pages in *Achaemenid History IV: Centre and Periphery*. Edited by Heleen Sancisi-Weerdenburg and Amélie Kuhrt. Leiden: Nederlands Instituut voor het Nabije Oosten.

Lichtheim, Miriam. 1978. *The New Kingdom*. Vol. 2 of *Ancient Egyptian Literature*. Berkeley and Los Angeles: University of California Press.

Limet, H. 1995. L'émigré dans la société mésopotamienne. Pages 165–179 in *Immigration and Emigration within the Ancient Near East: Festschrift E. Lipiński*. Edited by Karel van Lerberghe and Antoon Schoors. Leuven: Uitgeverij Peeters en Department Oriëntalistiek.

Lipiński, Edward. 1970. Recherches sur le Livre de Zacharie. *VT* 20:25–55.

———. 1973. Garden of Abundance, Image of Lebanon. *ZAW* 85:358–59.

Lipschits, Oded. 2003. Demographic Changes in Judah between the Seventh and the Fifth Centuries B.C.E. Pages 323–376 in Lipschits and Blenkinsopp 2003.

———. 2006. Achaemenid Imperial Policy, Settlement Processes in Palestine, and the Status of Jerusalem in the Middle of the Fifth Century B.C.E. Pages 19–52 in Lipschits and Oeming 2006.

Lipschits, Oded, and Joseph Blenkinsopp, eds. 2003. *Judah and the Judeans in the Neo-Babylonian Period*. Winona Lake, Ind.: Eisenbrauns

Lipschits, Oded, and Manfred Oeming, eds. 2006. *Judah and the Judeans in the Persian Period*. Winona Lake, Ind.: Eisenbrauns

Lohfink, Norbert. 1978. Die Gattung der "Historischen Kurzgeschichte" in den letzten Jahren von Juda und in der Zeit des Babylonischen Exils. *ZAW* 90:319–47.

Long, Gary Allan. 1996. A Lover, Cities, and Heavenly Bodies: Co-text and the Translation of Two Similies in Canticles (6:4c; 6:10d). *JBL* 115:703–9.

Loomba, Ania. 1998. *Colonialism/Postcolonialism*. London: Routledge

Luce, T. James. 1997. *The Greek Historians*. London: Routledge.

Lust, Johan. 1999. Exile and Diaspora: Gathering from Dispersion in Ezekiel. Pages 99–122 in *Lectures et relectures de la Bible: Festschrift P. M. Bogaert*. Edited by Jean-Marie Auwers and André Wénin. Leuven: Peeters.

Lux, Rüdiger. 2002. Das Zweiprophetenbuch. Pages 191–217 in "*Wort Jhwhs,*

das geschah—" (Hos 1,1): Studien zum Zwölfprophetenbuch. Edited by Erich
    Zenger. Freiburg: Herder.
Lyotard, Jean-François. 1984. The Postmodern Condition: A Report on Knowledge.
    Translated by Geoffrey Bennington and Brian Massumi. Theory and History
    of Literature 10. Minneapolis: University of Minnesota Press.
Macey, David. 2001. Frantz Fanon: A Biography. New York: Picador
Maier, Christl. 1995. Die 'fremde Frau' in Proverbien 1–9: Eine exegetische und
    sozialgeschichtliche Studie. OBO 144. Fribourg: Universitätsverlag; Göttin-
    gen: Vandenhoeck & Ruprecht.
———. 1998. Conflicting Attractions: Parental Wisdom and the "Strange Woman"
    in Proverbs 1–9. Pages 92–108 in Wisdom and the Psalms: A Feminist Com-
    panion to the Bible. Edited by Athalya Brenner and Carole R. Fontaine. FCB
    2/2. Sheffield: Sheffield Academic Press.
Malkki, Lisa H. 1997. National Geographic: The Rooting of Peoples and the Ter-
    ritorializing of National Identity among Scholars and Refugees. In Culture,
    Power, and Place: Explorations in Critical Anthropology. Edited by Akhil
    Gupta and James Ferguson. Durham, N.C.: Duke University Press.
Mannati, M. 1979. Les psaumes graduals constitutent-ils un genre littéraire dis-
    tinct à l'biblique? Sem 29:85–100.
Marbury, Herbert Robinson. 2003. The Separatist Rhetoric of the Ezra-Nehemiah
    Corpus: Its Political, Cultic, and Economic Significations. Ph.D. diss. Van-
    derbilt University.
Marguerat, Daniel, and Adrian Curtis, eds. 2000. Intertextualités: La Bible en
    échos. MdB 40. Geneva: Labor et Fides.
Marrs, Rick Roy. 1982. The Šyry-Hm'lwt (Psalms 120–134): A Philological and
    Stylistic Analysis. Ph.D. diss. Johns Hopkins University.
Mayer-Opificius, Ruth. 1984. Die geflügelte Sonne: Himmels- und Regendarstel-
    lung im Alten Vorderasien. UF 16:198–236.
McEvenue, Sean. 1981. The Political Structure in Judah from Cyrus to Nehemiah.
    CBQ 43:353–64.
McKane, William. 1970. Proverbs: A New Approach. OTL. Philadelphia: West-
    minster.
McKeating, Henry. 1993. Ezekiel. OTG. Sheffield: Sheffield Academic Press.
McKenzie, John L. 1968. Second Isaiah. AB 20. New York: Doubleday.
McKenzie, Steven L. 1999. The Chronicler as Redactor. Pages 70–90 in The
    Chronicler as Author: Studies in Text and Texture. Edited by M. Patrick
    Graham and Steven L. McKenzie. JSOTSup 263. Sheffield: Sheffield Aca-
    demic Press.
Mein, Andrew. 2001. Ezekiel as a Priest in Exile. Pages 199–213 in The Elusive
    Prophet: The Prophet as a Historical Person, Literary Character, and Anony-
    mous Artist. Edited by Johannes C. de Moor. OtSt 45. Leiden: Brill, 2001.
Meinhold, Arndt. 1991. Die Sprüche. Züricher Bibelkommentare 16. Zürich: The-
    ologischer.

Meir, Carl A. 1967. *Ancient Incubation and Modern Psychotherapy.* Translated by Monica Curtis. Evanston, Ill.: Northwestern University Press.

Memmi, Albert. 1973. The Impossible Life of Frantz Fanon. *The Massachusetts Review* 14/1:9–39.

Mendenhall, George E. 1973. *The Tenth Generation: The Origins of the Biblical Tradition.* Baltimore: Johns Hopkins University Press.

Merquior, José Guilherme. 1979. *The Veil and the Mask: Essays on Culture and Ideology.* London: Routledge.

Meshel, Ze'ev. 1992. Kuntillet 'Ajrud. *ABD* 4:103–9.

Mexican and U.S. Catholic Bishops. 2003. Strangers No Longer: Together on the Journey of Hope. Pastoral letter. Online: http://www.usccb.org/mrs/stranger. htm.

Meyers, Carol L., and Eric M. Meyers. 1987. *Haggai, Zechariah 1–8: A New Translation with Introduction and Commentary.* AB 25B. Garden City, N.Y.: Doubleday.

———. 1992. Jerusalem and Zion after the Exile: The Evidence of First Zechariah. Pages 121–35 in *Sha'arei Talmon: Studies in the Bible, Qumran and the Anicent Near East Presented to Shemaryahu Talmon.* Edited by Michael Fishbane, Emanuel Tov and Weston W. Fields. Winona Lake, Ind.: Eisenbrauns.

Meyers, Eric M. 1985. The Shelomith Seal and the Judean Restoration: Some Additional Considerations. *ErIsr* 18:*33–*38.

Michaeli, Frank. 1967. *Les livres des Chroniques, d'Esdras et de Néhémie.* CAT 16. Neuchatel: Delachaux et Niestlé.

Milgrom, Jacob. 1991. *Leviticus 1–16: A New Translation with Introduction and Commentary/.* AB 3. New York: Doubleday.

Millard, Matthias. 1984. *Die Komposition des Psalters: Ein formgeschichtlicher Ansatz.* FAT 9. Tübingen: Mohr Siebeck.

Miller, J. Maxwell, and John H. Hayes, 1986. *A History of Ancient Israel and Judah.* Philadelphia: Westminster.

Miller, Patrick D. 1969. A Note on the Meša' Inscription. *Or* 38:461–64.

———. 1973. *The Divine Warrior in Early Israel.* HSM 5. Cambridge: Harvard University Press. Repr., Atlanta: Society of Biblical Literature, 2006.

Miscall, Peter. 1995. Texts, More Texts, A Textual Reader and a Textual Writer. *Semeia* 69/70:247–60.

Mitchell, Christine. 2001. The Ideal Ruler as Intertext in 1–2 Chronicles and the *Cyropaedia.* Ph.D. diss. Carleton University.

Momigliano, Arnaldo. 1977. *Essays in Ancient and Modern Historiography.* Middletown, Conn.: Wesleyan University Press.

———. 1990. *The Classical Foundations of Modern Historiography.* Berkeley and Los Angeles: University of California Press.

Moor, Johannes C. de. 1997. Structure and Redaction: Isaiah 60,1–63,6. Pages 325–46 in *Studies in the Book of Isaiah: Festschrift Willem A. M. Beuken.*

Edited by Jacques van Ruiten and Marc Vervenne. BETL 132. Leuven: University Press.

Moore, Stephen D. 2001. Postcolonialism. Pages 182–88 in *Handbook of Postmodern Biblical Interpretation*. Edited by A. K. M. Adam. St. Louis: Chalice.

Moortgat, Anton. 1926. *Hellas und die Kunst der Achaemeniden*. Leipzig: Pfeiffer.

Morgenstern, Julian. 1949. Two Prophecies from 520–516 B.C. *HUCA* 22:365–431.

Moscati, Sabatino, Ann Britt Tilia, and Tano Citeroni. 1980. *Persepoli: Luce e silenzi di un impero scomparso*. Milan: Rusconi.

Mowinckel, Sigmund. 1921. *Psalmenstudien*. 6 vols. Kristiana: Dybwad.

———. 1962. *Psalms in Israel's Worship*. Translated by D. R. Ap-Thomas. Nashville: Abingdon.

Mullen, E. Theodore, Jr. 1993. *Narrative History and Ethnic Boundaries: The Deuteronomistic History and the Creation of Israelite National Identity*. SemeiaSt 24. Atlanta: Scholars Press.

Murphy, Roland E. 1974. A Form-Critical Consideration of Ecclesiastes VII. Pages 77–85 in vol. 1 of *Society of Biblical Literature 1974 Seminar Papers*. SBLSemPap 5. Cambridge, Mass.: Society of Biblical Literature.

———. 1988. Wisdom and Eros in Proverbs 1–9. *CBQ* 50: 600–603.

———. 1992. *Ecclesiastes*. WBC 23A. Dallas: Word.

Myers, Jacob M. 1965. *Ezra-Nehemiah*. AB 14. Garden City, NY: Doubleday.

Na'aman, Nadav. 2000. Royal Vassals or Governors? On the Status of Sheshbazzar and Zerubbabel in the Persian Empire. *Henoch* 22:35–44.

Naveh, Joseph. 1981. The Aramaic Ostraca from Tel Arad. Pages 153–76 in *Arad Inscriptions*. Edited by Yohanan Aharoni. Translated by Judith Ben-Or. Jerusalem: Israel Exploration Society.

Nelson, Richard D. 1981. Josiah in the Book of Joshua. *JBL* 100: 531–40.

———. 1997. *Joshua: A Commentary*. OTL. Louisville: Westminster John Knox.

Newsom, Carol A. 1989. Woman and the Discourse of Patriarchal Wisdom: A Study of Proverbs 1–9. Pages 142–59 in *Gender and Difference in Ancient Israel*. Edited by Peggy L. Day. Minneapolis: Fortress.

Nicholson, Ernest W. 1965. The Meaning of the Term 'am ha'arez in the Old Testament. *JSS* 10:59–66.

———. 1986. *God and His People: Covenant and Theology in the Old Testament*. Oxford: Clarendon.

Niehr, Herbert. 1999. Religio-Historical Aspects of the "Early Post-Exilic" Period. Pages 228–44 in *The Crisis of Israelite Religion: Transformation of Religious Tradition in Exilic and Post-Exilic Times*. Edited by Bob Becking and Marjo C. A. Korpel. OtSt 42. Leiden: Brill.

Nielsen, Flemming A. J. 1997. *The Tragedy in History: Herodotus and the Deuteronomistic History*. JSOTSup 251. Sheffield: Sheffield Academic Press.

Noth, Martin. 1960. *The History of Israel*. 2d ed. Translated by Peter R. Ackroyd. London: Black.

————. 1987. *The Chronicler's History.* Translated by Hugh G. M. Williamson. JSOTSup 50. Sheffield: Sheffield Academic Press.

Nötscher, Friedrich. 1969. *Das Angesicht Gottes schauen nach biblisher und babylonisher Auffassung.* Darmstadt: Wissenschaftliche Buchgessellschaft.

Oded, Bustenay. 1977. Judah and the Exile. Pages 435–88 in *Israelite and Judean History.* Edited by John H. Hayes and J. Maxwell Miller. Philadelphia: Westminster.

————. 1979. *Mass Deportations and Deportees in the Neo-Assyrian Empire.* Wiesbaden: Reichert.

————. 1995. Observations on the Israelite/Judean Exiles in Mesopotamia during the Eighth–Sixth Centuries B.C.E. Pages 205–12 in *Immigration and Emigration within the Ancient Near East: Festschrift E. Lipiński:* Edited by Karel van Lerberghe and Antoon Schoors. Leuven: Uitgeverij Peeters en Department Oriëntalistiek.

Olmstead, A. T. 1948. *History of the Persian Empire.* Chicago: University of Chicago Press.

Olyan, Saul M. 1996. Honor, Shame, and Covenant Relations in Ancient Israel. *JBL* 115:201–18.

Partin, Harry B. 1967. The Muslim Pilgrimage: Journey to the Center. Ph.D. diss. University of Chicago.

Pearce, Sarah. 1995. Josephus as Interpreter of Biblical Law: The Representation of the High Court of Deut. 17:8–12 according to Jewish Antiquities 4.218. *JJS* 46:30–42.

Peckham, Brian. 1993. *History and Prophecy: The Development of Late Judean Literary Traditions.* ABRL. New York: Doubleday.

Perdue, Leo G. 2000. *Proverbs.* IBC. Louisville: Westminster John Knox.

Pérez Firmat, Gustavo. 1994. *Life on the Hyphen: The Cuban-American Way.* Austin: University of Texas Press.

Pering, Birger. 1932–33. Die geflügelte Scheibe in Assyrien. *AfO* 8:281–96.

Perowne, J. J. Stewart. 1836. *The Book of Psalms.* London: Draper.

Perrot, Jean. 1974. Recherches dans le secteur de tépé de l'Apadana. *Cahiers de la délégation archéologique francaise en Iran* 4. Paris: Delegation Archeologique Francaise en Iran.

Petersen, David L. 1985. *Haggai and Zechariah 1–8.* OTL. Philadelphia: Westminster.

Petitjean, Albert. 1969. *Les oracles du proto-Zacharie: Un programme de restauration pour la communauté juive après l'exil.* Paris: Gabalda; Leuven: Editions Imprimerie Orientaliste.

Phillips, Judith R. 2000. Zechariah's Vision and Joseph in Egypt: An Ancient Dialogue About Jewish Identity. *Conservative Judaism* 53/1:51–61.

Plett, Heinrich. 1991. Intertextualities. Pages 3–29 in *Intertextuality.* Edited by Heinrich F. Plett. Berlin: de Gruyter.

Polaski, Donald C. 2001. *Authorizing an End: The Isaiah Apocalypse and Intertextuality.* BIS 50. Leiden: Brill.

Polignac, François de. 1984. *La Naissance de la cité grecque: Cultes, espace et société VIIIe-VIIe siècles avant J.-C.* Paris: Éditions la Découverte.

Polzin, Robert. 1976. *Late Biblical Hebrew: Toward an Historical Typology of Biblical Prose.* HMS 12. Missoula, Mont.: Scholars Press.

Pons, Jacques. 1986. Le vocabulaire d'Ézéchiel 20: Le prophète s'oppose à la vision deutéronomiste de l'histoire. Pages 214–33 in *Ezekiel and His Book: Textual and Literary Criticism and Their Interrelation.* Edited by Johan Lust. BETL 74. Leuven: Peeters.

Pope, Artur Upham. 1974. Art as an Essential of Iranian History. Pages 153–62 in *Hommage Universel.* Vol. 1 of *Commémoration Cyrus.* Acta Iranica 1. Leiden: Brill.

Porada, Edith. 1969. *The Art of Ancient Iran: Pre-Islamic Cultures.* New York: Greystone.

Porten, Bezalel. 1968. *Archives from Elephantine: The Life of an Ancient Jewish Military Colony.* Berkeley and Los Angeles: University of California Press.

———. 1984. The Diaspora: The Jews in Egypt. Pages 372–400 in *Introduction; The Persian Period.* Vol. 1. of *The Cambridge History of Judaism.* Edited by W. D. Davies and Louis Finkelstein. Cambridge: Cambridge University Press.

———. 2003. Settlement of the Jews at Elephantine and the Arameans at Syene. Pages 451–70 in Lipschits and Blenkinsopp 2003.

Porten, Bezalel, and Ada Yardeni. 1986. *Letters.* Vol. 1 of *Textbook of Aramaic Documents from Ancient Egypt.* Winona Lake, Ind.: Eisenbrauns.

Porter, John A. 1965. *The Vertical Mosaic: A Study of Social Class and Power in Canada.* Toronto: University of Toronto Press.

Posener, Georges. 1936. *La première domination Perse en Égypte: Recueil d'inscriptions hiéroglyphiques.* Cairo: L'institut Francais d'archéologie orientale.

Pury, Albert de, and Thomas Römer. 1995. Terres d'exil et terres d'accueil: Quelques réflexions sur le judaïsme postexilique face à la Perse et à l'Égypte. *Transeu* 9:25–34.

Rad, Gerhard von. 1972. *Wisdom in Israel.* Translated by James D. Martin. Valley Forge, Pa.: Trinity Press International.

Rappaport, Uriel. 1996. Les juifs et leurs voisins. *Annales-Histoire, Sciences Sociales* 51:955–74.

Rawlinson, Henry C. 1847. The Persian Cuneiform Inscription at Behistun, Decyphered and Translated. *JRAS* 10:1–349.

Redditt, Paul L. 1995. *Haggai, Zechariah, Malachi.* NCBC. Grand Rapids: Eerdmans.

Reisman, Daniel. 1873. Iddin-Dagan's Sacred Marriage Hymn. *JCS* 25:185–202.

Rendsburg, Gary A. 1990. *Linguistic Evidence for the Northern Origin of Selected Psalms.* SBLMS 43. Atlanta: Scholars Press.

Renkema, Johan. 1995. Does Hebrew YTWM really mean 'Fatherless'? *VT* 45:119–122.

Ringgren, Helmer. 1980. זָרַח *zārach*; מִזְרָח *mizrāch*. TDOT 4:141–43.

Roaf, Michael. 1974. The Subject Peoples on the Base of the Statue of Darius. *Cahiers de la Délégation Archéologique Française en Iran* 4:73–160.

———. 1980. Texts about the Sculptures and Sculptors of Persepolis. *Iran* 18:65–74.

———. 1983. *Sculptures and Sculptors at Persepolis. Iran* 21. London: The British Academy.

Robert, A. 1934–35. Les attaches littéraires Bibliques de Prov. I–IX. *RB* 43:42–68, 172–204, 374–84; 44: 344–65, 502–25.

Rooker, Mark F. 1990. *Biblical Hebrew in Transition.* JSOTSup 90. Sheffield: Sheffield Academic Press.

Root, Margaret Cool. 1979. *King and Kingship in Achaemenid Art: Essays on the Creation of an Iconography of Empire.* Acta Iranica 19. Leiden: Brill.

———. 1985. The Parthenon Frieze and the Apadana Reliefs at Persepolis: Reassessing a Programmatic Relationship. *AJA* 89:103–20.

———. 1989. The Persian Archer at Persepolis: Aspects of Chronology, Style and Symbolism. *REA* 91:33–50.

———. 1991. From the Heart: Powerful Persianisms in the Art of the Western Empire. Pages 1–29 in *Achaemenid History VI.* Edited by Heleen Sancisi-Weerdenburg and Amélie Kuhrt. Leiden: Nederlands Instituut voor het Nabije Oosten.

———. 1992. Art and Architecture (Persian Art). *ABD* 1:440–47.

Rose, Wolter H. 2000. *Zemah and Zerubbabel: Messianic Expectations in the Early Postexilic Period.* JSOTSup 304. Sheffield: Sheffield Academic Press.

Roth, Martha T. 1989a. *Babylonian Marriage Agreements 7th–3rd Centuries B.C.* AOAT 222. Neukirchen-Vluyn: Neukirchener.

———. 1989b. Marriage and Matrimonial Prestations in First Millennium B. C. Babylonia. Pages 245–64 in *Women's Earliest Records from Ancient Egypt and Western Asia: Proceedings of the Conference on Women in the Ancient Near East, Brown University, Providence, Rhode Island, November 5–7, 1987.* Edited by Barbara S. Lesko. BJS 166. Atlanta: Scholars Press.

———. 1989–90. The Material Composition of the Neo-Babylonian Dowry. *AfO* 36/37:1–55.

———. 1991. The Dowries of the Women of the Itti-Marduk-balāṭu Family. *JAOS* 111:19–37

Rubenstein, Jeffrey L. 1992. History of Sukkot during the Second Temple and Rabbinic Periods: Studies in the Continuity and Change of a Festival. Ph.D. diss. Columbia University.

Rudolph, Wilhelm. 1949. *Esra und Nehemia.* HAT 20. Tübingen: Mohr Siebeck.

———. 1970. *Haggai, Sacharja 1–8, Sacharja 9–14, Maleachi.* Gütersloh: Gütersloher Verlagshaus.

Ruiz, Jean-Pierre. 1997. Exile, History and Hope: A Hispanic Reading of Ezekiel 20. *The Bible Today* (March): 106–13.

———. 1998. Among the Exiles by the River Chebar: A U.S. Hispanic American Reading of Prophetic Cosmology in Ezekiel 1:1–3. *Journal of Hispanic/Latino Theology* 6/2:43–67.

Ruszkowski, Leszek. 2000. *Volk und Gemeinde im Wandel: Eine Untersuchung zu Jesaja 56–66*. FRLANT 191. Göttingen: Vandenhoeck & Ruprecht.

Sacchi, P. 2001. Re Vassalli O Governatori? Una Discussione. *Henoch* 23:147–152.

Safrai, Shmuel. 1981. *Die Wallfahrt im Zeitalter des Zweiten Tempels*. Forschungen zum jüdisch-christlichen Dialog 3. Neukirchen-Vluyn: Neukirchener.

Said, Edward W. 1981. Criticism between Culture and System. Pages 178–225 in idem, *The World, The Text and the Critic*. Cambridge: Harvard University Press.

———. 1983. The Mind of Winter: Reflections on Life in Exile. *Harper's Magazine* (September 1984): 49–55.

———. 1996. *Representations of the Intellectual*. New York: Random House.

Sami, Ali. 1967. *Persepolis = Takht-i-Jamshid*. 5th ed. Shiraz: Musavi Printing Office.

Sarre, Friedrich. 1925. *Die Kunst des Alten Persien*. Edited by William Cohn. Die Kunst des Ostens 5. Berlin: Cassirer.

Schmandt-Besserat, Denise, ed. 1980. *Ancient Persia: The Art of an Empire*. Malibu, Calif.: Undena.

Schmid, H. 1976. Die "Juden" im Alten Testament. Pages 17–29 in *Wort und Wirklichkeit: Studien zur Afrikanistik u. Orientalistik*. Edited by Brigitta Benzing, Otto Bocher, and Günter Mayer. Meisenheim am Glan: Hain.

Schmidt, Erich F. 1953. *Persepolis I: Structures, Reliefs, Inscriptions*. OIP 68. Chicago: University of Chicago Press.

———. 1957. *Persepolis II: Contents of the Treasury and Other Discoveries*. OIP 69. Chicago: University of Chicago Press.

———. 1970. *Persepolis III: The Royal Tombs and Other Monuments*. OIP 70. Chicago: University of Chicago Press.

Schmitt, Rüdiger. 1990. Bīsotūn, iii. Darius' Inscriptions. Pages 299–305 in vol. 4 of *Encyclopædia Iranica*. Edited by Ehsan Yarshater. London: Routledge.

———. 1991. *The Bisitun Inscriptions of Darius the Great: Old Persian Text*. Corpus Inscriptionum Iranicarum 1.1. London: Society of Oriental and African Studies.

Schneider, Heinrich. 1959. *Die Bücher Esra und Nehemiah*. HSAT 4.2. Bonn: Hanstein.

Schneiders, Sandra M. 1991. *The Revelatory Text: Interpreting the New Testament as Sacred Scripture*. San Francisco: Harper.

Schnutenhaus, Frank. 1964. Das Kommen und Erscheinen Gottes im Alten Testament. *ZAW* 76:1–22.

Schottroff, Willy. 1982. Zur Sozialgeschichte Israels in der Perserzeit. *VF* 27:46–68.

Schramm, Brooks. 1995. *The Opponents of Third Isaiah: Reconstructing the Cultic History of the Restoration.* JSOTSup 193. Sheffield: Sheffield Academic Press.

Schroer, Silvia. 1995. Wise and Counselling Women in Ancient Israel: Literary and Historical Ideals of the Personified Ḥokmâ. Pages 67–84 in *A Feminist Companion to Wisdom Literature.* Edited by Athalya Brenner. FCB 9. Sheffield: Sheffield Academic Press.

Schultz, Friedrich W. 1877. *The Book of Ezra.* Translated by C. A. Briggs. J. P. Lange Commentaries 7. New York: Scribner, Armstrong.

Schüssler Fiorenza, Elisabeth. 1999. *Rhetoric and Ethic: The Politics of Biblical Studies.* Minneapolis: Fortress.

Schwartz, Martin. 1985. The Old Eastern Iranian World View according to the Avesta. Pages 640–63 in vol. 2 of *The Cambridge History of Iran.* Edited by Ilya Geshevitch. Cambridge: Cambridge University Press.

Scott, R. B. Y. 1965. *Proverbs, Ecclesiastes: Introduction, Translation, and Notes.* AB 18. Garden City, N.Y.: Doubleday.

Scott, William R. 1993. The Booths of Ancient Israel's Autumn Festival. Ph.D. diss. Johns Hopkins University.

Scriba, Albrecht. 1995. *Die Geschichte des Motivkomplexes Theophanie: Seine Elemente, Einbindung in Geschehensabläufe und Verwendungsweisen in altisraelitischer, frühjüdischer und frühchristlicher Literatur.* FRLANT 167. Göttingen: Vandenhoeck & Ruprecht.

Segovia, Fernando F. 1995a. Cultural Studies and Contemporary Biblical Criticism: Ideological Criticism as Mode of Discourse. Pages 1–17 in *Social Location and Biblical Interpretation in Global Perspective.* Vol. 2 of *Reading from This Place.* Edited by Fernando F. Segovia and Mary Ann Tolbert. Minneapolis: Fortress.

———. 1995b. Toward a Hermeneutics of the Diaspora: A Hermeneutics of Otherness and Engagement. Pages 68–69 in *Social Location and Biblical Interpretation in the United States.* Vol. 1 of *Reading from This Place.* Edited by Fernando F. Segovia and Mary Ann Tolbert. Minneapolis: Fortress.

———. 1996. In the World but Not of It: Exile as a Locus for a Theology of the Diaspora. Pages 195–217 in *Hispanic/Latino Theology: Challenge and Promise.* Edited by Ada María Isasi-Díaz and Fernando F. Segovia. Minneapolis: Fortress.

———. 2000. Interpreting beyond Borders: Postcolonial Studies and Diasporic Studies in Biblical Criticism. In *Interpreting Beyond Borders.* Edited by Fernando F. Segovia. The Bible and Postcolonialism 3. Sheffield: Sheffield Academic Press.

Seitz, Christopher R. 1992. Third Isaiah. *ABD* 3:501–7.

———. 1996. How Is the Prophet Isaiah Present in the Latter Half of the Book? The Logic of Chapters 40–66 within the Book of Isaiah. *JBL* 115:219–40.

Sellers, Susan, ed. 1996. *The Hélène Cixous Reader.* New York: Routledge.

Sellin, Ernst, and Georg Fohrer. 1968. *Introduction to the Old Testament.* Translated by David E. Green. Nashville: Abingdon.

Sen, Amartya. 1981. *Poverty and Famines: An Essay on Entitlement and Deprivation.* Oxford: Clarendon.

Seow, C. L. 1993. Review of Gary A. Rendsburg, *Linguistic Evidence for the Northern Origin of Selected Psalms. JBL* 112:334–37.

———. 1996a. Linguistic Evidence and the Dating of Qohelet. *JBL* 115:643–66.

———. 1996b. The Socioeconomic Context of "The Preacher's" Hermeneutic. *PSB* 17:168–95.

———. 1997. Dangerous Seductress of Elusive Lover? The Woman of Ecclesiastes 7. Pages 23–33 in *Women, Gender, and Christian Community.* Edited by Jane Dempsey Douglass and James F. Kay. Louisville: Westminster John Knox.

Sérandour, A. 1995. Réflexions à propos d'un livre récent sur *Aggée-Zacharie 1–8. Transeu* 10:75–84.

Seybold, Klaus. 1978. *Die Wallfahrtspsalmen: Studien zur Entstehungsgeschichte von Psalm 120–134.* BTS 3. Neukirchen-Vluyn: Neukirchener.

Shahbazi, A. Shapur. 1974. An Achaemenid Symbol I: A Farewell to "Fravahr" and "Ahuramazda." *Archäologische Mitteilungen aus Iran* NS 7:135–44.

———. 1980. An Achaemenid Symbol II: Farnah (God Given) Fortune "Symbolized." *Archäologische Mitteilungen aus Iran* NS 13:119–47.

Shiloh, Yigal. 1984. *Excavations at the City of David.* Qedem 19. Jerusalem: The Hebrew University of Jerusalem.

Silverman, Michael H. 1985. *Religious Values in the Jewish Proper Names at Elephantine.* AOAT 217. Neukirchen-Vluyn: Neukirchener.

Skehan, Patrick W. 1971. *Studies in Israelite Poetry and Wisdom.* CBQMS 1. Washington, D.C.: Catholic Biblical Association.

Smart, James D. 1965. *History and Theology in Second Isaiah.* Philadelphia: Westminster.

Smith, Mark S. 1990. The Near Eastern Background of Solar Language for Yahweh. *JBL* 109:29–39.

———. 2002. *The Early History of God: Yahweh and the Other Deities in Ancient Israel.* 2d ed. Grand Rapids: Eerdmans.

Smith, Mark S., with Elizabeth Bloch-Smith. 1997. *Pilgrimage Pattern in Exodus.* JSOTSup 239. Sheffield: Sheffield Academic Press.

Smith, Morton. 1987. *Palestinian Parties and Politics That Shaped the Old Testament.* 2d ed. London: SCM.

Smith, Paul A. 1995. *Rhetoric and Redaction in Trito-Isaiah: The Structure, Growth and Authorship of Isaiah 56–66.* VTSup 62. Leiden: Brill.

Smith-Christopher, Daniel L. 1989. *The Religion of the Landless: The Social Context of the Babylonian Exile.* Bloomington, Ind.: Meyer Stone.

———. 1994. The Mixed Marriage Crisis in Ezra 9–10 and Nehemiah 13: A Study of the Sociology of the Post-Exilic Judaean Community. Pages 243–65 in *Second Temple Studies 2. Temple and Community in the Persian Period.*

Edited by Tamara Cohn Eskenazi and Kent Harold Richards. JSOTSup 175. Sheffield: Sheffield Academic Press.

———. 1997. Reassessing the Historical and Sociological Impact of the Babylonian Exile (597/587–539 BCE). Pages 7–36 in *Exile: Old Testament, Jewish, and Christian Conceptions*. Edited by James M. Scott. VTSup 56. Leiden: Brill.

———. 1999. Ezekiel on Fanon's Couch: A Postcolonialist Dialogue with David Halperin's *Seeking Ezekiel*. Pages 108–44 in *Peace and Justice Shall Embrace: Power and Theopolitics in the Bible: Essays in Honor of Millard Lind*. Edited by Ted Grimsrud and Loren L. Johns. Telford, Pa.: Pandora; Scottsdale, Pa.: Herald.

———. 2002. *A Biblical Theology of Exile*. OBT. Minneapolis: Fortress Press.

Soggin, J. Alberto. 1989. Introduction to the Old Testament: From Its Origins to the Closing of the Alexandrian Canon. 3rd ed. OTL. Louisville: Westminster John Knox.

Spivak, Gayatri Chakravorty. 1999. *A Critique of Post-colonial Reason: Toward a History of the Vanishing Present*. Cambridge: Harvard University Press.

Stähli, Hans-Peter. 1985. *Solare Elemente im Jahweglauben des Alten Testaments*. OBO 66. Fribourg: Universitätsverlag.

Starbuck, Scott R. A. 1989. Like Dreamers Lying in Wait, We Lament: A New Reading of Psalm 126. *Koinonia* 1/2:128–49.

Steck, Odil Hannes. 1986a. Der Grundtext in Jesaja 60 und sein Aufbau. *ZTK* 83:261–96.

———. 1986b. Heimkehr auf der Schulter oder/und auf der Hüfte: Jes 49,22b/60,4b. *ZAW* 98:275–77.

———. 1991. *Studien zu Tritojesaja*. BZAW 203. Berlin: de Gruyter.

Stern, Ephraim. 1982. *Material Culture of the Land of the Bible in the Persian Period 538–332 B.C.* Warminster: Aris & Phillips.

———. 1994. *Dor, Ruler of the Seas: Twelve Years of Excavations at the Israelite-Phoenician Harbor Town on the Carmel Coast*. Jerusalem: Israel Exploration Society.

Sternberg, Meir. 1985. *The Poetics of Biblical Narrative: Ideological Literature and the Drama of Reading*. Bloomington: Indiana University Press.

Stevenson, Kalinda Rose. 1996. *The Vision of Transformation: The Territorial Rhetoric of Ezekiel 40–48*. SBLDS 154. Atlanta: Scholars Press

Stolper, Matthew W. 1985. *Entrepreneurs and Empire: The Murašû Archive, the Murašû Firm, and Persian Rule in Babylonia*. Uitgaven van het Nederlands Historisch-Archaeologisch Instituut te Istanbul 54. Leiden: Nederlands Historisch-Archaeologisch Instituut te Istanbul.

Strassmaier, Johann N. 1890a. *Inschriften von Cambyses, König von Babylon (529–521 v. Chr.)* Babylonische Texte 8–9. Leipzig: Pfeiffer.

———. 1890b. *Inschriften von Cyrus, König von Babylon (538–529 v. Chr.)* Babylonische Texte 7. Leipzig: Pfeiffer.

Strawn, Brent A. 2005. *What Is Stronger Than a Lion? Leonine Image and Metaphor in the Hebrew Bible and the Ancient Near East.* OBO 212. Fribourg: Academic Press; Göttingen: Vandenhoeck & Ruprecht.

Stronach, David. 1974. La Statue de Darius le grand decouverte a Suse. *Cahiers de la Délégation Achéologique Française en Iran* 4:61–72.

———. 1978. *Pasargadae: A Report on the Excavations Conducted by the British Institute of Persian Studies from 1961–1963.* Oxford: Clarendon.

———. 1989. The Royal Garden at Pasargadae: Evolution and Legacy. Pages 475–502 in *Archaeologia Iranica et Orientalis: Miscellanea in Honorem Louis Vanden Berghe.* Edited by Leon de Meyer and E. Haerinck. Belgium: Gent.

Sugirtharajah, R. S. 1998a. Biblical Studies after the Empire: From a Colonial to a Postcolonial Mode of Interpretation. Pages 13–22 in *The Postcolonial Bible.* Edited by R. S. Sugirtharajah. The Bible and Postcolonialism 1. Sheffield: Sheffield Academic Press.

———. 1998b. A Postcolonial Exploration of Collusion and Construction in Biblical Interpretation. Pages 91–116 in *The Postcolonial Bible.* Edited by R. S. Sugirtharajah. The Bible and Postcolonialism 1. Sheffield: Sheffield Academic Press.

———. 2001. *The Bible and the Third World: Precolonial, Colonial and Postcolonial Encounters.* Cambridge: Cambridge University Press.

———. 2002. *Postcolonial Criticism and Biblical Interpretation.* Oxford: Oxford University Press.

———, ed. 2005. *The Postcolonial Bible Reader.* Oxford: Blackwell.

Sweeney, Marvin A. 2000. *King Josiah of Judah: The Lost Messiah of Judah.* New York: Oxford University Press.

Sykes, Seth. 1997. Time and Space in Haggai-Zechariah 1–8: A Bakhtinian Analysis of a Prophetic Chronicle. *JSOT* 76:97–124.

Tate, W. Randolph. 1997. *Biblical Interpretation: An Integrated Approach.* Rev. ed. Peabody, Mass.: Hendrickson.

Taylor, J. Glen. 1993. *Yahweh and the Sun: Biblical and Archaeological Evidence for Sun Worship in Ancient Israel.* JSOTSup 111. Sheffield: JSOT Press.

Thomas, D. Winton, ed. 1959. *Documents from Old Testament Times.* New York: Harper & Row.

Thompson, John B. 1984. *Studies in the Theory of Ideology.* Berkeley and Los Angeles: University of California Press.

Throntveit, Mark A. 1992. *Ezra-Nehemiah.* IBC. Louisville: John Knox.

Tigay, Jeffrey H. 1986. *You Shall Have No Other Gods: Israelite Religion in the Light of Hebrew Inscriptions.* HSM 31. Atlanta: Scholars Press.

Tilia, Ann Britt. 1972. *Studies and Restorations at Persepolis and Other Sites of Fārs.* Istituto italiano per il Medio ed Estremo Oriente Reports and Memoirs XVI. Rome: Istituto italiano per il Medio ed Estremo Oriente.

Tollefson, Kenneth D., and Hugh G. M. Williamson 1992. Nehemiah as Cultural Revitalization: An Anthropological Perspective. *JSOT* 56:41–68.

Tolman, Herbert Cushing. 1908. *Ancient Persian Lexicon*. Vanderbilt Oriental Series 6. New York: American Book Company.

———. 1910. *Cuneiform Supplement*. Vanderbilt Oriental Series 7. New York: American Book Company.

Toorn, Karel van der. 1989. Female Prostitution in Payment of Vows in Ancient Israel. *JBL* 108:193–205.

Torrey, Charles Cutler. 1928. *The Second Isaiah: A New Interpretation*. New York: Charles Scribner's Sons.

Trible, Phyllis. 1993. Love Lyrics Redeemed. Pages 100–120 in *A Feminist Companion to the Song of Songs*. Edited by Athalya Brenner. FCB 1. Sheffield: Sheffield Academic Press.

Tucker, Robert C., ed. 1978. *The Marx-Engels Reader*. 2d ed. New York: Norton.

Tull, Patricia. 2000. Intertextuality and the Hebrew Scriptures. *CurBS* 8:59–90.

Turner, Victor W. 1969. *Ritual Process: Structure and Anti-structure*. Chicago: Aldine.

———. 1973a. The Center Out There: Pilgrim's Goal. *HR* 12:191–230.

———. 1973b. Pilgrimage and Communitas. *Studia missionalia* 23:305–27.

Turner, Victor, and Edith Turner. 1978. *Image and Pilgrimage in Christian Culture: Anthropological Perspectives*. New York: Columbia University Press.

Uehlinger, Christoph. 1997. "Powerful Persianisms" in Glyptic Iconography of Persian Period Palestine. Pages 134–82 in *The Crisis of Israelite Religion: Transformation of Religious Tradition in Exilic and Post-Exilic Times*. Edited by Bob Becking and Marjo C. A. Korpel. OtSt 42. Leiden: Brill.

———, ed. 2000. *Images as Media: Sources for the Cultural History of the Near East and the Eastern Mediterranean (1st Millennium BCE)*. OBO 175. Fribourg: Universitätsverlag; Göttingen: Vandenhoeck & Ruprecht.

———. 2001. Bildquellen und 'Geschichte Israels': Grundsätzliche Überlegungen und Fallbeispiele. Pages 25–77 in *Steine, Bilder, Texte: Historische Evidenz ausserbiblischer und biblischer Quellen*. Edited by Christof Hardmeier. Leipzig: Evangelische Verlagsanstalt.

Ussishkin, David. 2006. The Borders and *De Facto* Size of Jerusalem in the Persian Period. Pages 147–66 in Lipschits and Oeming 2006.

Van de Mieroop, Marc. 1999. *Cuneiform Texts and the Writing of History*. London: Routledge.

Van Leeuwen, Raymond C. 1997. The Book of Proverbs. *NIB* 5:17–264.

Van Seters, John. 1983. *In Search of History: Historiography in the Ancient World and the Origins of Biblical History*. New Haven: Yale University Press.

———. 1984. Joshua 24 and the Problem of Tradition in the Old Testament. Pages 139–58 in *In the Shelter of Elyon: Essays on Ancient Palestinian Life and Literature in Honor of G. W. Ahlström*. Edited by W. Boyd Barrick and John R. Spencer. JSOTSup 31. Sheffield: JSOT Press.

Vanderhooft, David Stephen. 1999. *The Neo-Babylonian Empire and Babylon in the Latter Prophets*. HSM 59. Atlanta: Scholars Press.

Veeser, H. Aram, ed. 1996. *Confessions of the Critic*. New York: Routledge.

Vink, J. G. 1969. The Date and Origin of the Priestly Code in the Old Testament. Pages 1–144 in *The Priestly Code and Seven Other Studies*. Edited by P. A. H. de Boer. OtSt 15. Leiden: Brill.

Volz, Paul. 1932. *Jesaia II: Übersetzt und erklärt*. KAT 9.2. Leipzig: Deichert.

Walser, Gerold. 1966. *Die Völkerschaften auf den Reliefs von Persepolis: Historische Studien über den sogenanten Tributzug an der Apadanatreppe*. Berlin: Mann.

Wanke, Gunther. 1984. Prophecy and Psalms in the Persian Period. Pages 162–88 in *Introduction; The Persian Period*. Vol. 1 of *The Cambridge History of Judaism*. Edited by W. D. Davies and Louis Finkelstein. Cambridge: Cambridge University Press.

Washington, Harold C. 1994a. The Strange Woman ('iššâ zarâ/nokrîyyâ) of Proverbs 1–9 and Post-Exilic Judaean Society. Pages 217–42 in *Second Temple Studies 2: Temple and Community in the Persian Period*. Edited by Tamara Cohn Eskenazi and Kent Harold Richards. JSOTSup 175. Sheffield: JSOT Press.

———. 1994b. *Wealth and Poverty in the Instruction of Amenemope and the Hebrew Proverbs*. SBLDS 142. Atlanta: Scholars Press.

———. 1995. The Strange Woman. Pages 157–84 in *A Feminist Companion to Wisdom Literature*. Edited by Athalya Brenner. FCB 9. Sheffield: Sheffield Academic Press.

Watts, John D.W. 1987. *Isaiah 34–66*. WBC 25. Waco, Tex.: Word.

Weeks, Stuart D. E. 2002. Biblical Literature and the Emergence of Jewish Nationalism. *BibInt* 10:144–57.

Weems, Renita J. 1995. *Battered Love: Marriage Sex and Violence in the Hebrew Prophets*. Minneapolis: Fortress.

———. 1997. Song of Songs. *NIB* 5:361–434.

Weinberg, Joel P. 1992. *The Citizen-Temple Community*. Translated by Daniel L. Smith-Christopher. JSOTSup 151. Sheffield: Sheffield Academic Press.

———. 1996. *Der Chronist in seiner Mitwelt*. BZAW 239. Berlin: de Gruyter.

Wellhausen, Julius. 1973. *Prolegomena to the History of Israel*. Translated by J. Sutherland Black and Allan Menzies. Gloucester, Mass.: Smith.

Westbrook, Raymond. 1988. *Old Babylonian Marriage Law*. AfO 23. Horn, Austria: Berger.

Westermann, Claus. 1969. *Isaiah 40–66*. David M. H. Stalker. OTL. Philadelphia: Westminster.

Wette, Wilhelm M. L. de. 1836. *Kommentar über die Psalmen*. Heidelberg: Mohr Siebeck.

Whybray, R. Norman. 1975. *Isaiah 40–66*. NCB. London: Oliphants.

———. 1989. *Ecclesiastes*. OTG. Sheffield: Sheffield Academic Press.

———. 1990. The Sage in the Israelite Royal Court. Pages 133–41 in *The Sage in Israel and the Ancient Near East*. Edited by John G. Gammie and Leo G. Perdue. Winona Lake, Ind.: Eisenbrauns.

————. 1994. *Proverbs*. NCBC. Grand Rapids: Eerdmans.

Wilber, Donald N. 1969. *Persepolis: The Archaeology of Parsa, Seat of the Persian Kings*. New York: Crowell.

Willey, Patricia Tull. *Remember the Former Things: The Recollection of Previous Texts in Second Isaiah*. SBLDS 161. Atlanta: Scholars Press.

Williamson, Hugh G. M. 1985. *Ezra, Nehemiah*. WBC 16. Waco, Tex.: Word.

————. 1991. Ezra and Nehemiah in Light of the Texts from Persepolis. *BBR* 1:41–61.

————. 1998. Judah and the Jews. Pages 145–63 in *Studies in Persian History: Essays in Memory of David M. Lewis*. Edited by Maria Brosius and Amélie Kuhrt. Leiden: Nederlands Instituut voor het Nabije Oosten.

Wills, Lawrence M. 1990. *The Jew in the Court of the Foreign King: Ancient Jewish Court Legends*. Minneapolis: Fortress.

Wilson, Gerald H. 1993. Shaping the Psalter: A Consideration of Editorial Linkage in the Book of Psalms. Pages 72–82 in *The Shape and Shaping of the Psalter*. Edited by J. Clinton McCann. JSOTSup 159. Sheffield: Sheffield Academic Press.

Wright, John W. 2006. Remapping Yehud: The Borders of Yehud and the Genealogies of Chronicles. Pages 67–89 in Lipschits and Oeming 2006.

Yaron, Reuven. 1961. *Introduction to the Law of the Aramaic Papyri*. Oxford: Clarendon.

Yee, Gale A. 1989. "I Have Perfumed My Bed with Myrrh": The Foreign Woman ('ISSA ZARA) in Proverbs 1–9. *JSOT* 43:54–62.

————. 1995. Judges and the Dismembered Body. Pages 146–70 in *Judges and Method: New Approaches to Biblical Studies*. Edited by Gale A. Yee. Minneapolis: Fortress.

————. 2003. *Poor Banished Children of Eve: Woman as Evil in the Hebrew Bible*. Minneapolis: Fortress.

Yoder, Christine Roy. 2001. *Wisdom as a Woman of Substance: A Socioeconomic Reading of Proverbs 1–9 and 31:10–31*. BZAW 304. Berlin: de Gruyter.

Young, T. Cuyler, Jr. 1992. Persepolis. *ABD* 5:236.

Zaidman, Louise Bruit, and Pauline Schmitt Pantel. 1989. *La Religion grecque*. Paris: Colin.

————. 1995. *Religion in the Ancient Greek City*. Translated by Paul Cartledge. New York: Cambridge University Press.

Zimmerli, Walther. 1950. Zur Sprache Tritojesajas. *Schweizerische Theologische Umschau* 20:110–22.

————. 1963. *Gottes Offenbarung: Gesammelte Aufsätze zum Alten Testament*. Munich: Kaiser.

————. 1979. *Ezekiel 1: A Commentary on the Book of the Prophet Ezekiel 1–24*. Translated by Ronald E. Clements. Hermeneia. Philadelphia: Fortress.

Zornberg, Avivah Gottlieb. 1995. *Genesis: The Beginning of Desire*. Philadelphia: Jewish Publication Society.

CONTRIBUTORS

Richard Bautch is Associate Professor of Humanities at St. Edward's University, Austin, and co-chair of the task force on biblical hermeneutics in the Catholic Biblical Association. His study of penitential texts from the Persian Period has been published as *Developments in Genre between Post-exilic Penitential Prayers and the Psalms of Communal Lament* (Society of Biblical Literature, 2003).

Jon L. Berquist is Executive Editor for Biblical Studies at Westminster John Knox Press in Louisville, Kentucky. His writings on the Persian period include *Judaism in Persia's Shadow: A Social and Historical Approach*. In recent years he has also taught at New Brunswick Theological Seminary in New Brunswick, New Jersey. He has served as co-chair of SBL's Constructions of Ancient Space Seminar and is presently co-chair of AAR's Bible, Theology, and Postmodernity Group.

Alice W. Hunt is Associate Dean for Academic Affairs at Vanderbilt University Divinity School and Assistant Professor of Hebrew Bible at Vanderbilt's Divinity School and Graduate Department of Religion in Nashville, Tennessee. She is currently working on a project on the Bible and the immigration issue. Her recent book, *Missing Priests: The Zadokites in History and Tradition* (T&T Clark, 2006) focuses on issues of historiography in biblical studies.

David Janzen is Assistant Professor of Religious Studies at North Central College, outside of Chicago. His research interests focus on anthropological approaches to the literature of the Persian period and biblical literature regarding sacrifice. Recent publications include *The Social Meanings of Sacrifice in the Hebrew Bible* (de Gruyter, 2004) and *Witch-Hunts, Purity and Social Boundaries* (Sheffield Academic Press, 2002).

John Kessler is Professor of Old Testament and Chair of Biblical Studies at Tyndale Seminary, Toronto, Canada. He has published a series of works dealing with various aspects of the literature, sociology, and ideologies of Yehud. He is currently working on a general introduction to the theological streams within the Hebrew Bible, entitled *Ever Flowing Streams*, as well as *A Journey to the Source*, a guide for those undertaking the academic study of the Bible for the first time. He is a great lover of art, music, and life.

Melody D. Knowles is Associate Professor of Hebrew Scriptures at McCormick Theological Seminary. She is currently writing on the use of history in the Psalms. Her publications include *Centrality Practiced: Jerusalem in the Religious Practice of Yehud and the Diaspora in the Persian Period* (Society of Biblical Literature, 2006) and *Contesting Texts: Jews and Christians in Conversation about the Bible* (editor and co-author of the introduction with John Pawlikowski, Esther Menn, and Timothy Sandoval; Fortress, 2006).

Jennifer L. Koosed is an Assistant Professor of Religious Studies at Albright College in Reading, Pennsylvania. She has recently published a book on Ecclesiastes called *(Per)mutations of Qohelet: Reading the Body in the Book* (Continuum, 2006). Her research interests also include the Bible in popular culture.

Herbert Robinson Marbury is Assistant Professor of Hebrew Bible at Vanderbilt University. His area of specialization focuses on the history of the Second Temple period. His current research interests include ethics of the Hebrew Bible and African American biblical hermeneutics. He is currently working on a monograph on the Jerusalem priesthood in Persian Yehud. Prior to joining the faculty at Vanderbilt Divinity School, he served as chaplain at Clark Atlanta University and as a United Methodist pastor.

Christine Mitchell is Professor (without rank) of Hebrew Scriptures at St. Andrew's College in Saskatoon, Saskatchewan, Canada. She has written articles on Chronicles, Haggai, and Xenophon; her most recent article is "Power, Eros, and Biblical Genres," appearing in *Bible and Critical Theory* 3 (2007) and *Bakhtin and Genre Theory in Biblical Studies* (Society of Biblical Literature, 2007). Her current project is a comparative postcolonial reading of Haggai, Zechariah, Malachi, and Persian imperial inscriptions.

Julia M. O'Brien is Paul H. and Grace L. Stern Professor of Old Testament at Lancaster Theological Seminary in Lancaster, Pennsylvania. While most of her writing has been on the Minor Prophets, including a Sheffield volume on Nahum (2002) and the Abingdon Old Testament commentary on Nahum–Malachi (2004), her primary interest remains with the social and ethical implications of biblical interpretation.

Donald C. Polaski is Visiting Assistant Professor of Religious Studies at The College of William & Mary, Williamsburg, Virginia. He is currently working on a monograph, *Envisioning Writing: Texts and Power in Early Judaism*, which examines the development of textuality as authoritative in early Jewish discourse. He is also co-author, with three colleagues, of *Unmasking Identity and Power: An Introduction to the Hebrew Bible*, a soon-to-be-published Hebrew Bible introductory textbook.

Jean-Pierre Ruiz is Associate Professor of Biblical Studies at St. John's University in New York, where he also serves as Director of the Master of Arts in Liberal Studies. He is also a Senior Research Fellow of the Vincentian Center for Church and Society, and he serves as Editor in Chief of the *Journal of Hispanic/Latino Theology*. His current research focuses on migration in/and the Bible.

Brent A. Strawn is Associate Professor of Old Testament in the Candler School of Theology and Graduate Division of Religion at Emory University, Atlanta, Georgia. He is the author of *What Is Stronger Than a Lion? Leonine Image and Metaphor in the Hebrew Bible and the Ancient Near East* (2005) and recently co-edited *Qumran Studies: New Approaches, New Questions* (2007).

Printed in the United States
103716LV00004B/25/A